Spelling Connections

J. Richard Gentry, Ph.D.

ZB Zaner-Bloser

Author

J. Richard Gentry, Ph. D.

Reviewers

Paula Boales, Killeen ISD, Killeen, TX
Sherry Durham, Ed. D., Lufkin ISD, Lufkin, TX
Karyn L. Huskisson, Klein Instructional Center, Spring, TX
Carmen Ramos, San Benito CISD, San Benito, TX
Susan Shogan, Round Rock ISD, Round Rock, TX
Linda Stout, Crawford ISD, Crawford, TX

ELL and Spanish Consultants

Ellen Riojas Clark, Ph.D., Professor, College of Education
  and Human Development, Division of Bicultural-Bilingual
  Studies, The University of Texas at San Antonio, TX
Bertha Pérez, Ed.D., Professor Emeritus of Literacy,
  College of Education and Human Development,
  The University of Texas at San Antonio, TX
Rocio Reyes-Moore, Spanish Language Productions,
  Alexandria, OH

ISBN 978-0-7367-6867-2

Zaner-Bloser, Inc.
1-800-421-3018
www.zaner-bloser.com
Printed in the United States of America   12 13 14 15 25170 6 5 4

SUSTAINABLE FORESTRY INITIATIVE

Certified Chain of Custody
Promoting Sustainable Forestry
www.sfiprogram.org
SFI-01042

Table of Contents

Word Sorting

A word sort helps you become a Word Detective. When you sort, you look for patterns in your spelling words. You see how words are the same and how they are different. Word sorting can help you remember how to spell words.

Buddy Sort using the word sort cards

Word sort on an interactive whiteboard

There are different kinds of word sorts you can use with your spelling words.

- **Individual Sort**—Use word sorting to practice your spelling words.
- **Buddy Sort**—Do a word sort with a partner.
- **Speed Sorts on Your Own**—Time yourself as you sort your spelling words. Then do it again and try to improve on the number of seconds it takes to complete the word sort.
- **Speed Sorts With a Team**—See which team can complete the sort in the shortest time and with the greatest accuracy.

Spell Check

Spell check helps find misspelled words.

When you write on a computer, spell check can help you find spelling mistakes.

If you type **yuo** when you meant to type **you,** then spell check will let you know you made a mistake. It will even ask if you meant to type **you**.

But if you type **sick** and you meant to type **sock,** spell check cannot help. Why? Because **sick** and **sock** are both words, and spell check doesn't know you typed the wrong word.

Look, Say

1 **Look** at the word.

2 **Say** the letters in the word. Think about how each sound is spelled.

Cover, See

3 **Cover** the word with your hand or close your eyes.

4 **See** the word in your mind. Spell the word to yourself.

Write, Check

5 **Write** the word.

6 **Check** your spelling against the spelling in the book.

Taking a Test

1. **Get** ready for the test. Make sure your paper and pencil are ready.

2. **Listen** carefully as your teacher says each word and uses it in a sentence. Don't write before you hear the word **and** the sentence.

3. **Write** the word carefully. Make sure your handwriting is easy to read. If you want to print your words, ask your teacher.

4. **Use** a pen to correct your test. Look at the word as your teacher says it.

5. **Say** the word aloud. Listen carefully as your teacher spells the word. Say each letter aloud. Check the word one letter at a time.

6. **Circle** any misspelled parts of the word.

7. **Look** at the correctly written word. Spell the word again. Say each letter out loud.

8. **Write** any misspelled words correctly.

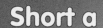

Short a

Read the spelling words and sentences.

1.	ask	I **ask** Pat for help.
2.	sat	Mom **sat** on the sofa.
3.	fan	The **fan** keeps us cool.
4.	map	The **map** shows our town.
5.	hand	I use my **hand** to wave.
6.	cap	Take the **cap** off your head!
7.	sad	The bad news made us **sad**.
8.	fat	We love our old **fat** dog.
9.	bat	I hit the ball with the **bat**.
10.	as	Hop and jump **as** I do.

Think & Sort the spelling words.

1–2. Write the words that begin with the **short a** sound.

3–10. Write the words that have the **short a** sound between two consonants.

Remember

The **short a** sound can be spelled **a: bat**.

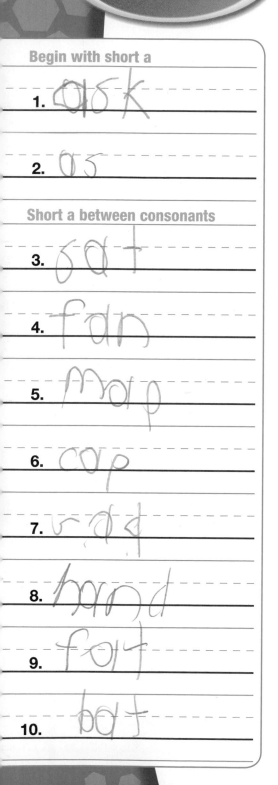

Begin with short a

1. ask

2. as

Short a between consonants

3. sat

4. fan

5. map

6. cap

7. sad

8. hand

9. fat

10. bat

TEKS 2.23A Use phonological knowledge to match sounds to letters to construct unknown words.
2.23C Spell high-frequency words from a commonly used list.

Connections to PHONICS

Ending Sounds

1–3. Write the rhyming words that end with **t**.

Word Structure

Replace the underlined letters to write a spelling word.

4. ca<u>t</u>   **5.** <u>s</u>and

Rhyming Words

Write a spelling word for each set of clues.

6. Wave this to keep cool. Its name rhymes with **man**.

7. Use this to find your way. Its name rhymes with **tap**.

8. If you feel this way, you are not glad. Its name rhymes with **glad**.

Use the Dictionary

9–10. A dictionary lists words in a-b-c order. Write the two spelling words that begin with the letter **a** in a-b-c order.

Dictionary Check Check a-b-c order in your **Spelling Dictionary**.

Ending Sounds

1. sot

2. bot

3. folt

Word Structure

4. fоth

5. won

Rhyming Words

6. cap map

7. sot fat

8. Ran man

Use the Dictionary

9.

10.

 TEKS 2.23A Use phonological knowledge to match sounds to letters to construct unknown words.
2.23C Spell high-frequency words from a commonly used list.

15

ask	sat	fan	map	hand
cap	sad	fat	bat	as

Complete the Analogies

An analogy compares pairs of things that are connected in some way. For example, you know that socks and mittens are both things to wear. Here is an analogy about things you wear: **Sock** is to **foot** as **mitten** is to **hand**.

Write a spelling word to complete each analogy.

1. **Smile** is to **happy** as **frown** is to _____.
2. **Short** is to **tall** as **skinny** is to _____.
3. **Foot** is to **shoe** as **head** is to _____.
4. **Hide** is to **hid** as **sit** is to _____.
5. **Catch** is to **glove** as **hit** is to _____.

Use Context Clues

Write a spelling word to complete each sentence.

6. We can't do this alone. Let's _____ Matt for some help.
7. This is my little sister's glove. It does not fit my _____.
8. How do you get to the zoo? We need a _____ to find the way.
9. We use the _____ on a hot day.
10. If I do _____ the coach says, maybe I will score a goal!

Complete the Analogies

1. _____
2. _____
3. _____
4. _____
5. _____

Use Context Clues

6. _____
7. _____
8. _____
9. _____
10. _____

TEKS 2.23C Spell high-frequency words from a commonly used list.

Connections to WRITING

Proofread a Story

To show where changes are needed, you can use proofreading marks. The symbol ≡ means make a capital letter. The symbol / means make a small letter. Find eight misspelled words in the story below. Rewrite the story using correct spelling. Make the corrections shown by the proofreading marks.

My Ball Game

I put on my /Baseball kap. I grab my batt. i put my glove on my hannd. I ast my dad to drive me to the park. He says yes. He is az big a baseball fen as I am! last year he satt and watched all my /Games.
We will be sadd when baseball is over.

NARRATIVE Writing Prompt

Write a Story

Write a story about something you did with a friend. Use as many spelling words as you can.

- Use the writing process: prewrite, draft, revise, edit, and publish.
- First, tell who was there and what happened. Then tell what happened next. Finally, tell how everything worked out.
- Use complete sentences with correct capitalization, punctuation, grammar, and spelling.
- Circle two words you checked for correct spelling in a dictionary.

Transfer

Think of two more words with the **short a** sound at the beginning and three more words with the sound between two consonants. Write the words in your Spelling Journal. Circle the vowel **a** in each word.

 TEKS 2.23A Use phonological knowledge to match sounds to letters to construct unknown words.
2.23C Spell high-frequency words from a commonly used list. **2.23F** Use resources to find correct spellings.

Word Study

can	fan	sat	bat	basket
dad	map	cap	cabin	napkins
man	hand	sad	fancy	salad
ask	as	fat	hatch	wagon

Pattern Power

1. _____

2. _____

3. _____

4. _____

5. _____

Meaning Mastery

6. _____

7. _____

8. _____

9. _____

10. _____

Pattern Power

Follow the directions. Use words from the list.

1–2. Write two words that rhyme with **lap**.

3–5. Write three words that rhyme with **cat**.

Meaning Mastery

Write the word that matches each meaning.

6. pieces of cloth to wipe your mouth

7–8. two words that name things used for carrying items

9. Write the word that comes before **far** in the **Spelling Dictionary**.

10. Write the word that comes before **cake** in the **Spelling Dictionary**.

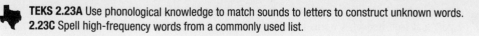

TEKS 2.23A Use phonological knowledge to match sounds to letters to construct unknown words.
2.23C Spell high-frequency words from a commonly used list.

Science

Word Hunt

Read the paragraph below. Look for words with the **short a** sound.

Some bats are big, but others are as small as your hand. A bat has a furry body like a mouse. Each front leg has a flap of skin like a bird's wing. Bats are the only mammals that can fly. Baby bats are born like other mammals. They don't hatch from eggs like birds do. Bats come out of their caves at night and fan out into the sky like a big black cloud. They catch and eat thousands of bugs. Then the bats land in trees and hang down from their feet to nap. On a clear night, ask an adult to take you outside to look for bats.

1. _____

2. _____

3. _____

4. _____

5. _____

6. _____

7. _____

8. _____

WORD SORT

1–2. Write the words that were made by adding letters to the **short a** word **and**.

3–4. Write the **short a** words that rhyme with **match**.

5–6. Write the **short a** words that rhyme with **pan**.

7–8. Write the **short a** words that rhyme with **tap**.

TEKS 2.23A Use phonological knowledge to match sounds to letters to construct unknown words.
2.23C Spell high-frequency words from a commonly used list.

Connections to THINKING

Read the spelling words and sentences.

1. send   I **send** mail to Dan.
2. bell   The **bell** rings at noon.
3. well   We all feel **well** today.
4. help   Please **help** me carry this bag.
5. fell   Anna **fell** when she ran.
6. went   I **went** to the store.
7. spell   We can **spell** many words.
8. next   The party is **next** week.
9. tell   Would you **tell** me a story?
10. end   How does the story **end**?

Think & Sort the spelling words.

1. Write the word that begins with the **short e** sound.

2–10. Write the words that have the **short e** sound between two consonants.

Remember

The **short e** sound can be spelled **e: bell**.

Beginning short e

1. _____

Short e between two consonants

2. _____

3. _____

4. _____

5. _____

6. _____

7. _____

8. _____

9. _____

10. _____

 TEKS 2.23A Use phonological knowledge to match sounds to letters to construct unknown words.
2.23C Spell high-frequency words from a commonly used list.

Short e Spelling Pattern

Write a spelling word that completes the sentence. The spelling word will have the same **short e** spelling pattern as the underlined word. The spelling word will rhyme with the underlined word.

1. We _____ into the <u>tent</u>.

2. Did Jim <u>bend</u> the _____ of the straw?

Word Math

Follow the directions to write spelling words.

3. went – nt + ll = _____

4. nest – s + x = _____

Word Structure

Replace the underlined letters to write a spelling word.

5. s<u>a</u>nd   **7.** f<u>a</u>ll

6. sp<u>i</u>ll   **8.** b<u>u</u>ll

Double consonants, as in the word **bell,** are complex because two letters make one sound. Circle the complex consonants in the words you wrote on this page.

Use the **Dictionary**

Find the word in the **Spelling Dictionary** that has each word in its definition. Write the word and the page number where you find it.

9. aid   **10.** say

Short e Spelling Pattern

1. _____

2. _____

Word Math

3. _____

4. _____

Word Structure

5. _____

6. _____

7. _____

8. _____

Use the Dictionary

9. _____

10. _____

TEKS 2.23A Use phonological knowledge to match sounds to letters to construct unknown words. **2.23Bi** Spell words with common orthographic patterns and rules: complex consonants. **2.23C** Spell high-frequency words from a commonly used list.

send	bell	well	help	fell
went	spell	next	tell	end

Use Antonyms

Write the spelling word that is opposite in meaning to each word below.

1. receive

2. ill

3. hurt

4. came

5. begin

6. ask

Multiple Meanings

Which spelling word has both meanings?

7. just after; nearest

8. a period of time; putting letters together in the right order

Check your answers in the **Spelling Dictionary,** and write the page numbers where you find them.

Use Synonyms

Write the words that mean almost the same as the words below.

9. dropped

10. alarm

Use Antonyms

1.

2.

3.

4.

5.

6.

Multiple Meanings

7.

8.

Use Synonyms

9.

10.

TEKS2.23C Spell high-frequency words from a commonly used list.

Connections to WRITING

Proofread a Paragraph

The symbol ∧ means add something. The symbol ℯ means take out something. Proofread the paragraph below for eight misspelled words. Then rewrite the paragraph. Write the spelling words correctly and make the corrections shown by the proofreading marks.

I Could Help

Last week i wennt to the park with a friend. My Friend fel and got hurt. I tried to think of what to do nexst. Should I sand someone to get hellp? Should I tel an adult? In the ennd, I told an adult. I couldn't make my my friend wel, but at least I could help.

Proofreading Marks

≡	Capital Letter
/	Small Letter
∧	Add
ℯ	Delete
⊙	Add a Period
⊬	Indent

EXPOSITORY Writing Prompt
Write a Paragraph

Write a paragraph to tell about a way to help a friend. Use as many spelling words as you can.

- Use the writing process: prewrite, draft, revise, edit, and publish.
- Brainstorm and pick a topic for your writing.
- Begin with a sentence that tells the main idea.
- Add details in the next sentences.
- Write an ending in the last sentence.
- Use complete sentences with correct capitalization, punctuation, grammar, and spelling.
- Circle two words you checked for correct spelling in a dictionary.

Transfer
Think of five more words with the **short e** sound. Write the words in your Spelling Journal and circle the **e** in each word.

TEKS 2.23A Use phonological knowledge to match sounds to letters to construct unknown words. **2.23C** Spell high-frequency words from a commonly used list. **2.23F** Use resources to find correct spellings.

23

best	well	bell	end	melon
let	went	help	elephant	celery
pen	next	fell	lemon	lettuce
send	tell	spell	sketch	vegetable

Pattern Power

1.
2.
3.
4.
5.
6.
7.

Meaning Mastery

8.
9.
10.

Pattern Power

Follow the directions. Use words from the list.

1–5. Write the words that have the **ell** spelling pattern and circle the double consonants.

6–7. Write the words that rhyme with **mend**.

Meaning Mastery

Write the word that matches each meaning. Circle the letter that spells **short e** in each word.

8. a small and sour yellow fruit

9. an animal with tusks and a trunk

10. juicy, round fruit with a hard rind

TEKS 2.23A Use phonological knowledge to match sounds to letters to construct unknown words. **2.23Bi** Spell words with common orthographic patterns and rules: complex consonants. **2.23C** Spell high-frequency words from a commonly used list.

Social Studies

Word Hunt

Read the paragraphs below. Look for words with the **short e** sound.

It was the end of the school year. Leta and Ted went by an empty lot on their way home.

"Let's tell our neighbors to help clean this lot and plant a garden," said Leta.

"I'll send e-mails to everyone," said Ted.

The planting of the garden went well. Soon vegetables were growing. Celery, lettuce, and melons filled the rows. Each day people came to tend the garden.

Leta and Ted gave a picnic at the end of the summer. People came to have fun and get their crops. They agreed to have another garden the next summer.

1. _____

2. _____

3. _____

4. _____

5. _____

6. _____

7. _____

8. _____

1–2. Write the **short e** words that have the **ell** pattern.

3–5. Write the **short e** words that have the **end** pattern.

6–8. Write the words that have two syllables with the **short e** sound in the first syllable.

TEKS 2.23A Use phonological knowledge to match sounds to letters to construct unknown words.
2.23C Spell high-frequency words from a commonly used list.

Connections to THINKING

Read the spelling words and sentences.

1. hit — I use a bat to **hit** the ball.
2. fill — Please **fill** my cup.
3. will — I **will** eat later.
4. wind — The **wind** is blowing hard.
5. miss — I **miss** Ben when he is gone.
6. milk — A cow gives **milk**.
7. win — Our team can **win** this game.
8. hill — He rides a bike up the **hill**.
9. bill — I pay the **bill** for the meal.
10. fit — The shoes **fit** me just right.

Think & Sort the spelling words.

1–4. Write the words that rhyme with **mill**.
5–6. Write the words that rhyme with **it**.
7–10. Write the other words that have the **short i** sound.

Remember

The **short i** sound can be spelled **i: hill**.

Rhyme with mill

1. _____
2. _____
3. _____
4. _____

Rhyme with it

5. _____
6. _____

Other short i words

7. _____
8. _____
9. _____
10. _____

 TEKS 2.23A Use phonological knowledge to match sounds to letters to construct unknown words.
2.23C Spell high-frequency words from a commonly used list.

Connections to PHONICS

Short i Rhyming Words

Write a spelling word that rhymes with the underlined word to complete each sentence.

1. There is <u>still</u> time to run up that _____.

2. <u>Jill</u> _____ help us dig this hole.

3. Keep your <u>chin</u> up. We can _____ this game!

4. Use your <u>mitt</u> to catch the ball she _____.

Word Structure

5. Change the first letter in **silk** to make this spelling word.

6. Change one letter in **wand** to make this spelling word.

7. Change the last letter in **film** to make this spelling word.

Double consonants, as in the word **hill,** are complex because two letters make one sound. Circle the complex consonants in the words you wrote on this page.

Find these words in your **Spelling Dictionary**. Write the word that comes <u>after</u> each word.

8. fishing **9.** bike **10.** mime

Short i Rhyming Words

1. _____
2. _____
3. _____
4. _____

Word Structure

5. _____
6. _____
7. _____

Use the Dictionary

8. _____
9. _____
10. _____

TEKS 2.23A Use phonological knowledge to match sounds to letters to construct unknown words. **2.23Bi** Spell words with common orthographic patterns and rules: complex consonants. **2.23C** Spell high-frequency words from a commonly used list.

hit	fill	will	wind	miss
milk	win	hill	bill	fit

Multiple Meanings

Write the word that can be used twice in each sentence.

1. He had a _____ when his shirt did not _____.
2. The vet's _____ was costly to treat the duck's _____.
3. Her strong _____ _____ serve her well.
4. The near _____ made us see how much we would _____ our cat.
5. After she _____ the home run, she got _____ on her back.

Use Antonyms

Antonyms are words that mean the opposite. Write a spelling word that is an antonym for each word below.

6. lose _____
7. empty _____

Word Categorization

Write the spelling word that belongs in each group.

8. valley, mountain, _____
9. water, juice, _____
10. breeze, air, _____

Multiple Meanings

1.
2.
3.
4.
5.

Use Antonyms

6.
7.

Word Categorization

8.
9.
10.

TEKS 2.23C Spell high-frequency words from a commonly used list.

Connections to WRITING

Proofread a Poster

The symbol ⊙ means add a period. The symbol ⌗ means indent. Find eight misspelled words in the poster below. Rewrite the poster using correct spelling. Make the corrections shown by the proofreading marks.

Grant School Baseball Game

What: Teachers Against Kids

Where: Grant Park

When: May 15 at 10 A.M⊙

⌗ Come to the hil. This game well surely be a hitt! Watch the best ̷team winn! don't mis it! We'd like to fil the stands with fans. We'll play whether there's winnd or rain. after the game, there will be free cookies and milc.

PERSUASIVE Writing Prompt
Write a Poster

Write a poster for an event. Use as many spelling words as you can.

- Use the writing process: prewrite, draft, revise, edit, and publish.
- Brainstorm and choose an event to write about.
- Tell what the event is, when and where the event will happen, and why people should come.
- Read your writing. Circle two words that may be misspelled. Use a dictionary to check the spelling.

Transfer

Think of six more words with the **short i** sound. The words can have **i** at the beginning or in the middle of the word. Write the words in your Spelling Journal. Circle the vowel **i** in each word.

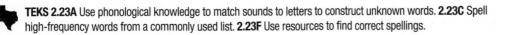
TEKS 2.23A Use phonological knowledge to match sounds to letters to construct unknown words. **2.23C** Spell high-frequency words from a commonly used list. **2.23F** Use resources to find correct spellings.

Word Study

big	will	fill	fit	crisp
bit	wind	win	fish	twist
spin	miss	hill	kitten	nibble
hit	milk	bill	little	wiggle

Circle any double consonants in the words you write.

Use Antonyms

Write the spelling word that is the opposite of each word below.

1. huge
2. soggy
3. hit
4. unfit

Word Categorization

5–6. Write the spelling words that name animals.

Use Synonyms

Write the word that means the same as the words below.

7. small bite
8. spin or turn
9. white drink
10. paper money

Use Antonyms

1.

2.

3.

4.

Word Categorization

5.

6.

Use Synonyms

7.

8.

9.

10.

TEKS 2.23Bi Spell words with common orthographic patterns and rules: complex consonants.
2.23C Spell high-frequency words from a commonly used list.

Math

 Word Hunt

Read the poem below. Look for words with the **short i** sound.

> Start the race by running fast
> Will you win or come in last?
> Knit a scarf bit by bit.
> How long before the scarf will fit?
> You will know as math skills grow!
>
> The grill is ready for the meat,
> So how much time before we eat?
> How many gallons do you think
> It takes to fill your kitchen sink?
> You will know as math skills grow!
>
> Pour the batter in the tin.
> How many muffins will fit in?
> How many coins are needed still
> To leave a tip and pay the bill?
> You will know as math skills grow!

1. _____

2. _____

3. _____

4. _____

5. _____

6. _____

7. _____

WORD SORT

1–6. Write the **short i** words that have the **ill** pattern.

7. Write the two-syllable word with **short i** in the first syllable.

TEKS 2.23A Use phonological knowledge to match sounds to letters to construct unknown words.
2.23Bi Spell words with common orthographic patterns and rules: complex consonants.
2.23C Spell high-frequency words from a commonly used list.

Rhyme with hog

1. _____

2. _____

3. _____

Rhyme with hot

4. _____

5. _____

6. _____

Other short o words

7. _____

8. _____

9. _____

10. _____

Connections to THINKING

Read the spelling words and sentences.

1.	dog	The **dog** likes its bone.
2.	doll	I play with a **doll**.
3.	stop	We **stop** at the red light.
4.	cot	You can sleep on a **cot**.
5.	log	This **log** is from that tree.
6.	fog	We cannot see in the **fog**.
7.	spot	The dog has one black **spot**.
8.	pond	Fish live in the **pond**.
9.	nod	I **nod** when I mean yes.
10.	lot	Two cups is a **lot** of milk!

Think & Sort the spelling words.

1–3. Write the words that rhyme with **hog**.

4–6. Write the words that rhyme with **hot**.

7–10. Write the other words that have the **short o** sound.

Remember

The **short o** sound can be spelled **o: cot**.

TEKS 2.23A Use phonological knowledge to match sounds to letters to construct unknown words.
2.23C Spell high-frequency words from a commonly used list.

Sound Matching

Write a spelling word for each set of letter sounds.

1. It begins like **cap** and ends like **lot**. _____

2. It begins like **let** and ends like **dog**. _____

3. It begins like **spin** and ends like **pot**. _____

4. It begins like **fit** and ends like **log**. _____

Word Structure

5. Change the vowel in **step** to make this spelling word.

6. Change the last two letters in **post** to make this spelling word.

7. Change the first two letters in **call** to make this spelling word.

Use the Dictionary

The words in a dictionary are in a-b-c order.

8–10. Write these words in a-b-c order.

    nod   dog   lot

Dictionary Check Check the a-b-c order of the words in your **Spelling Dictionary**.

Sound Matching
1.
2.
3.
4.

Word Structure
5.
6.
7.

Use the Dictionary
8.
9.
10.

 TEKS 2.23A Use phonological knowledge to match sounds to letters to construct unknown words.
2.23C Spell high-frequency words from a commonly used list.

33

| dog | fog | doll | spot | stop |
| pond | cot | nod | log | lot |

Word Categorization

Word Categorization

Write the spelling word that fits in each group.

1. cat, bird, _____

2. lake, puddle, _____

3. rain, snow, _____

4. bed, crib, _____

5. toy, game, _____

6. wood, twig, _____

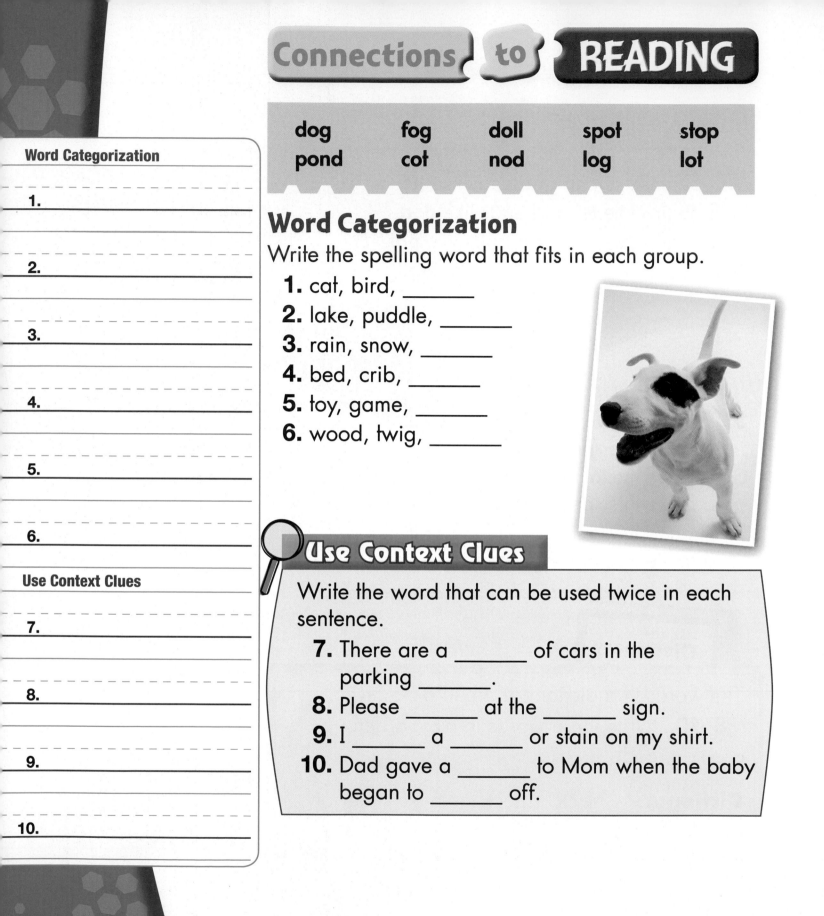

Use Context Clues

Use Context Clues

Write the word that can be used twice in each sentence.

7. There are a _____ of cars in the parking _____.

8. Please _____ at the _____ sign.

9. I _____ a _____ or stain on my shirt.

10. Dad gave a _____ to Mom when the baby began to _____ off.

Word Categorization

1. _____

2. _____

3. _____

4. _____

5. _____

6. _____

Use Context Clues

7. _____

8. _____

9. _____

10. _____

TEKS 2.23C Spell high-frequency words from a commonly used list.

Connections to WRITING

Proofread a Poem

Proofread the poem below for eight misspelled words. Then rewrite the poem. Write the spelling words correctly and make the corrections shown by the proofreading marks.

Proofreading Marks

≡	Capital Letter
/	Small Letter
∧	Add
ℒ	Delete
⊙	Add a Period
⊬	Indent

By the Pond

There is a ponnd near my home where my doag

and i stopp.

We rest on a cott and watch the small fish go plop⊙

A lott of Deer come to drink in the morning fogg.

And there's often a big frog perched on of a logg.

I come here a lot. It's my special spott.

Write a Poem

Write a poem about a place where you like to go. Use as many spelling words as you can.

- Use the writing process: prewrite, draft, revise, edit, and publish.
- List poem ideas. Then choose one.
- Tell what your place looks and sounds like. Tell how you feel about it.
- Add rhyme to your poem if you can.
- Read your writing. Circle two words that may be misspelled. Use a dictionary to check the spelling.

Transfer

Think of six more words with the **short o** sound. Write the words in your Spelling Journal. Circle the vowel **o** in each word.

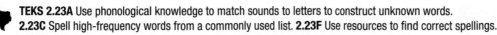

TEKS 2.23A Use phonological knowledge to match sounds to letters to construct unknown words.
2.23C Spell high-frequency words from a commonly used list. **2.23F** Use resources to find correct spellings.

Word Study

body	stop	doll	nod	smock
got	fog	cot	block	model
mom	pond	log	octopus	hobby
dog	lot	spot	popcorn	bonnet

Circle any double consonants in the words you write.

Pattern Power

Follow the directions. Use words from the list.

1–5. Write the two-syllable words that have the **short o** sound.

Word Building

Replace the underlined letter in each of these words to write a spelling word.

6. p<u>o</u>d

7. d<u>u</u>ll

8. <u>f</u>ond

9. bl<u>a</u>ck

10. sm<u>a</u>ck

Pattern Power

1.

2.

3.

4.

5.

Word Building

6.

7.

8.

9.

10.

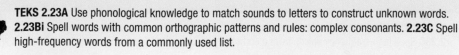

TEKS 2.23A Use phonological knowledge to match sounds to letters to construct unknown words. **2.23Bi** Spell words with common orthographic patterns and rules: complex consonants. **2.23C** Spell high-frequency words from a commonly used list.

Science

Word Hunt

Read the paragraphs below. Look for words with the **short o** sound.

Mom took Tom, little Mimi, and Spot the dog to the pond. Their hobby was watching animals. When they got there they couldn't see much, because there was a lot of fog. Then the sun came out. Mom put a pretty bonnet on Mimi.

Tom saw a frog sitting on a log. He saw a lot of insects flying on top of the pond. Suddenly he saw a large body floating in the pond.

"Do you think it's an octopus?" he asked Mom. Mom answered, "No, an octopus would not live in a pond." They looked again. It was a big rock!

1. _____

2. _____

3. _____

4. _____

5. _____

6. _____

7. _____

8. _____

1–3. Write the **short o** words that begin or end with a consonant blend.

4. Write the **short o** word that rhymes with **sock**.

5–8. Find four words with more than one syllable that have a **short o** in the first syllable.

TEKS 2.23A Use phonological knowledge to match sounds to letters to construct unknown words.
2.23C Spell high-frequency words from a commonly used list.

Connections to THINKING

Read the spelling words and sentences.

1.	jug	The **jug** has water in it.
2.	mud	Rain turns dirt to **mud**.
3.	just	I have **just** one cat.
4.	hunt	I **hunt** for my missing glasses.
5.	club	Tina will join our **club**.
6.	drum	Sam plays the **drum** well.
7.	jump	I can **jump** two feet.
8.	dust	Juan will **dust** the old table.
9.	rub	I **rub** the cat's back.
10.	cup	Ann drinks a **cup** of milk.

Think & Sort the spelling words.

1–2. Write the words that rhyme with **tub**.

3–4. Write the words that rhyme with **rust**.

5–10. Write the other words that have the **short u** sound.

Remember

The **short u** sound can be spelled **u: cup**.

Rhyme with tub

1. _____

2. _____

Rhyme with rust

3. _____

4. _____

Other short u words

5. _____

6. _____

7. _____

8. _____

9. _____

10. _____

TEKS 2.23A Use phonological knowledge to match sounds to letters to construct unknown words.
2.23C Spell high-frequency words from a commonly used list.

Sound Blending

1. Write the word that starts like **job** and ends like **rust**.

2. Write the word that starts like **dog** and ends like **must**.

3. Write the word that starts like **ring** and ends like **tub**.

4. Write the word that starts like **class** and ends like **cub**.

Sounds and Letters

Write the spelling word that ends with the same two letters and sounds as these words.

5. lamp   **6. pup**   **7. plum**

Word Structure

Replace the underlined letters to write spelling words.

8. j<u>o</u>g   **9.** h<u>i</u>nt

Use the
Dictionary

A dictionary tells you the meanings of words. Write the spelling word for this meaning and the page where you find it in your **Spelling Dictionary**.

10. soft, wet dirt

Sound Blending

1. _____

2. _____

3. _____

4. _____

Sounds and Letters

5. _____

6. _____

7. _____

Word Structure

8. _____

9. _____

Use the Dictionary

10. _____

TEKS 2.23A Use phonological knowledge to match sounds to letters to construct unknown words.
2.23C Spell high-frequency words from a commonly used list.

39

jug	mud	just	hunt	club
drum	jump	dust	rub	cup

Use Synonyms

Write the word that means the same or nearly the same as the underlined word or words.

1. Pam will <u>leap</u> over the fence.
2. We <u>look hard</u> for the missing cat.
3. That baby is <u>only</u> six months old.
4. We like to play in the <u>wet dirt</u>.

Complete the Analogies

Write a spelling word to complete each analogy.

5. **Food** is to **plate** as **milk** is to _____.
6. **Blow** is to **horn** as **beat** is to _____.

Use Context Clues

Write a spelling word to complete each sentence.

7. Pour the water into my glass from that big _____.
8. My cat likes for me to _____ its back.
9. Our _____ meets in the tree house every week.
10. Before my aunt and uncle come, Mom wants me to _____ the tables.

Use Synonyms
1. ____
2. ____
3. ____
4. ____

Complete the Analogies
5. ____
6. ____

Use Context Clues
7. ____
8. ____
9. ____
10. ____

TEKS 2.23C Spell high-frequency words from a commonly used list.

Connections to WRITING

Proofread a Letter

Find eight misspelled words in the letter below. Rewrite the letter using correct spelling. Make the corrections shown by the proofreading marks.

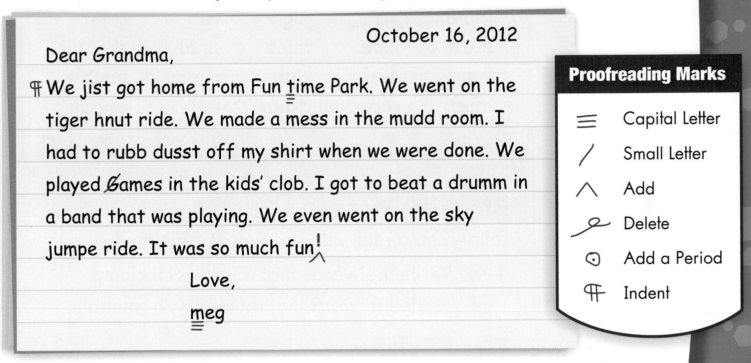

October 16, 2012

Dear Grandma,

¶ We jist got home from Fun time Park. We went on the tiger hnut ride. We made a mess in the mudd room. I had to rubb dusst off my shirt when we were done. We played Games in the kids' clob. I got to beat a drumm in a band that was playing. We even went on the sky jumpe ride. It was so much fun!

Love,

meg

Proofreading Marks

≡	Capital Letter
/	Small Letter
∧	Add
ℯ	Delete
⊙	Add a Period
¶	Indent

DESCRIPTIVE Writing Prompt

Write a Letter

Write a letter that tells about a special day. Use as many spelling words as you can.

- Choose the person who will receive your letter. Write **Dear** and the person's name in the greeting. Put a comma after the greeting.
- In the body or main part of your letter, tell what you did or where you went.
- End with a closing, such as **Your friend**. Put a comma after the closing and sign your name.
- Check for correct grammar, capitals, and punctuation.
- Use a dictionary to check your spelling.

Transfer

Think of six more words with the **short u** sound. Write the words in your Spelling Journal. Circle the vowel **u** in each word.

TEKS 2.23A Use phonological knowledge to match sounds to letters to construct unknown words. **2.23C** Spell high-frequency words from a commonly used list. **2.23F** Use resources to find correct spellings.

Word Study

bump	just	jug	rub	gruff
must	jump	hunt	until	stump
rug	dust	club	sunny	tumble
mud	cup	drum	ugly	puddle

Rhyming Words

Follow the directions. Use words from the list.

1–3. Write the words that rhyme with **clump**.

4. Write the word that rhymes with **mumble**.

Word Building

Replace the underlined letter in each word to write a word from the list.

5. j<u>o</u>g   **6.** c<u>a</u>p   **7.** p<u>a</u>ddle

Use Antonyms

Write the word from the list that means the opposite of each word.

8. cloudy   **9.** pretty   **10.** kind

Rhyming Words

1.

2.

3.

4.

Word Building

5.

6.

7.

Use Antonyms

8.

9.

10.

TEKS 2.23A Use phonological knowledge to match sounds to letters to construct unknown words.
2.23C Spell high-frequency words from a commonly used list.

Social Studies

Word Hunt

Read the paragraphs below. Look for words with the **short u** sound.

Bud and Ming have a summer club. "We just like to have fun on the long, sunny days," they say. On hot days, they run and jump into Bud's pool to cool off. Then they eat lunch under a tree, where they munch on a bunch of grapes and drink cups of lemonade. They hide lucky coins and then hunt for them. On rainy days they jump in mud puddles. Then they have to rub off all the mud and dust.

"We'll have the club until school starts," says Bud.

Ming says, "We must have the club again next summer!"

1. _____
2. _____
3. _____
4. _____
5. _____
6. _____
7. _____
8. _____

WORD SORT

Write the **short u** words that have each pattern.

1–3. **ust**

4–6. **unch**

7. **ump**

8. **unt**

TEKS 2.23A Use phonological knowledge to match sounds to letters to construct unknown words.
2.23C Spell high-frequency words from a commonly used list.

43

Assessment

Each assessment word in the box fits one of the spelling patterns you have studied over the past five weeks. Read the spelling patterns. Then write each assessment word under the unit number it fits.

Unit 1

1–2. The **short a** sound can be spelled **a: bat**.

Unit 2

3–4. The **short e** sound can be spelled **e: bell**.

Unit 3

5–6. The **short i** sound can be spelled **i: hill**.

Unit 4

7–8. The **short o** sound can be spelled **o: cot**.

Unit 5

9–10. The **short u** sound can be spelled **u: cup**.

Words for Assessment

fond

belt

silk

moss

nap

yell

spun

gill

mad

mug

Unit 1

1. _____

2. _____

Unit 2

3. _____

4. _____

Unit 3

5. _____

6. _____

Unit 4

7. _____

8. _____

Unit 5

9. _____

10. _____

Review

Unit 1: Short a

ask	map	fan	hand	as

Write a spelling word to complete each sentence. The spelling word will rhyme with the underlined word.

1. May I _____ what's on your <u>mask</u>?

2. Put your _____ in the <u>sand</u>.

3. John <u>has</u> the same name _____ his dad.

4. Heidi <u>ran</u> to get the _____.

5. Hold the _____ in your <u>lap</u>.

Unit 2: Short e

tell	send	next	went	well

Write the spelling word that rhymes with each word or group of words.

6. spend, lend, bend

7. bent, dent, rent

8. text

9–10. Write the spelling words that rhyme with each other.

Unit 1

1. _____
2. _____
3. _____
4. _____
5. _____

Unit 2

6. _____
7. _____
8. _____
9. _____
10. _____

Unit 3

1. _____

2. _____

3. _____

4. _____

5. _____

Unit 4

6. _____

7. _____

8. _____

9. _____

10. _____

Unit 3: Short i

| will | milk | miss | wind | hit |

Replace one letter in each word to write a spelling word.

1. hot

2. wand

3. well

4. mess

5. silk

Unit 4: Short o

| fog | lot | dog | pond | stop |

Remove a letter or letters from each word below to write a spelling word.

6. plot

7. frog

8. stopper

9. ponder

10. doggy

Unit 5: Short u

| cup | jump | mud | just | dust |

Change one letter in each underlined word to write a spelling word.

1. The wind brought a lot of <u>rust</u>.

2. The cause was a <u>must</u> one.

3. How deep is the <u>mad</u>?

4. Can you <u>lump</u> the puddle?

5. You may drink from this <u>cap</u>.

1.

2.

3.

4.

5.

Spelling Study Strategy

Spelling Tic-Tac-Toe

Here's a game you can play with a friend.

1. Write your spelling words in a list. Ask your friend to do the same. Trade lists.

2. Draw a tic-tac-toe board on a piece of paper. Decide who will use **X** and who will use **O**.

3. Ask your partner to call out the first word on your list. Spell it aloud. If you spell it correctly, make an **X** or an **O** (whichever you are using) on the tic-tac-toe board. If you misspell it, you lose your turn.

4. Take turns until you have practiced all the words or have won the game.

Directions: Read the introduction and the passage that follows. Then read each question and fill in the space in front of the correct answer.

Izzie is on a baseball team. She wrote this story about trying to hit a home run for her mother's birthday. She wants you to review her paper. As you read, think about ways Izzie can make her story better.

Izzie at Bat

(1) I had this great idea before yesterday's baseball game. (2) I would het a home run for my mother! (3) It was her birthday, and she is my biggest fan.

(4) Mom sat in the frunt row wearing a blue cap. (5) I gave her a nod when it was my turn at bat. (6) Then I picked up a very fat bat so I wouldn't mis the ball. (7) But the bat was juss too heavy. (8) Every time I swung it, I fell over!

(9) On my nixt turn at bat, I hit the ball hard, but it landed in some mud near my mom. (10) She tried to jomp out of the way, but mud splashed her feet and legs. (11) "Just wait until I get another turn!" I yelled.

(12) Soon it was the last inning. (13) I rubbed some dust on my hand as I wint to the plate. (14) Smack went my bat, sending the ball soaring into the outfield. (15) I raced to first base, sure that it was a home run. (16) Then a dawg appeared out of nowhere, leaping high in the air to make a great catch. (17) At least my mom's birthday was exciting!

GO ON

1 What change, if any, should be made in sentence 2?

- ⬭ Change *would* to **wood**
- ⬭ Change *het* to **hit**
- ⬭ Change *mother* to **muther**
- ⬭ Make no change

2 What change, if any, should be made in sentence 3?

- ⬭ Change *birthday* to **berthday**
- ⬭ Change *is* to **as**
- ⬭ Change *fan* to **fin**
- ⬭ Make no change

3 What change, if any, should be made in sentence 4?

- ⬭ Change *sat* to **satt**
- ⬭ Change *frunt* to **front**
- ⬭ Change *cap* to **cop**
- ⬭ Make no change

4 What change, if any, should be made in sentence 5?

- ⬭ Change *I* to **i**
- ⬭ Change *nod* to **nad**
- ⬭ Change *bat* to **bit**
- ⬭ Make no change

5 What change should be made in sentence 6?

- ⬭ Change *picked* to **packed**
- ⬭ Change *fat* to **fit**
- ⬭ Change *mis* to **miss**
- ⬭ Change *ball* to **boll**

6 What change, if any, should be made in sentence 7?

- ⬭ Change *bat* to **batt**
- ⬭ Change *was* to **wus**
- ⬭ Change *juss* to **just**
- ⬭ Make no change

7 What change, if any, should be made in sentence 9?

- ⬭ Change *nixt* to **next**
- ⬭ Change *landed* to **lended**
- ⬭ Change *mud* to **mod**
- ⬭ Make no change

8 What change, if any, should be made in sentence 10?

- ⬭ Change *jomp* to **jump**
- ⬭ Change *splashed* to **spleshed**
- ⬭ Change *legs* to **lags**
- ⬭ Make no change

9 What change should be made in sentence 13?

- ⬭ Change *dust* to **dost**
- ⬭ Change *hand* to **hant**
- ⬭ Change *wint* to **went**
- ⬭ Change *plate* to **playt**

10 What change should be made in sentence 16?

- ⬭ Change *then* to **thin**
- ⬭ Change *dawg* to **dog**
- ⬭ Change *catch* to **cetch**
- ⬭ Change *make* to **maik**

Grammar, Usage, and Mechanics
What Is a Sentence?

A **sentence** tells one complete thought. It begins with a capital letter and ends with an end mark. A sentence has two parts.

The **subject** tells what the sentence is about:

> **The bus** came late.

The **predicate** tells what happened:

> The bus **came late**.

Practice Activity

A. Is each group of words a sentence? Write **yes** or **no**.

1. went to the store   **2.** I will get milk.

3. You need a bun.   **4.** A big ham

5. The dog cannot come in.

B. Write a complete sentence by adding a word from the box. Tell whether the missing word is the subject (**S**) or the predicate (**P**).

milk	jump	fog

6. _____ comes in the morning. **S** or **P**

7. Frogs and rabbits _____. **S** or **P**

8. _____ builds strong bones. **S** or **P**

Practice Activity A

1. _____

2. _____

3. _____

4. _____

5. _____

Practice Activity B

6. _____

7. _____

8. _____

The Writing Process: Narrative
Writing a Personal Narrative

PREWRITING
Sometimes people write stories about themselves called personal narratives. What did you do last summer? Make a list of the events in order. Look for personal narratives in books or have an adult help you search for them on the Internet.

DRAFTING
Use your list of events to write your own personal narrative. Use as many spelling words as you can.

REVISING
Read your narrative. Have you included a beginning, a middle, and an end? Write your final draft.

EDITING
Use the **Editing Checklist** to proofread your narrative. Use proofreading marks. Circle two words that may be misspelled. Use a dictionary to check the spelling.

PUBLISHING
Make a copy of your personal narrative and share it with your readers.

EDITING CHECKLIST

Spelling
- ✓ Circle words that contain the spelling patterns and rules learned in Units I–5.
- ✓ Check the circled words in your **Spelling Dictionary**.
- ✓ Check for other spelling errors.

Capital Letters
- ✓ Capitalize important words in the title.
- ✓ Capitalize the first word in each sentence.
- ✓ Capitalize proper nouns.

Punctuation
- ✓ End each sentence with the correct punctuation.
- ✓ Use commas, apostrophes, and quotation marks correctly.

 TEKS 2.23A Use phonological knowledge to match sounds to letters to construct unknown words.
2.23F Use resources to find correct spellings.

51

End with ll

1. _____
2. _____
3. _____
4. _____
5. _____
6. _____
7. _____

End with lk

8. _____
9. _____
10. _____

Connections to THINKING

Read the spelling words and sentences.

1.	chalk	I use **chalk** to write.
2.	fall	Winter comes after **fall**.
3.	wall	I cannot see over that **wall**.
4.	talk	We **talk** on the phone.
5.	ball	Throw me the **ball**.
6.	walk	Let's **walk** to the store.
7.	small	A frog is a **small** animal.
8.	tall	Matt is six feet **tall**.
9.	call	Did you **call** my name?
10.	all	I drank **all** my milk.

Think & Sort the spelling words.

1–7. Write the words that have the vowel sound in **ball** and end with **ll**.

8–10. Write the words that have the vowel sound in **ball** and end with **lk**.

Remember

The vowel sound you hear in **ball** and **talk** can be spelled **a**.

TEKS 2.23A Use phonological knowledge to match sounds to letters to construct unknown words.
2.23C Spell high-frequency words from a commonly used list.

Connections to PHONICS

You will use each spelling word once on this page.

Blend Sounds

Replace the vowel in each word to make a spelling word.

1. will

2. cell

3. bill

Sound and Letter Patterns

When two of the same consonants end a word, we say the consonants are complex. Answers for 4–7 will end with double, or complex, consonants. Circle the complex consonants in each word.

4. Write the spelling word that has three letters and ends with a double consonant.

5–6. Use your answer to number 4 to write two more rhyming words that have four letters.

7. Now use your answer to number 4 to write a rhyming word with five letters.

Use the Dictionary

Find these words in your **Spelling Dictionary**. Write the word that comes <u>after</u> each one.

8. chain   **9.** tale   **10.** wait

Blend Sounds

1. _____

2. _____

3. _____

Sound and Letter Patterns

4. _____

5. _____

6. _____

7. _____

Use the Dictionary

8. _____

9. _____

10. _____

TEKS 2.23A Use phonological knowledge to match sounds to letters to construct unknown words.
2.23Bi Spell words with common orthographic patterns and rules: complex consonants.
2.23C Spell high-frequency words from a commonly used list.

53

chalk	fall	wall	talk	ball
walk	small	tall	call	all

Word Categorization

Write the spelling word that fits each group.

1. say, speak, _____
2. run, jog, _____
3. bat, glove, _____

Complete the Analogies

Write a spelling word to complete each analogy.

4. **March** is to **September** as **spring** is to _____.
5. **Empty** is to **full** as **none** is to _____.
6. **Paper** is to **pen** as **chalkboard** is to _____.
7. **Big** is to **large** as **high** is to _____.
8. **Elephant** is to **big** as **mouse** is to _____.

Use Context Clues

Write a spelling word to complete each sentence.

9. After math, we will line up along the classroom _____.
10. Listen for the nurse to _____ your name.

Remember that the double consonant at the end of **ball** makes only one sound. Circle the double consonants in the words you wrote.

Word Categorization

1. _____
2. _____
3. _____

Complete the Analogies

4. _____
5. _____
6. _____
7. _____
8. _____

Use Context Clues

9. _____
10. _____

TEKS 2.23Bi Spell words with common orthographic patterns and rules: complex consonants.
2.23C Spell high-frequency words from a commonly used list.

Connections to WRITING

Proofread a Paragraph

Proofread the paragraph below for eight misspelled words. Then rewrite the paragraph. Write the spelling words correctly and make the corrections shown by the proofreading marks.

Proofreading Marks

☰	Capital Letter
/	Small Letter
∧	Add
ℒ	Delete
⊙	Add a Period
⊮	Indent

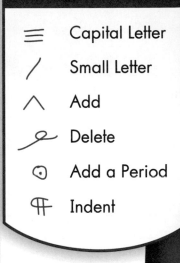

jones Field

We play boll at Jones Field. It is is a short wolk from my house. It is a smoll field, but the Grass is nice. My friends al like to play there Some can even hit the ball over the toll Jones field wol. I often cawl my Friends to tok about the fun we have at Jones Field.

DESCRIPTIVE Writing Prompt
Write a Paragraph

Write a paragraph to describe a place where you like to play. Use as many spelling words as you can.

- Use the writing process: prewrite, draft, revise, edit, and publish.
- Tell where the place is, what you do there, and what makes it special.
- Check your draft for complete sentences, correct spelling, grammar, capital letters, and punctuation.
- Read your writing. Circle two words that may be misspelled. Use a dictionary to check the spelling.

Transfer

Think of three more words that end with the **all** or the **alk** spelling pattern. These can be new words you used in your descriptive paragraph. Write the words in your Spelling Journal. Circle the spelling pattern **all** or **alk** in each word.

TEKS 2.23A Use phonological knowledge to match sounds to letters to construct unknown words. **2.23Bi** Spell words with common orthographic patterns and rules: complex consonants. **2.23C** Spell high-frequency words from a commonly used list. **2.23F** Use resources to find correct spellings.

Word Study

talk	all	ball	crosswalk	stalk
walk	chalk	tall	mall	stall
small	fall	almost	squall	
call	wall	crawl		

Pattern Power

1.

2.

3.

4.

Word Categorization

5.

6.

7.

Word Building

8.

9.

10.

Pattern Power

Use words from the box and follow these directions.

1–2. Write the five-letter words that have the **alk** spelling pattern.

3–4. Write the five-letter words that have the **all** spelling pattern.

Word Categorization

Write the word or words that best fit each group.

5. nearly, just about, _____

6–7. run, _____, _____

Word Building

Replace the underlined letter in each word to write a word from the box.

8. f_i_ll   **9.** tal_e_   **10.** _t_alk

TEKS 2.23Bi Spell words with common orthographic patterns and rules: complex consonants.
2.23C Spell high-frequency words from a commonly used list.

Art

Read the paragraphs below. Look for words with the vowel sound in **ball**.

Kurt Wenner is an artist. He crawls on the ground to make chalk drawings on sidewalks. Crowds watch him work fast. They like what he has done.

You can be an artist, too. Get some chalk and paper towels. Find a walkway and start. Make a castle with a wall. Draw a town with small houses. Add green lawns. Sketch a tall tree. Draw a hawk in the sky. Choose almost anything. Use towels to blend colors.

People will walk by. They will always stop to talk. They will all call you a sidewalk artist, too.

1. _____
2. _____
3. _____
4. _____
5. _____
6. _____
7. _____
8. _____

WORD SORT

1–2. Write the two-syllable words that have the **alk** pattern.

3. Write the word with the **all** pattern that means the opposite of **large**.

4–8. Write the words that have the **aw** pattern.

TEKS 2.23Bi Spell words with common orthographic patterns and rules: complex consonants.
2.23C Spell high-frequency words from a commonly used list.

Consonant Blends

Read the spelling words and sentences.

1.	flat	I made a **flat** pancake.
2.	glass	I fill the **glass** with milk.
3.	plant	The **plant** grows in a pot.
4.	dress	Amy wears a red **dress**.
5.	front	Sit in the **front** seat.
6.	bring	May I **bring** you some food?
7.	grass	She cuts the **grass**.
8.	glad	I feel **glad** to be here.
9.	clap	We **clap** to the beat.
10.	class	Our **class** has ten boys in it.

Think & Sort the spelling words.

1–4. Write the words that begin with consonant + **r** blends.

5–10. Write the words that begin with consonant + **l** blends.

Remember

A **consonant blend** is two or more consonants together that make more than one sound: **gl** in **glad** and **dr** in **dress**. Many consonants blend with **l** and **r**.

Consonant + r blends

1.

2.

3.

4.

Consonant + l blends

5.

6.

7.

8.

9.

10.

TEKS 2.23A Use phonological knowledge to match sounds to letters to construct unknown words. **2.23Bi** Spell words with common orthographic patterns and rules: complex consonants. **2.23C** Spell high-frequency words from a commonly used list.

Sound and Letter Patterns

Follow the directions to write a spelling word.
Circle the consonant blends.

1. chant – ch + pl = _____
2. mad – m + gl = _____
3. sing – s + br = _____
4. pass – p + gr = _____
5. tap – t + cl = _____

Consonant Blends

Write the spelling word that begins with
the same consonant blend as the three words
in each group. Circle the consonant blend that
begins your word.

6. from, frog, frost, _____
7. drop, drive, drink, _____

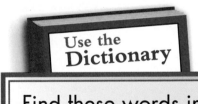
Use the Dictionary

Find these words in your **Spelling Dictionary**.
Write the word that comes <u>before</u> each one.
Circle the consonant blend that begins each word.

8. glossy   9. clean   10. fluffy

Sound and Letter Patterns

1. _____
2. _____
3. _____
4. _____
5. _____

Consonant Blends

6. _____
7. _____

Use the Dictionary

8. _____
9. _____
10. _____

 TEKS 2.23A Use phonological knowledge to match sounds to letters to construct unknown words.
2.23Bi Spell words with common orthographic patterns and rules: complex consonants. **2.23C** Spell
high-frequency words from a commonly used list.

59

flat	glass	plant	dress	front
bring	grass	glad	clap	class

Use Antonyms

Antonyms are words that mean the opposite. Write the antonym for each word. Circle the consonant blends.

1. take   **2.** sad   **3.** back

Multiple Meanings

Use the same spelling word in both blanks to complete this sentence.

4. We will _____ a large _____ next to the house.

Word Categorization

Write the spelling word that belongs in each group.

5. mug, cup, _____

6. level, even, _____

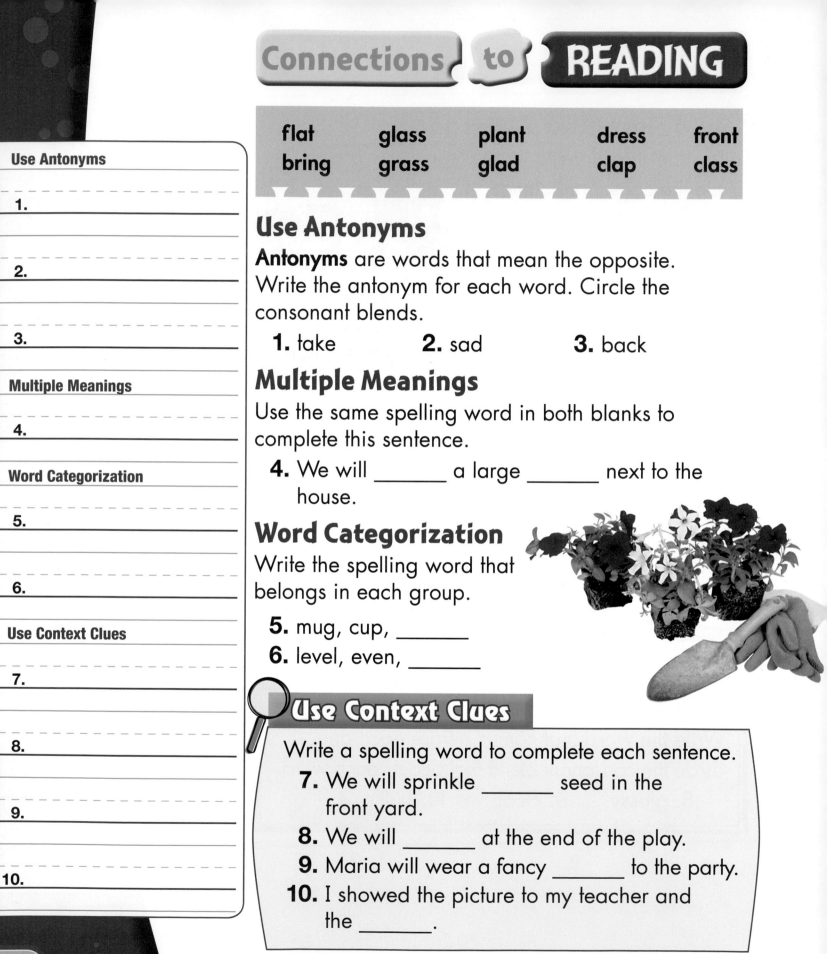

Use Context Clues

Write a spelling word to complete each sentence.

7. We will sprinkle _____ seed in the front yard.

8. We will _____ at the end of the play.

9. Maria will wear a fancy _____ to the party.

10. I showed the picture to my teacher and the _____.

Use Antonyms

1. _____

2. _____

3. _____

Multiple Meanings

4. _____

Word Categorization

5. _____

6. _____

Use Context Clues

7. _____

8. _____

9. _____

10. _____

TEKS 2.23C Spell high-frequency words from a commonly used list.

Connections to WRITING

Proofread an E-Mail Message

Proofread the e-mail message below for eight misspelled words. Then rewrite the message. Write the spelling words correctly and make the corrections shown by the proofreading marks.

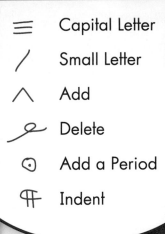

Send	Save as a Draft	Cancel	Attach Files

From: JG99@kids.com

To: Patti@fastmail.com

Subject: School Cleanup

Patti∧

The school cleanup is on f̲riday. Our clas is meeting at 8 a.m⊙ We will cut the gras in fornt and pick up glas. We will also plannt some F/lowers. Dess in i̶n̶ old clothes and birng trash bags. I am gladd you can help.

José

EXPOSITORY Writing Prompt
Write an E-mail Message

Write an e-mail message to a friend. Ask your friend to do something with you. Use as many spelling words as you can.

- Use the writing process: prewrite, draft, revise, edit, and publish.
- Tell the time, the place, and what to bring.
- Check your draft for correct spelling, grammar, capital letters, and punctuation.
- Use a print dictionary or an online dictionary to check your spelling.

Transfer
Think of six more words that begin with a **consonant blend**. Find words with **consonant + r** blends and **consonant + l** blends. These can be words you used in your e-mail. Write the words in your Spelling Journal. Circle the consonant blend in each word.

 TEKS 2.23A Use phonological knowledge to match sounds to letters to construct unknown words. **2.23Bi** Spell words with common orthographic patterns and rules: complex consonants. **2.23C** Spell high-frequency words from a commonly used list.

Word Study

broom	front	flat	clap	fluffy
cluck	grass	glass	cliff	frisky
frog	glad	dress	grand	glossy
plant	class	bring	platter	grumpy

Use Synonyms

A **synonym** is a word that means the same or nearly the same as another word. Write the word from the list that means the same as these words.

1. soft   **3.** large dish

2. student group   **4.** shiny

Check your answers in a dictionary.

Pattern Power

5–6. Write the two-syllable words that have a consonant + **r** blend.

Word Endings

Remove the endings from these words to make a word in the list.

7. planting   **9.** clapping

8. bringing   **10.** flattest

Use Synonyms

1.

2.

3.

4.

Pattern Power

5.

6.

Word Endings

7.

8.

9.

10.

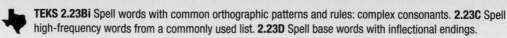

TEKS 2.23Bi Spell words with common orthographic patterns and rules: complex consonants. **2.23C** Spell high-frequency words from a commonly used list. **2.23D** Spell base words with inflectional endings.

Science

Word  Hunt

Read the paragraphs below. Look for words with consonant blends.

Our class read about plants, trees, and grass. We learned that they grow in many different kinds of places. Only a few plants grow in dry, flat deserts. Plants need to put down roots. People plow the soil to make it loose where rocky ground is hard.

Plants need warm, sunny days to grow well. They need water that rain can bring. Plants get food from water, the soil, and the sunshine.

We planted a grand garden at school. It was soon full of fresh vegetables and fruit. We are glad our plants got what they needed.

1. _____

2. _____

3. _____

4. _____

5. _____

6. _____

7. _____

8. _____

WORD SORT

1–4. Write the words that have a **gr blend**.

5–8. Write the words that have a **pl blend**.

TEKS 2.23Bi Spell words with common orthographic patterns and rules: complex consonants.
2.23C Spell high-frequency words from a commonly used list.

63

Connections to THINKING

Read the spelling words and sentences.

1.	wink	Can you **wink** at me?
2.	sing	We **sing** songs in class.
3.	sink	Do not let the boat **sink**.
4.	king	A **king** may wear a crown.
5.	long	That dog has a **long** tail.
6.	ring	The **ring** is made of gold.
7.	hang	I **hang** the shirt on the line.
8.	bank	We get money at the **bank**.
9.	wing	The bird's **wing** is broken.
10.	drink	I **drink** a lot of water.

Think & Sort the spelling words.

1–4. Write the words that include the consonant blend **nk**.

5–10. Write the words that include the consonant digraph **ng**.

Remember

A **consonant blend** is two or more consonants together that make more than one sound.

A **consonant digraph** is two consonants together that make one new sound.

nk

1. _____
2. _____
3. _____
4. _____

ng

5. _____
6. _____
7. _____
8. _____
9. _____
10. _____

TEKS 2.23A Use phonological knowledge to match sounds to letters to construct unknown words. 2.23Bi Spell words with common orthographic patterns and rules: complex consonants. 2.23C Spell high-frequency words from a commonly used list.

Segment Sounds

Follow the directions to write a spelling word.

1. Change the **nk** in **wink** to make this spelling word.
2. Change the **t** in **kit** to make this spelling word.
3. Change the **a** in **sang** to make this spelling word.
4. Change the **nk** in **rink** to make this spelling word.

Word Structure

Follow the directions to write the spelling words.

5. Change one letter in **drank** to make this word.
6. Change one letter in **hand** to make this word.
7. Change two letters in **ball** to make this word.
8. Change two letters in **lost** to make this word.

Use the Dictionary

A dictionary lists words in a-b-c order. Write the word that comes <u>after</u> each of these words in your **Spelling Dictionary**.

9. sing   10. wing

Circle the **ng** consonant digraph in the words that you wrote.

Segment Sounds
1.
2.
3.
4.

Word Structure
5.
6.
7.
8.

Use the Dictionary
9.
10.

TEKS 2.23A Use phonological knowledge to match sounds to letters to construct unknown words.
2.23Bi Spell words with common orthographic patterns and rules: complex consonants.
2.23C Spell high-frequency words from a commonly used list.

wink	sing	sink	king	long
ring	hang	bank	wing	drink

Use Synonyms

Write the spelling word that could replace the underlined word or words.

1. An overloaded boat might <u>go down below the water</u>.

2. The <u>person who rules</u> put on his fancy robes for the party.

3. We need to draw a <u>circle</u> around the right word.

Make Inferences

Write the spelling word with the **ng** consonant digraph that completes each sentence.

4. We had to wait in line for a very _____ time.

5. Chang ate a drumstick, and Sam ate a _____.

Use Context Clues

Write a spelling word to complete each sentence.

6. The class will _____ for the king.

7. Ebony will _____ her picture next to mine.

8. I saw you _____ at me!

9. A cool _____ would be good right now.

10. I want to thank the man at the _____.

Use Synonyms

1.

2.

3.

Make Inferences

4.

5.

Use Context Clues

6.

7.

8.

9.

10.

TEKS 2.23Bi Spell words with common orthographic patterns and rules: complex consonants.
2.23C Spell high-frequency words from a commonly used list.

Connections to WRITING

Proofread an Ad

Proofread the ad below for eight misspelled words. Then rewrite the ad. Write the spelling words correctly and make the corrections shown by the proofreading marks.

> **Rent my Rowboat
> Just $5 a Day!**
>
> It is 10 feet log and will not singk. It is on the bak of the Haley River. You can row in it and fish and snig! You can winnk at people as you go by. You can eat and drinke as you float along. You will feel like a keeng with a golden rig.
>
> **Call Em at 555-2440.**

PERSUASIVE Writing Prompt

Write an Ad

Write an ad for something you might sell or rent to someone. Use as many spelling words as you can.

- Use the writing process: prewrite, draft, revise, edit, and publish.
- Tell who would want to buy your item. Add features that would appeal to your audience, tell what it costs and how and where to get it.
- Check your draft for correct spelling, grammar, capital letters, and punctuation.
- Circle two words that may be misspelled. Use a dictionary to check the spelling.

Transfer

Think of six more words that have **ng** or **nk**. These can be new words you used in your ad. Write the words in your Spelling Journal. Circle the **ng** or **nk** in each word.

TEKS. 2.23A Use phonological knowledge to match sounds to letters to construct unknown words. **2.23Bi** Spell words with common orthographic patterns and rules: complex consonants. **2.23C** Spell high-frequency words from a commonly used list. **2.23F** Use resources to find correct spellings.

Word Study

bending	king	wink	wing	blink
doing	long	sink	belong	cranky
going	bank	ring	kingdom	finger
sing	drink	hang	think	swing

Categorizing Words

Categorizing Words

1.

2.

3.

4.

5.

Use words from the box to complete the activities.
Write the word that belongs to each group.

1. queen, prince, _____

2. chant, hum, _____

3. bracelet, necklace, _____

4. slide, seesaw, _____

5. arm, fin, _____

Rhyming Words

Rhyming Words

6.

7.

Write the word that rhymes.

6. thank, sank, _____

7. rang, bang, _____

Pattern Power

Pattern Power

8.

9.

10.

8–10. Write the five-letter words with the
ink pattern.

TEKS 2.23Bi Spell words with common orthographic patterns and rules: complex consonants. **2.23C** Spell high-frequency words from a commonly used list.

Social Studies

Word Hunt

Read the story below. Look for words with the **ng** and **nk** patterns.

If you want to buy something, you need money. Hugo wanted to buy a bike of his own. He found out how much the one he wanted cost. He had been saving for a long time, but he didn't have enough in the bank.

To earn money, Hugo asked his Dad if there were any jobs he could do around the house and how much they would be worth. "We'll think of something for you," Dad said, as he winked at Hugo. "Those dishes in the sink need to be washed. You can weed the garden, and you can fix the wing on your sister's airplane."

Hugo finally earned money and got his bikc. He thanked his parents for helping him.

1. _____
2. _____
3. _____
4. _____
5. _____
6. _____
7. _____
8. _____

WORD SORT

1–3. Write the words with more than four letters that have the **nk** pattern.

4–8. Write the words that have the **ng** digraph.

TEKS 2.23Bi Spell words with common orthographic patterns and rules: complex consonants.
2.23C Spell high-frequency words from a commonly used list.

Connections to THINKING

Read the spelling words and sentences.

Short a
1.

Short e
2.
3.

Short i
4.
5.
6.

Short u
7.
8.
9.
10.

1. give   I **give** the pen to Emma.
2. come   Can you **come** out to play?
3. does   What **does** that robot do?
4. done   He has **done** well in school.
5. been   Have you **been** to the park?
6. head   Take that hat off your **head**.
7. some   We stopped to eat **some** lunch.
8. live   Do you **live** on my street?
9. have   We **have** fun in gym every day.
10. said   Alex **said** he can walk home.

Think & Sort the spelling words.

1. Write the word with the **short a** sound.

2–3. Write the words with the **short e** sound.

4–6. Write the words with the **short i** sound.

7–10. Write the words with the **short u** sound.

Remember

Some short vowel sounds are spelled with two vowels: **ai** in **said, ee** in **been,** and **ave** in **have**.

TEKS 2.23A Use phonological knowledge to match sounds to letters to construct unknown words.
2.23C Spell high-frequency words from a commonly used list.

Segment Sounds

Write a spelling word for each set of letter sounds.

1. It begins like **dog** and ends like **one**. _____
2. It begins like **sun** and ends like **come**. _____
3. It begins like **hang** and rhymes with **bed**. _____

Sounds and Letters

4. Write the spelling word that spells the **short a** sound **a-consonant-e**.
5. Write the spelling word that can have a **short i** sound or a **long i** sound.
6. Write the spelling word that ends with a /**z**/ sound but not the letter **z**.
7. Write the spelling word that begins with the /**k**/ sound.

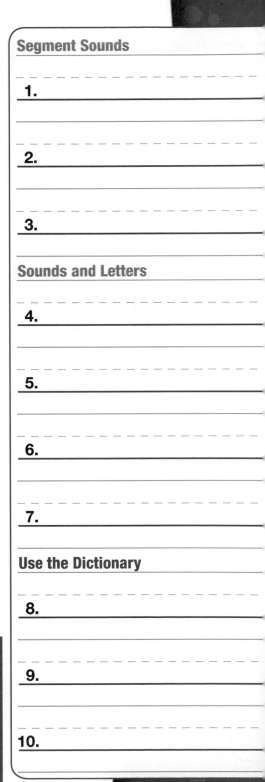

Segment Sounds

1. _____

2. _____

3. _____

Sounds and Letters

4. _____

5. _____

6. _____

7. _____

Use the Dictionary

8. _____

9. _____

10. _____

Use the Dictionary

A dictionary lists words in a-b-c order. Write the word that comes <u>before</u> each of these words in your **Spelling Dictionary**.

8. glad   **9.** beeswax   **10.** salad

 TEKS 2.23A Use phonological knowledge to match sounds to letters to construct unknown words.
2.23C Spell high-frequency words from a commonly used list.

71

give	come	does	done	been
head	some	live	have	said

Word Meaning

Write a spelling word that fits each clue.

1. This word can mean the opposite of "take away."
2. It is part of the body.
3. It means "do" and is used with **he, she,** and **it**.
4. This word can mean the opposite of "go."

Word Categorization

Write the spelling word that belongs in each group.

5. be, being, _____
6. say, saying, _____
7. do, did, _____
8. _____, lived, living

Use Context Clues

Write the spelling word that completes the sentence.

9. What do you _____ in your lunch box today?
10. Julio and I will play _____ songs for you.

Word Meaning

1.
2.
3.
4.

Word Categorization

5.
6.
7.
8.

Use Context Clues

9.
10.

TEKS 2.23C Spell high-frequency words from a commonly used list.

Connections to WRITING

Proofread an Invitation

Proofread the invitation below for eight misspelled words. Then rewrite the invitation. Write the spelling words correctly and make the corrections shown by the proofreading marks.

Proofreading Marks

≡ Capital Letter

/ Small Letter

∧ Add

⌇ Delete

⊙ Add a Period

⫪ Indent

> **You Are Invited!**
>
> **What?**   I am going to giv a party. We will play som games and hafe fun.
>
> **Where?**   I liv at 237 Brown Street.
>
> **When?**   Please kum at 3:00 on june 24. The party will be dun at at 4:00.
>
> **Why?**   I have bin wanting to have a Party all summer. Mom and dad finally sed I could have one!

EXPOSITORY Writing Prompt

Write an Invitation

You are having a party! Write a party invitation to tell your friends about it. Use as many spelling words as you can.

- Use the writing process: prewrite, draft, revise, edit, and publish.
- Be sure to tell what will happen, where it will happen, and when it will happen.
- Check your draft for correct spelling, grammar, capital letters, and punctuation.
- Circle two words that may be misspelled. Use a dictionary to check the spelling.

Transfer

Think of six more words that have short vowel sounds. Try to find words that have the **short vowel sound** spelled with more than one letter, such as **said** and with vowel-consonant-e, such as **come**. Write the words in your Spelling Journal. Circle the letter or letters that spell the **short vowel sound** in each word.

TEKS 2.23A Use phonological knowledge to match sounds to letters to construct unknown words.
2.23C Spell high-frequency words from a commonly used list. **2.23F** Use resources to find correct spellings.

Word Study

and	been	give	live	glove
fix	some	come	become	gone
leg	have	done	love	shiver
does	said	head	nothing	shovel

Pattern Power

Use words from the box and follow these directions.

1–4. Write the words that have the **short vowel sound** spelled with two vowels together.

5–7. Write the two-syllable words that have the **short vowel sound** in the first syllable.

Word Building

Replace the underlined letters in each word to write a word from the box.

8. <u>e</u>nd

9. <u>st</u>ove

10. l<u>o</u>g

Pattern Power

1. _____

2. _____

3. _____

4. _____

5. _____

6. _____

7. _____

Word Building

8. _____

9. _____

10. _____

 TEKS 2.23A Use phonological knowledge to match sounds to letters to construct unknown words.
2.23C Spell high-frequency words from a commonly used list.

Math

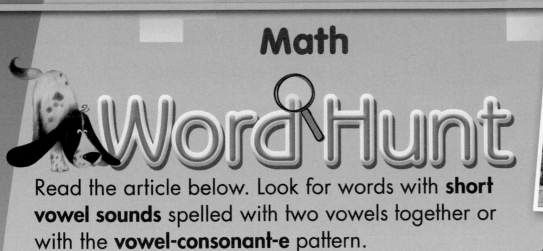

Word Hunt

Read the article below. Look for words with **short vowel sounds** spelled with two vowels together or with the **vowel-consonant-e** pattern.

Do you love to live on the beach during the summer? Many beach-goers have said that nothing is more fun than to build a sand castle. Head for the beach. Come with a shovel and a bucket. Bring containers to form cubes, domes, and cones.

Find a good spot away from the tide. Spread out the sand. Wet some sand and pack it to form a base. Pack sand in a bucket, cup, or cone. Make shapes to build walls and towers. Use water to fix cracks. Does your work look done? Wait! You can add shapes like circles and diamonds. Add some seashells. A pile of sand has now become a wonderful castle.

1. _____
2. _____
3. _____
4. _____
5. _____
6. _____
7. _____
8. _____

WORD SORT

1–5. Write the words that have a **short vowel sound** spelled with two vowels together in the word.

6–8. Write words in the first paragraph that spell a **short vowel sound** with **vowel + consonant + e**.

TEKS 2.23A Use phonological knowledge to match sounds to letters to construct unknown words.
2.23C Spell high-frequency words from a commonly used list.

Connections to THINKING

Read the spelling words and sentences.

1.	cute	That baby has a **cute** face.
2.	wave	The children **wave** good-bye.
3.	robe	My **robe** keeps me warm.
4.	late	Don't be **late** for school.
5.	mule	A **mule** is a big, slow animal.
6.	tape	I **tape** the sign to the wall.
7.	joke	The **joke** was very funny.
8.	fire	Wood burns in a **fire**.
9.	pipe	Water runs through that **pipe**.
10.	base	Sean ran to first **base**.

Think & Sort the spelling words.

1–4. Write the words with the **a-consonant-e** pattern.

5–6. Write the words with the **i-consonant-e** pattern.

7–8. Write the words with the **o-consonant-e** pattern.

9–10. Write the words with the **u-consonant-e** pattern.

Remember

Long vowel sounds can be spelled with the **vowel-consonant-e** pattern.

a-consonant-e

1. _____
2. _____
3. _____
4. _____

i-consonant -e

5. _____
6. _____

o-consonant-e

7. _____
8. _____

u-consonant-e

9. _____
10. _____

TEKS 2.23A Use phonological knowledge to match sounds to letters to construct unknown words. **2.23Biii** Spell words with common orthographic patterns and rules: long vowels. **2.23C** Spell high-frequency words from a commonly used list.

Blend Sounds

Use the clues to find the words. Write the spelling words.

1. four letters, three sounds, rhymes with **date** __1.__
2. four letters, three sounds, starts like **come** __2.__
3. four letters, three sounds, rhymes with **tire** __3.__
4. four letters, three sounds, starts like **top** __4.__

Vowel Sounds

Write the spelling words that have the same vowel sound as the words in each group.

5–6. road, pole, _____, _____

7. music, cute, _____

Find these words in your **Spelling Dictionary**. Write the word that comes <u>before</u> each of them.

8. baseball   9. we   10. plain

Blend Sounds
1.
2.
3.
4.

Vowel Sounds
5.
6.
7.

Use the Dictionary
8.
9.
10.

TEKS 2.23A Use phonological knowledge to match sounds to letters to construct unknown words. **2.23Biii** Spell words with common orthographic patterns and rules: long vowels. **2.23C** Spell high-frequency words from a commonly used list.

cute	wave	robe	late	mule
tape	joke	fire	pipe	base

Rhyme Time

The circus is coming. It's going to be great!
We need to get ready. We cannot be **1.** .
A clown will be riding (she doesn't need fuel),
She'll come into town on the back of a **2.** .
Her face will be painted, and there's no dispute.
The clothes she'll be wearing really are **3.** .
So get ready now, your place I will save.
When she comes by we will give a big **4.** .

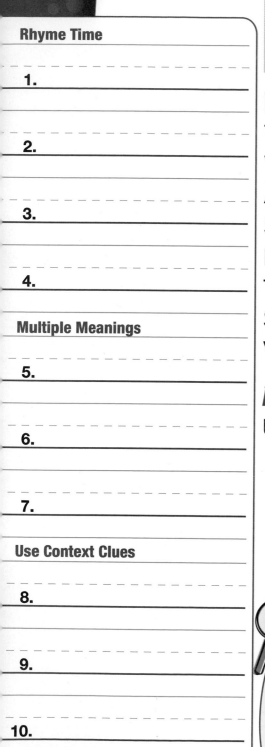

Multiple Meanings

Use the same word on both blanks.

5. We will _____ the sign up with _____.
6. Dad decided to _____ up the _____ to keep warm.
7. Angelo will _____ his story on his run to third _____.

Use Context Clues

Write a spelling word to complete each sentence.

8. Water dripped slowly out of the _____.
9. I didn't find that _____ funny at all.
10. The judge wore a long, black _____.

Rhyme Time

1.
2.
3.
4.

Multiple Meanings

5.
6.
7.

Use Context Clues

8.
9.
10.

TEKS. 2.23C Spell high-frequency words from a commonly used list.

Connections to WRITING

Proofread a Story

Find eight misspelled words in the story below. Rewrite the story using correct spelling. Make the corrections shown by the proofreading marks.

¶Ben was lait to his baseball game⊙ He needed to tap his sore hand first. Ben gave the coach a wav when he got to the field. Ben looked at first bays. There was a myule standing there! No one knew what to do. <u>s</u>hould they call the ~~P~~olice? Should they call a fyre truck? A farmer from nearby came and ~~and~~ took the cut animal home. Now it's a big joak that a mule had been playing in Ben's place!

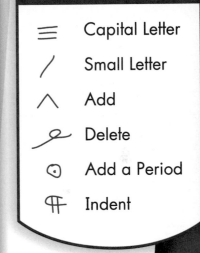

Proofreading Marks

≡	Capital Letter
/	Small Letter
∧	Add
℮	Delete
⊙	Add a Period
¶	Indent

NARRATIVE Writing Prompt

Write a Story

Write a made-up story that seems real. Use as many spelling words as you can.

- Use the writing process: prewrite, draft, revise, edit, publish.
- Make sure your story has a beginning, a middle, and an end.
- Tell the story events in order.
- Use complete sentences and check your spelling, grammar, capital letters, and punctuation.
- Read your story. Circle two words that may be misspelled. Use a dictionary to check the spelling.

Transfer

Think of six more words that have long vowels spelled **vowel-consonant-e.** Write the words in your Spelling Journal. Circle the letter or letters that spell the **long vowel sound** in each word.

TEKS 2.23A Use phonological knowledge to match sounds to letters to construct unknown words. **2.23Biii** Spell words with common orthographic patterns and rules: long vowels. **2.23C** Spell high-frequency words from a commonly used list. **2.23F** Use resources to find correct spellings.

Word Study

bone	late	wave	pipe	chute
made	joke	robe	broke	crate
ride	fire	mule	face	twine
cute	base	tape	size	zone

Pattern Power

Use words from the box and follow these directions.

1. Write the word that begins like **ride** and ends with **o-consonant-e**.

2. Write the five-letter word that ends with **o-consonant-e**.

3–4. Write two words that rhyme with **chase**.

Meaning Mastery

Write the word that matches each meaning.

5. a box used for storage

6. amount of space a thing takes up

Change the Vowel Sound

Change each word into a long vowel word in the box by adding **e**.

7. rid   **8.** rob   **9.** twin   **10.** tap

Pattern Power

1.

2.

3.

4.

Meaning Mastery

5.

6.

Change the Vowel Sound

7.

8.

9.

10.

80

TEKS 2.23A Use phonological knowledge to match sounds to letters to construct unknown words. **2.23Biii** Spell words with common orthographic patterns and rules: long vowels. **2.23C** Spell high-frequency words from a commonly used list.

Technology

Word Hunt

Read the article below. Look for words with **long vowels** spelled **vowel-consonant-e**.

Do you want to plan a trip? Use the Internet. Let's go to Bryce Canyon. Type the name of the place or website to search. Click to open the site.

Plans can be made online. Click on the link "Plan Your Visit." Find out if it's too late to book a spot in a base camp. Read about a trail ride on a mule. Plan a hike. You can print a map of the trail. Learn fire safety rules.

The "Nature and Science" link shows animals you might see, such as a cute squirrel. "For Kids" shows things kids can do and links to games.

Print or save information. The Internet can help you plan any trip.

1. _____
2. _____
3. _____
4. _____
5. _____
6. _____
7. _____
8. _____

WORD SORT

1–6. Write the words with **long i** spelled **i-consonant-e**.

7–8. Write the words with **long u** spelled **u-consonant-e**.

TEKS 2.23A Use phonological knowledge to match sounds to letters to construct unknown words. **2.23Biii** Spell words with common orthographic patterns and rules: long vowels. **2.23C** Spell high-frequency words from a commonly used list.

Assess for Transfer

Units 7–11

Unit 7

1. _____

2. _____

Unit 8

3. _____

4. _____

Unit 9

5. _____

6. _____

7. _____

Unit 10

8. _____

Unit 11

9. _____

10. _____

Assessment

Write each assessment word under the unit number it fits. Use each word once.

Unit 7

1–2. The vowel sound you hear in **ball** and **talk** can be spelled **a**.

Unit 8

3–4. A **consonant blend** is two or more consonants together that make more than one sound.

Unit 9

5–7. A **consonant blend** is two or more consonants together that make more than one sound. A **consonant digraph** is two consonants together that make one new sound.

Unit 10

8. Some short vowel sounds are spelled with two vowels together.

Unit 11

9–10. Long vowel sounds can be spelled with the **vowel-consonant-e** pattern.

Words for Assessment

cove

dead

sung

hate

salt

grip

tank

hall

flap

ink

Unit 7: Vowel Sound: al

all	talk	small	walk	call

Write the spelling word that matches the clues. Use each word once.

1. This word begins like **smell** and rhymes with **tall**.

2. This word has four letters and rhymes with **hall**.

3. This word begins with a vowel and rhymes with **fall**.

4. This word begins like **wind** and rhymes with **chalk**.

5. This word begins like **tip** and rhymes with **stalk**.

Unit 8: Consonant Blends

glad	grass	plant	front	class

Write the spelling word that begins with the same consonant blend as the two words in each group. Circle the consonant blend that begins your word.

6. grin, green, _____

7. place, plug, _____

8. frost, fresh, _____

9. glow, glide, _____

10. clean, clip, _____

Unit 7

1. _____

2. _____

3. _____

4. _____

5. _____

Unit 8

6. _____

7. _____

8. _____

9. _____

10. _____

Unit 9

1.

2.

3.

4.

5.

Unit 10

6.

7.

8.

9.

10.

Unit 9: Blend: nk, Digraph: ng

| bank | sing | drink | long | king |

Change the vowel in each word to make a spelling word.

1. bunk

2. sang

3. drank

4. lung

5. Replace the **ss** in **kiss** to make a spelling word.

Unit 10: Short Vowel Sounds

| said | some | been | does | have |

Write a spelling word by adding the missing letters.

6. h ___ v ___

7. d ___ ___ s

8. b ___ ___ n

9. s ___ m ___

10. s ___ ___ d

Unit 11: Vowel-Consonant-e

late	joke	fire	cute	base

Write the spelling word that has the same vowel sound pattern as the words in each group.

1. hope, nose, _____

2. smile, kite, _____

3. mule, huge, _____

4. same, take, _____

5. grade, save, _____

Unit 11

1. _____

2. _____

3. _____

4. _____

5. _____

Spelling Study Strategy

Sorting by Sounds and Spellings

1. Work in groups of five. Choose spelling words from Units 7–11.

2. Have each person write one of these labels on a piece of paper: (1) Vowel Sound: **al**; (2) **gl, gr, pl, fl, fr, cl, dr, br**; (3) **ng, nk**; (4) Short Vowel Sound; (5) Vowel-Consonant-e.

3. Each person writes a spelling word on the paper with the label that fits the word's spelling pattern.

4. Go over each list together and check the spelling.

Standardized Test Practice

Directions: Read the introduction and the passage that follows. Then read each question and fill in the space in front of the correct answer.

Erin wrote this story about a lonely king who loses his mule. She wants you to review her paper. As you read, think about ways Erin can make her story better.

The King's Mule

(1) Kign Erd ruled a small country. (2) He loved his people but he was lonely. (3) He did not have a queen, but he did have a favorite muel. (4) Every day, he put on his robe and walked into the tall gras in front of the castle. (5) He would rub the mule's hed and talk to it like a friend.

(6) One day the mule was missing. (7) The king decided to call oll of his people together. (8) "I will give my beautiful glass ring to whoever finds the mule," he sed.

(9) No one could find the mule because the king's maid Nia had hidden it behind a wall. (10) She had been lonely, too. (11) Nia wanted the king to tolk to her, not the mule. (12) But now the king had a long face and wasn't talking at all.

(13) The maid decided to brign the mule back, and she told the king why she had hidden it. (14) The king was so gladd to find someone else who was lonely. (15) He had found his queen, and he gave Nia the ring as he had promised.

GO ON

1 What change, if any, should be made in sentence 1?

- ◯ Change *Kign* to **King**
- ◯ Change *ruled* to **rooled**
- ◯ Change *small* to **smoll**
- ◯ Make no change

2 What change, if any, should be made in sentence 3?

- ◯ Change *did* to **ded**
- ◯ Change *have* to **hav**
- ◯ Change *muel* to **mule**
- ◯ Make no change

3 What change should be made in sentence 4?

- ◯ Change *robe* to **rob**
- ◯ Change *tall* to **tawl**
- ◯ Change *gras* to **grass**
- ◯ Change *front* to **frunt**

4 What change, if any, should be made in sentence 5?

- ◯ Change *rub* to **rubb**
- ◯ Change *hed* to **head**
- ◯ Change *like* to **liek**
- ◯ Make no change

5 What change, if any, should be made in sentence 7?

- ◯ Change *king* to **kign**
- ◯ Change *call* to **coll**
- ◯ Change *oll* to **all**
- ◯ Make no change

6 What change should be made in sentence 8?

- ◯ Change *give* to **giv**
- ◯ Change *glass* to **glas**
- ◯ Change *ring* to **rin**
- ◯ Change *sed* to **said**

7 What change, if any, should be made in sentence 9?

- ◯ Change *find* to **finde**
- ◯ Change *hidden* to **hiden**
- ◯ Change *wall* to **woll**
- ◯ Make no change

8 What change, if any, should be made in sentence 11?

- ◯ Change *wanted* to **wonted**
- ◯ Change *tolk* to **talk**
- ◯ Change *mule* to **muel**
- ◯ Make no change

9 What change, if any, should be made in sentence 13?

- ◯ Change *brign* to **bring**
- ◯ Change *back* to **bake**
- ◯ Change *told* to **tolled**
- ◯ Make no change

10 What change, if any, should be made in sentence 14?

- ◯ Change *gladd* to **glad**
- ◯ Change *find* to **fined**
- ◯ Change *so* to **soe**
- ◯ Make no change

STOP

Grammar, Usage, and Mechanics
Sentences That Tell, Sentences That Ask

A **telling sentence** makes a statement.
It ends with a period.

> The grass is wet.

An **asking sentence** asks a question.
It ends with a question mark.

> Is the grass wet?

Both kinds of sentences begin with a capital letter.

Practice Activity

A. What kind of sentence is each one below?
Write **telling** or **asking**.

1. Does Mom know?
2. Who has a ball?
3. The dogs are cute.
4. I will come, too.
5. Did Dan call?
6. The farm is flat.

| said | walk | plant | joke |

B. Write the word that completes each sentence.

7. Did you tell that funny _____?

8. Juan _____, "Yes, I will."

9. We can _____ home together.

10. Will the _____ grow soon?

Practice Activity A

1.

2.

3.

4.

5.

6.

Practice Activity B

7.

8.

9.

10.

The Writing Process: Narrative
Writing a Friendly Letter

PREWRITING
A fun way to tell stories is to write a friendly letter. You can write a letter to a friend, a family member, or a pen pal. Think about a story that will be fun to read. Make a list of the events in order.

DRAFTING
Use your list of events to write a friendly letter. Make sure your letter has all five parts: heading, greeting, body, closing, and signature. Use spelling words.

REVISING
Read your letter. Check to see if you included all of the events on your list. Did you include all five parts of a friendly letter? Now write your final draft.

EDITING
Use the **Editing Checklist** to proofread your letter. Use proofreading marks. Circle two words that may be misspelled. Use a dictionary to check your spelling.

PUBLISHING
Make a copy of your friendly letter. Ask an adult to help you address and mail your letter.

EDITING CHECKLIST

Spelling
✓ Circle words that contain the spelling rules and patterns learned in Units 7–11.
✓ Check the circled words in your **Spelling Dictionary**.
✓ Check for other spelling errors.

Capital Letters
✓ Capitalize important words in the title.
✓ Capitalize the first word in each sentence.
✓ Capitalize proper nouns.

Punctuation
✓ End each sentence with the correct punctuation.
✓ Use commas, apostrophes, and quotation marks correctly.

 TEKS 2.23A Use phonological knowledge to match sounds to letters to construct unknown words.
2.23F Use resources to find correct spellings.

Connections to THINKING

Read the spelling words and sentences.

a-consonant-e	
1.	
2.	
3.	

ai

| 4. | |
| 5. | |

ay

6.	
7.	
8.	
9.	
10.	

1. safe — This is a **safe** place.
2. day — What **day** of the week is it?
3. rain — I can't run fast in the **rain**.
4. say — Please **say** yes.
5. play — Will you **play** catch with me?
6. ate — Who **ate** the last plum?
7. stay — Let's **stay** here for an hour.
8. save — Everyone can help **save** water.
9. may — You **may** come in.
10. wait — I **wait** for the mail to come.

Think & Sort the spelling words.

1–3. Write the words with **long a** spelled **a-consonant-e**.

4–5. Write the words with **long a** spelled **ai**.

6–10. Write the words with **long a** spelled **ay**.

Remember

The **long a** sound can be spelled in different ways: **a-consonant-e** in **safe**, **ai** in **rain**, and **ay** in **day**.

TEKS 2.23A Use phonological knowledge to match sounds to letters to construct unknown words. **2.23Biii** Spell words with common orthographic patterns and rules: long vowels. **2.23C** Spell high-frequency words from a commonly used list.

Segmentation

Write the spelling word that fits each clue.

1. It begins like **race** and ends like **tin**.

2. It begins like **stop** and ends like **pay**.

3. It begins like **wave** and ends like **sit**.

4. It begins like **dark** and ends like **say**.

5. It begins like **plan** and ends like **way**.

Rhyming Words

Complete the sentence with a word that rhymes with the underlined word.

6. Ask Mother if we _____ <u>play</u> outside.

7. Trey _____ his whole <u>plate</u> of fruits and vegetables.

Use the
Dictionary

8–10. Write these spelling words in a-b-c order.

save   safe   say

Dictionary Check Check a-b-c order in your **Spelling Dictionary**.

Segmentation
1.
2.
3.
4.
5.
Rhyming Words
6.
7.
Use the Dictionary
8.
9.
10.

 TEKS 2.23A Use phonological knowledge to match sounds to letters to construct unknown words. **2.23Biii** Spell words with common orthographic patterns and rules: long vowels. **2.23C** Spell high-frequency words from a commonly used list.

| safe | day | rain | say | play |
| ate | stay | save | may | wait |

Antonyms

Write the **long a** word that is the opposite of the underlined word in each sentence.

1. Owls are usually sleeping during the <u>night</u>.
2. Willa wants to <u>spend</u> her money.
3. You <u>go</u> here while I get more napkins.
4. We will <u>work</u> at the park after school.

Use Context Clues

Write the spelling words that complete the story.

D.J. wanted to go outside, but it was raining very hard. There was thunder, too. She did not want to **5.** for the **6.** to stop. She asked, "Please, Dad, **7.** I go outside?"

"No," she heard her dad **8.** ."It is not a good time to be outside. Stay inside where you are **9.** from the storm."

"I know!" said D.J. "Remember the last storm when we played checkers and **10.** popcorn? We can do that today!"

Antonyms

1.
2.
3.
4.

Use Context Clues

5.
6.
7.
8.
9.
10.

 TEKS 2.23Biii Spell words with common orthographic patterns and rules: long vowels.
2.23C Spell high-frequency words from a commonly used list.

Connections to WRITING

Proofread a Speech

Find eight misspelled words in the speech below. Rewrite the speech using correct spellings. Make the corrections shown by the proofreading marks.

¶ Our class collects cans one dey every week. We give

up our playy time after school and stae an extra hour.

We use the Money we make to sayve the rane forest.

don't wate to join us. Then you can saiy that you

helped save land! You maa like it so much that you'll

want to do more.

Proofreading Marks

≡	Capital Letter
/	Small Letter
∧	Add
℘	Delete
⊙	Add a Period
¶	Indent

PERSUASIVE Writing Prompt

Write a Speech

Think about something that you really like to do or that you think is important. Write a speech to get others to join you. Use as many spelling words as you can.

- Use the writing process: prewrite, draft, revise, edit, and publish.
- Choose a topic you feel strongly about. Tell how you feel and give reasons you feel that way. Try to get the audience to agree with you.
- Check your draft for complete sentences, correct spelling, grammar, capital letters, and punctuation.
- Circle two words that may be misspelled. Use a dictionary to check the spelling.

Transfer

Think of three more words that have the **long a** sound spelled **a-consonant-e**, **ay,** or **ai**. Write the words in your Spelling Journal. Circle the letter or letters that make the **long a** sound.

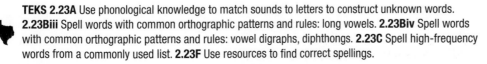

TEKS 2.23A Use phonological knowledge to match sounds to letters to construct unknown words. **2.23Biii** Spell words with common orthographic patterns and rules: long vowels. **2.23Biv** Spell words with common orthographic patterns and rules: vowel digraphs, diphthongs. **2.23C** Spell high-frequency words from a commonly used list. **2.23F** Use resources to find correct spellings.

Extend & Transfer

Word Study

ape	say	safe	save	daisy
bake	play	day	always	plate
game	may	ate	plain	spray
rain	wait	stay	space	stain

Pattern Power

Write words that fit each spelling pattern.

1–2. gate, date, _____, _____

3. gave, pave, _____

Antonyms

Write the **long a** word from the list that means the opposite of each word below.

4. go   **5.** never   **6.** dangerous

Inflectional Endings

Remove the ending from these words and write the base word from the list.

7. raining   **9.** waiting

8. spraying   **10.** playing

Circle the vowel digraphs in the answers you wrote.

Pattern Power

1.

2.

3.

Antonyms

4.

5.

6.

Inflectional Endings

7.

8.

9.

10.

94

TEKS 2.23A Use phonological knowledge to match sounds to letters to construct unknown words. **2.23Biii** Spell words with common orthographic patterns and rules: long vowels. **2.23Biv** Spell words with common orthographic patterns and rules: vowel digraphs, diphthongs. **2.23C** Spell high-frequency words from a commonly used list. **2.23D** Spell base words with inflectional endings.

Social Studies

Word Hunt

Read the Native American tale below. Look for words with **long a** spelled **a-consonant-e, ai,** and **ay**.

> Long ago, people grew corn that they made into meal. The people would save the cornmeal in a crate. Late each night, someone came and took the cornmeal. The next day people saw prints made by a huge dog. The people needed to keep the meal safe. So one night they decided to stay up and wait for the dog. As the tale is told, a huge dog came down from space. It ate the cornmeal. When the people ran to chase it, the dog flew away. A trail of cornmeal fell from its mouth across the sky. Each grain became a star. That spray of stars is the Milky Way.

1. _____
2. _____
3. _____
4. _____
5. _____
6. _____
7. _____
8. _____

1–3. Write three words that end with **ate**.

4–6. Write three words with **long a** spelled **ai**.

7–8. Write the four-letter words that end with **ay**.

TEKS 2.23A Use phonological knowledge to match sounds to letters to construct unknown words. **2.23Biii** Spell words with common orthographic patterns and rules: long vowels. **2.23Biv** Spell words with common orthographic patterns and rules: vowel digraphs, diphthongs. **2.23C** Spell high-frequency words from a commonly used list.

Read the spelling words and sentences.

1.	sea	Fish swim in the **sea**.
2.	week	The school **week** begins today.
3.	eat	You may **eat** this apple.
4.	beef	Dad likes **beef** for dinner.
5.	neat	Please keep your room **neat**.
6.	need	I **need** to drink some water.
7.	seat	Have a **seat** on the sofa.
8.	seem	Those people **seem** nice.
9.	read	I can **read** this book.
10.	seen	Have you **seen** my cat?

Think & Sort the spelling words.

1–5. Write the words with **long e** spelled **ee**.

6–10. Write the words with **long e** spelled **ea**.

Remember

The **long e** sound can be spelled in different ways: **ee** in **seen** and **ea** in **eat**.

ee

1.

2.

3.

4.

5.

ea

6.

7.

8.

9.

10.

TEKS 2.23A Use phonological knowledge to match sounds to letters to construct unknown words. **2.23Biii** Spell words with common orthographic patterns and rules: long vowels. **2.23Biv** Spell words with common orthographic patterns and rules: vowel digraphs, diphthongs. **2.23C** Spell high-frequency words from a commonly used list.

Sound and Letter Patterns

Remember that a vowel digraph is two vowels together that make one sound. Write the spelling word. Then circle the letters that make the **long e** sound.

1. seen – n + m = _____

2. sea – a + en = _____

3. really – lly + d = _____

4. weed – d + k = _____

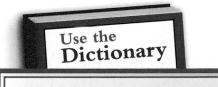

Beginning and Ending Sounds

5. Write the spelling word that ends with the **long e** sound.

6. Write the spelling word that begins like **need** and ends like **meat**.

7. Write the spelling word that begins with the **long e** sound.

8. Write the spelling word that begins like **sea** and ends like **beat**.

Use the Dictionary

Write the word that comes <u>before</u> each of these words in the **Spelling Dictionary**.

9. been   **10.** next

Sound and Letter Patterns
1.
2.
3.
4.

Beginning and Ending Sounds
5.
6.
7.
8.

Use the Dictionary
9.
10.

TEKS 2.23A Use phonological knowledge to match sounds to letters to construct unknown words. **2.23Biii** Spell words with common orthographic patterns and rules: long vowels. **2.23Biv** Spell words with common orthographic patterns and rules: vowel digraphs, diphthongs. **2.23C** Spell high-frequency words from a commonly used list.

sea	week	eat	beef	neat
need	seat	seem	read	seen

Use Analogies

Write a spelling word to complete each analogy.

1. **Pig** is to **pork** as **cow** is to _____.
2. **Cup** is to **drink** as **fork** is to _____.
3. **Fat** is to **thin** as **messy** is to _____.
4. **Soil** is to **water** as **land** is to _____.
5. **Video** is to **watch** as **book** is to _____.

Use Context Clues

Write the spelling words that complete the paragraph.

Dad and I take a bus ride when we want to see Grandma. We can go any day of the **6.**. I like to ride in the back **7.**. From the window, I have **8.** trucks, bridges, and tall buildings. When we **9.** to go home, we take the bus again. Does it **10.** like riding on a bus is fun? It is!

Circle the vowel digraphs in the answers you wrote.

Use Analogies

1. _____
2. _____
3. _____
4. _____
5. _____

Use Context Clues

6. _____
7. _____
8. _____
9. _____
10. _____

 TEKS 2.23Biv Spell words with common orthographic patterns and rules: vowel digraphs, diphthongs.
2.23C Spell high-frequency words from a commonly used list.

Connections to WRITING

Proofread a Book Report

Proofread the book report below for eight misspelled words. Then rewrite the book report. Write the spelling words correctly and make the corrections shown by the proofreading marks.

A Seea Story

¶You should reed this book! It is called <u>Sea Life</u>. It is by Ian whitelaw. It tells about sea animals You have never sean. Some are so strange! They don't even seam real. You will learn what they look like and what they eet It is so good, I read this ~~this~~ book twice a weeke. you really nead to take a seet and read this book!

Proofreading Marks

≡   Capital Letter

/   Small Letter

∧   Add

℘   Delete

⊙   Add a Period

¶   Indent

PERSUASIVE Writing Prompt

Write a Book Report

Write a book report to tell your classmates about a book you have read. Use as many **long e** spelling words as you can.

* Use the writing process: prewrite, draft, revise, edit, and publish.
* Give the title and author, tell what the book is about, and tell why it is worth reading.
* Use complete sentences with correct capitalization, punctuation, grammar, and spelling.
* Circle two words that may be misspelled. Use a dictionary to check the spelling.

Transfer
Think of three more words that have the **long e** sound spelled **ee** or **ea**. Write the words in your Spelling Journal. Circle the letters that make the **long e** sound.

TEKS 2.23A Use phonological knowledge to match sounds to letters to construct unknown words. **2.23Biii** Spell words with common orthographic patterns and rules: long vowels. **2.23Biv** Spell words with common orthographic patterns and rules: vowel digraphs, diphthongs. **2.23C** Spell high-frequency words from a commonly used list. **2.23F** Use resources to find correct spellings.

Word Study

beet	eat	sea	seen	easel
deep	need	beef	beaver	seek
easy	seem	neat	stream	sneeze
week	read	seat	street	teach

Rhyming Words

Rhyming Words

Write one or two words from the list above that rhyme with the words given. Use words with the **ee** spelling for **long e**.

1–2. meet, feet, _____, _____

   3. keep, beep, _____

   4. freeze, please, _____

Meaning Mastery

Meaning Mastery

Write the word that matches each meaning.

   5. the meat of a cow or steer

   6. clean, tidy

Inflectional Endings

Inflectional Endings

Remove the ending from each word and write the base word from the list.

   7. needed   **9.** seated

   8. seeming   **10.** teaching

Rhyming Words

1.

2.

3.

4.

Meaning Mastery

5.

6.

Inflectional Endings

7.

8.

9.

10.

TEKS 2.23A Use phonological knowledge to match sounds to letters to construct unknown words. **2.23Biii** Spell words with common orthographic patterns and rules: long vowels. **2.23Biv** Spell words with common orthographic patterns and rules: vowel digraphs, diphthongs. **2.23C** Spell high-frequency words from a commonly used list. **2.23D** Spell base words with inflectional endings.

Science

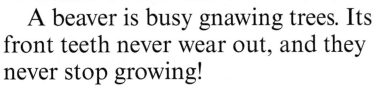

Word Hunt

Read the paragraphs below. Look for words with **long e** spelled **ee** and **ea**.

A beaver is busy gnawing trees. Its front teeth never wear out, and they never stop growing!

A beaver uses branches, rocks, and mud to build a home called a lodge. Have you seen one in a pond? The beaver can reach the lodge by swimming under the water. Its back feet are like flippers.

A beaver builds dams, too. A dam blocks a stream and forms a pond. The pond becomes a home for fish, frogs, turtles, ducks, and otters.

Trees are a meal, too. The beaver eats bark, twigs, and leaves. If you see one beaver, others are close by. They like to keep together. They work and live as a team.

1. _____

2. _____

3. _____

4. _____

5. _____

6. _____

7. _____

8. _____

WORD SORT

1. Write a two-syllable word with **long e** spelled **ea** in the first syllable.

2–3. Write two words that rhyme with **cream**.

4–8. Write the words with the **long e** sound spelled **ee**.

TEKS 2.23A Use phonological knowledge to match sounds to letters to construct unknown words.
2.23Biii Spell words with common orthographic patterns and rules: long vowels. **2.23Biv** Spell words with common orthographic patterns and rules: vowel digraphs, diphthongs. **2.23C** Spell high-frequency words from a commonly used list.

Connections to THINKING

Read the spelling words and sentences.

1. my — I put **my** seat next to yours.

2. try — I will **try** to call later.

3. mile — Mom runs one **mile** each day.

4. cry — I **cry** when I feel bad.

5. fry — Jan will **fry** the meat.

6. nice — That **nice** man helped me.

7. by — This story is **by** Ron.

8. sky — The **sky** is gray today.

9. fine — What a **fine** day for a picnic!

10. dry — The shirt can **dry** in the sun.

Think & Sort the spelling words.

1–7. Write the words with **long i** spelled **y**.

8–10. Write the words with **long i** spelled **i-consonant-e**.

Remember

The **long i** sound can be spelled in different ways: **y** in **sky** and **i-consonant-e** in **fine**.

y

1. _____

2. _____

3. _____

4. _____

5. _____

6. _____

7. _____

i-consonant-e

8. _____

9. _____

10. _____

TEKS 2.23A Use phonological knowledge to match sounds to letters to construct unknown words.
2.23Biii Spell words with common orthographic patterns and rules: long vowels. **2.23C** Spell high-frequency words from a commonly used list.

Segmentation

Write a spelling word for each set of sound clues.

1. It begins like **nut** and ends like **ice**.

2. It begins like **me** and ends like **by**.

3. It begins like **fin** and ends like **line**.

Word Structure

Change the underlined letter to make a spelling word. Write the word.

4. d<u>a</u>y   **5.** s<u>a</u>y

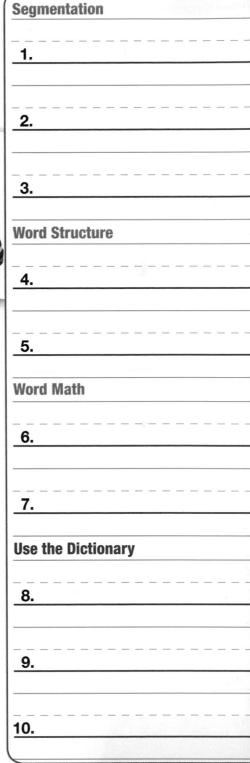

Word Math

Follow the directions to write a spelling word.

6. while – wh + m = _____

7. fly – fl + cr = _____

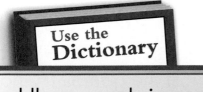
Use the
Dictionary

Find these words in your **Spelling Dictionary**.
Write the entry that comes <u>after</u> each one.

8. frown   **9.** trucks   **10.** busy

Segmentation
1.
2.
3.
Word Structure
4.
5.
Word Math
6.
7.
Use the Dictionary
8.
9.
10.

 TEKS 2.23A Use phonological knowledge to match sounds to letters to construct unknown words.
2.23Biii Spell words with common orthographic patterns and rules: long vowels. **2.23C** Spell
high-frequency words from a commonly used list.

my	try	mile	cry	fry
nice	by	sky	fine	dry

Use Synonyms

Write the **long i** spelling word that could best take the place of the underlined word or words.

1. The book is <u>next to</u> the vase.

2. I will <u>do my best</u> to win the race.

3. That <u>kind</u> person helped me when I fell.

4. I always feel <u>great</u> when I play ball.

5. These clothes are <u>not wet</u>.

Use Context Clues

Write the **long i** spelling word that completes each sentence.

6. Crack the egg and throw away the shell. Then put the egg in a pan to _____.

7. That book does not belong to you. It is _____ book.

8. It is more than five blocks to school. It is at least a _____ away.

9. I know you are sad we lost the game. Try not to _____.

10. Let go of the balloon. Watch it drift off into the _____.

Use Synonyms

1. _____
2. _____
3. _____
4. _____
5. _____

Use Context Clues

6. _____
7. _____
8. _____
9. _____
10. _____

TEKS 2.23Biii Spell words with common orthographic patterns and rules: long vowels.
2.23C Spell high-frequency words from a commonly used list.

Connections to WRITING

Proofread a Paragraph

Find eight misspelled words in the paragraph below. Rewrite the paragraph using correct spelling. Make the corrections shown by the proofreading marks.

Camping Is fun

¶You can have a fyne time camping if you do these things. First, go when it is dri. Find a place where you can look up at the ski. Keep warm bi making a Fire. If you bring the right food and gear you can even triy cooking over the fire. maybe you can fri the fish you catch. Follow mi advice, and you will have a nise time.

Proofreading Marks

≡   Capital Letter

/   Small Letter

∧   Add

℘   Delete

⊙   Add a Period

¶   Indent

EXPOSITORY Writing Prompt
Write a Paragraph to Inform

Write a paragraph for your classmates that tells about something you like to do. Tell how to do it right and use as many **long i** spelling words as you can.

- Use the writing process: prewrite, draft, revise, edit, and publish.
- Name what you like to do in your opening sentence. Then give more details. Tell where to do it. Also tell when and how to do it.
- Use complete sentences with correct capitalization, punctuation, grammar, and spelling.
- Circle two words that may be misspelled. Use a dictionary to check the spelling.

Transfer

Think of three more words that have the **long i** sound spelled **i-consonant-e** or **y**. Write the words in your Spelling Journal. Circle the letters that spell the **long i** sound.

TEKS 2.23A Use phonological knowledge to match sounds to letters to construct unknown words.
2.23Biii Spell words with common orthographic patterns and rules: long vowels. **2.23C** Spell high-frequency words from a commonly used list. **2.23F** Use resources to find correct spellings.

Pattern Power

1.

2.

3.

4.

5.

Word Building

6.

7.

8.

9.

10.

bike	try	mile	dry	mime
hide	nice	cry	alike	nylon
line	by	fry	housefly	pry
my	fine	sky	prize	spice

Pattern Power

Use words from the list above to complete these exercises.

1–2. Write the two words that have the **ice** pattern.

3–4. Write the words with two syllables that have **long i** spelled **y**.

5. Write the **long i** word that begins like **crop**.

Word Building

Replace the underlined letter in each word to write a word from the box.

6. m_u_le

7. hi_k_e

8. b_a_ke

9. ali_v_e

10. pri_d_e

TEKS 2.23A Use phonological knowledge to match sounds to letters to construct unknown words.
2.23Biii Spell words with common orthographic patterns and rules: long vowels. **2.23C** Spell high-frequency words from a commonly used list.

Word Hunt

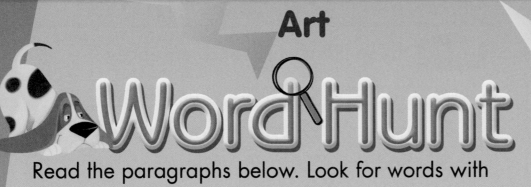

Read the paragraphs below. Look for words with **long i** spelled **i-consonant-e** and **y**.

Do you like to fly a kite? It is fun to see a kite glide across the sky. In Japan and China, painted kites are an art form. It seems that no two kites are alike. They can be any shape, like birds, fish, or dragons. There are small and large kites. A kite that is seven feet tall and just as wide is bigger than you are!

The shape and size of a kite is important. The kite must be able to rise in the wind.

Some kite makers want to share their art. Places like China and India have a Kite Day. You can have one, too. Give a prize for the best kite.

1. _____

2. _____

3. _____

4. _____

5. _____

6. _____

7. _____

8. _____

WORD SORT

1–2. Write two words that rhyme with **hide**.

3–4. Write two words that rhyme with **my**.

5–6. Write two words that rhyme with **bike**.

7–8. Write two words that rhyme with **size**.

TEKS 2.23A Use phonological knowledge to match sounds to letters to construct unknown words. **2.23Biii** Spell words with common orthographic patterns and rules: long vowels. **2.23C** Spell high-frequency words from a commonly used list.

o

1.

2.

3.

4.

oa

5.

6.

ow

7.

8.

9.

10.

Connections to THINKING

Read the spelling words and sentences.

1. old   She is eight years **old**.
2. know   Do you **know** the answer?
3. road   Sarah lives on this **road**.
4. cold   It can be **cold** in March.
5. grow   We will **grow** beans here.
6. hold   I can **hold** this big book.
7. low   The nest is on a **low** branch.
8. told   I **told** the story to Ken.
9. own   I **own** a bike and a helmet.
10. coat   My **coat** keeps me warm.

Think & Sort the spelling words.

1–4. Write the words with **long o** spelled **o**.

5–6. Write the words with **long o** spelled **oa**.

7–10. Write the words with **long o** spelled **ow**.

Remember

The **long o** sound can be spelled in different ways: **o** in **old**, **oa** in **coat**, and **ow** in **low**.

TEKS 2.23A Use phonological knowledge to match sounds to letters to construct unknown words.
2.23Biii Spell words with common orthographic patterns and rules: long vowels. **2.23Biv** Spell words with common orthographic patterns and rules: vowel digraphs, diphthongs. **2.23C** Spell high-frequency words from a commonly used list.

Connections to PHONICS

Sound and Letter Patterns

Follow the directions to write a spelling word.

1. tip – ip + old = _____

2. row – w + ad = _____

Rhyme Time

Write the spelling word that rhymes with the underlined word.

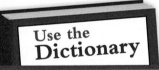

3. When do you think that it will <u>snow</u>?
I can guess, but I don't _____.

4. The pencil mark on the wall will <u>show</u>
Just how much Jamal did _____.

5. Fill the cup, so I've been <u>told</u>,
Then we'll see what it will _____.

Blend Sounds

Blend the sounds to write the spelling word.

6. Blend **o** with **ld**.

7. Blend **l** with **ow**.

8. Blend **ow** with **n**.

Use the
Dictionary

9–10. A dictionary lists words in a-b-c order.
Write the two spelling words that begin with the
letter **c** in a-b-c order.

Dictionary Check Check a-b-c order in your
Spelling Dictionary.

Circle the vowel digraphs in the answers you wrote
on this page.

TEKS 2.23A Use phonological knowledge to match sounds to letters to construct unknown words.
 2.23Biii Spell words with common orthographic patterns and rules: long vowels. **2.23Biv** Spell words
with common orthographic patterns and rules: vowel digraphs, diphthongs. **2.23C** Spell high-frequency
words from a commonly used list.

Sound and Letter Patterns

1. _____

2. _____

Rhyme Time

3. _____

4. _____

5. _____

Blend Sounds

6. _____

7. _____

8. _____

Use the Dictionary

9. _____

10. _____

old	know	road	cold	grow
hold	low	told	own	coat

Use Antonyms

Write the **long o** spelling word that means the opposite of each word below.

1. young _____

2. high _____

3. hot _____

4. shrink _____

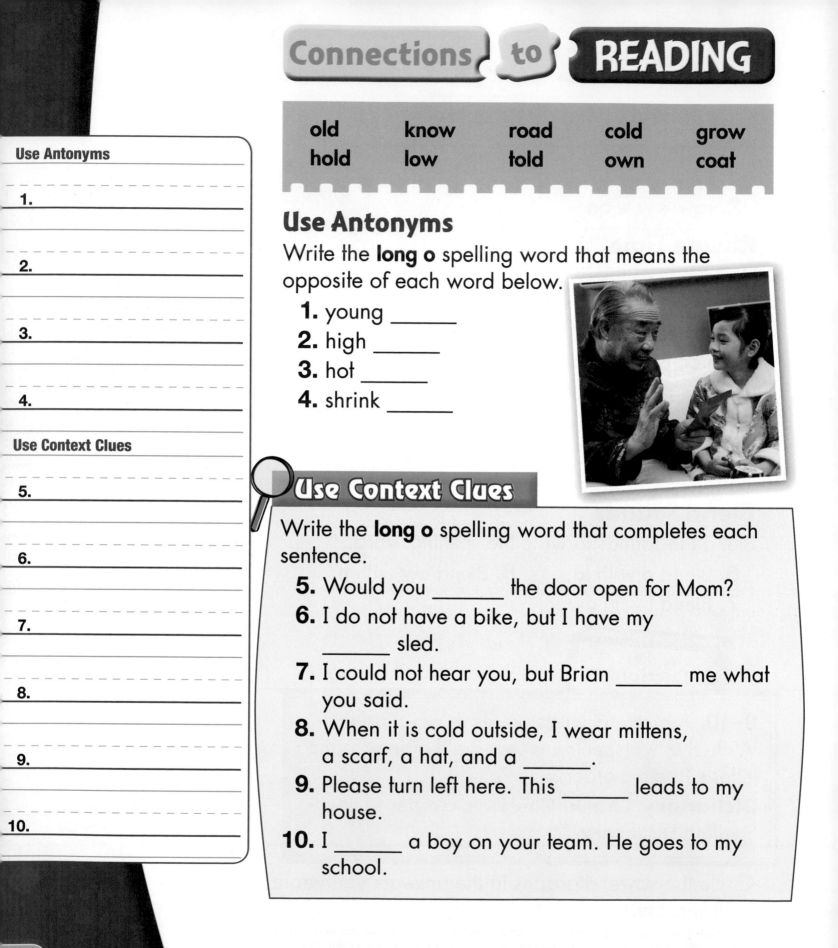

Use Context Clues

Write the **long o** spelling word that completes each sentence.

5. Would you _____ the door open for Mom?

6. I do not have a bike, but I have my _____ sled.

7. I could not hear you, but Brian _____ me what you said.

8. When it is cold outside, I wear mittens, a scarf, a hat, and a _____.

9. Please turn left here. This _____ leads to my house.

10. I _____ a boy on your team. He goes to my school.

Use Antonyms

1. _____

2. _____

3. _____

4. _____

Use Context Clues

5. _____

6. _____

7. _____

8. _____

9. _____

10. _____

 TEKS 2.23Biii Spell words with common orthographic patterns and rules: long vowels. **2.23C** Spell high-frequency words from a commonly used list.

Connections to WRITING

Proofread a Story

Find eight misspelled words in the paragraph below. Rewrite the paragraph using correct spelling. Make the corrections shown by the proofreading marks.

A Seal Story

¶Sam Seal got out of the water. He was coald. Pete

penguin said, "You need a cote! I knoaw where to get

you one!"

   "Holed on," Sam toald Pete⊙"I've already got my

oan! Every year I shed my owld one and growe a new

one. It's wet‸smooth. Most of the ⊤ime it keeps me very
       and

warm."

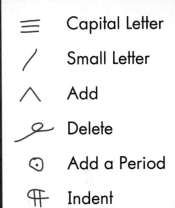

Proofreading Marks

≡	Capital Letter
/	Small Letter
∧	Add
ℓ	Delete
⊙	Add a Period
¶	Indent

NARRATIVE Writing Prompt

Write a Story

Write a story with animal characters. Tell what they say and do. Use as many spelling words as you can.

- Use the writing process: prewrite, draft, revise, edit, and publish.
- Begin the story with the names of characters. Tell the setting or place where the story happens. Describe the problem in the story.
- The middle of the story tells the things the characters do to solve the problem.
- The end tells how everything works out.
- Circle two words that may be misspelled. Use a dictionary to check the spelling.

Transfer

Think of three more words that have the **long o** sound spelled **o, oa,** or **ow**. Write the words in your Spelling Journal. Circle the letters that make the **long o** sound.

TEKS 2.23A Use phonological knowledge to match sounds to letters to construct unknown words. **2.23Biii** Spell words with common orthographic patterns and rules: long vowels. **2.23Biv** Spell words with common orthographic patterns and rules: vowel digraphs, diphthongs. **2.23C** Spell high-frequency words from a commonly used list. **2.23F** Use resources to find correct spellings.

Word Study

ago	know	road	low	coach
go	told	cold	below	follow
no	own	grow	foam	golden
old	coat	hold	odor	roast

Pattern Power

1.

2.

3.

Use Antonyms

4.

5.

Word Building

6.

7.

8.

9.

10.

Pattern Power

Use words from the box to complete these exercises.

1–2. Write the two-syllable words that end with **ow**.

3. Write the two-syllable word that has the **old** pattern.

Use Antonyms

Write a word from the box that means the opposite of each word below.

4. hot

5. high

Word Building

Add **oa** or **ow** to write a word from the box.

6. r __ __ d

9. c __ __ ch

7. __ __ n

10. gr __ __

8. f __ __ m

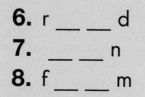**TEKS 2.23Biii** Spell words with common orthographic patterns and rules: long vowels. **2.23Biv** Spell words with common orthographic patterns and rules: vowel digraphs, diphthongs. **2.23C** Spell high-frequency words from a commonly used list.

Technology

Word Hunt

Read the paragraph below. Look for words with **long o** spelled **o, oa,** and **ow**.

Do you know a lot about computers? How do you move around on the screen? Do you hold the mouse and move it to change your place? Have you been told that you can also use special keys to move? First, look over your screen. Where do you want to go? Then follow these steps. To go up, press the Up arrow. You go up one line. To go down, press the Down arrow. You go one line below the line you were on. Press Home and you go to the beginning of the line. Now your goal can be to coach your friends. Show them how to use special keys, too.

1. _____
2. _____
3. _____
4. _____
5. _____
6. _____
7. _____
8. _____

WORD SORT

Follow the directions. Write each word only once.

1–5. Write the words with **long o** spelled **ow**.

6. Write a word with two syllables that begins with **long o** spelled **o**.

7–8. Write two words with **long o** spelled **oa**.

TEKS 2.23A Use phonological knowledge to match sounds to letters to construct unknown words. **2.23Biii** Spell words with common orthographic patterns and rules: long vowels. **2.23Biv** Spell words with common orthographic patterns and rules: vowel digraphs, diphthongs. **2.23C** Spell high-frequency words from a commonly used list.

113

/k/ spelled k and ck

1. _____

/k/ spelled c and k

2. _____

3. _____

/k/ spelled c

4. _____

/k/ spelled k

5. _____

6. _____

/k/ spelled ck

7. _____

8. _____

9. _____

10. _____

Connections to THINKING

Read the spelling words and sentences.

1. cook — The **cook** stirs the soup.
2. sick — Pete is **sick** with the flu.
3. cave — Many bats live in that **cave**.
4. kiss — I **kiss** the baby on her cheek.
5. rock — Never throw a **rock**.
6. cake — Please give me a piece of **cake**.
7. kick — I can **kick** the ball hard.
8. lock — Does the key fit this **lock**?
9. look — We **look** at the stars above.
10. luck — Good **luck** in the race!

Think & Sort the spelling words.

1. Write the word with the /**k**/ sound spelled with both **k** and **ck**.

2–3. Write the words with the /**k**/ sound spelled with both **c** and **k**.

4. Write the word with the /**k**/ sound spelled **c**.

5–6 Write the words with the /**k**/ sound spelled **k**.

7–10. Write the words with the /**k**/ sound spelled **ck**.

Remember

The /**k**/ sound can be spelled in different ways:
c in **cave**, **k** in **look**, and **ck** in **sick**.

TEKS 2.23A Use phonological knowledge to match sounds to letters to construct unknown words. **2.23Bi** Spell words with common orthographic patterns and rules: complex consonants. **2.23C** Spell high-frequency words from a commonly used list.

Connections to PHONICS

Word Structure

1. Write the spelling word that begins with the /**k**/ sound and contains a double consonant.

2. Write the spelling word that contains the **long a** sound and has the /**k**/ sound just once.

3. Write the spelling word that begins and ends with the /**k**/ sound and contains a double vowel.

Sound Blending

Write a spelling word for each set of letter sounds you blend.

4. This word starts like **safe** and rhymes with **kick**.

5. This word starts like **lake** and rhymes with **book**.

6. This word starts like **came** and rhymes with **make**.

7. This word starts like **rub** and rhymes with **block**.

Use the Dictionary

Find these words in your **Spelling Dictionary**. Write the entry that comes <u>before</u> each one.

8. lunch   **9.** log   **10.** king

Word Structure

1. _____

2. _____

3. _____

Sound Blending

4. _____

5. _____

6. _____

7. _____

Use the Dictionary

8. _____

9. _____

10. _____

TEKS 2.23A Use phonological knowledge to match sounds to letters to construct unknown words. **2.23Bi** Spell words with common orthographic patterns and rules: complex consonants. **2.23C** Spell high-frequency words from a commonly used list.

cook	sick	cave	kiss	rock
cake	kick	lock	look	luck

Complete the Sentences

Write the spelling word that will complete each sentence.

1. Did you remember to _____ the door when you left the house?

2. I can _____ beef and corn for our dinner tonight.

3. How many candles are on your birthday _____?

Use Context Clues

Write spelling words to complete the paragraph.

On January 24, 1848, James Marshall saw some shiny flakes in the river. He hit them with a **4.** . The flakes changed shape! Marshall had found gold. Soon people came from far and near to **5.** for gold. They slept in tents. Some tried to find a warm, dry, dark **6.** . No wonder many miners got **7.** . Most people had no **8.** finding gold. But some miners struck it rich. They would **9.** up their heels when they found gold. They would even **10.** the gold!

Complete the Sentences

1. _____

2. _____

3. _____

Use Context Clues

4. _____

5. _____

6. _____

7. _____

8. _____

9. _____

10. _____

 TEKS 2.23C Spell high-frequency words from a commonly used list.

Proofread a Diary Entry

Find eight misspelled words in the diary entry below. Rewrite the entry using correct spelling. Make the corrections shown by the proofreading marks.

December 16, 2012

Dear Diary,

¶ This year I was sicke on my Birthday. It was bad luk. Dad was going to cooke my favorite meal. Mom was going to bake a cacke that looked like a cav. We were all going to go outside to kik the soccer ball. Instead, I felt so so bad I could barely luk at food. mom gave me a kis to make me feel better.

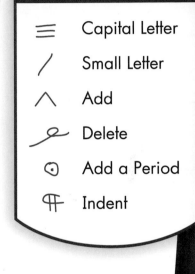

Proofreading Marks

☰	Capital Letter
/	Small Letter
∧	Add
℘	Delete
⊙	Add a Period
¶	Indent

Write a Diary Entry

Write a diary entry. Tell about your day yesterday. Use as many spelling words as you can.

- Use the writing process: prewrite, draft, revise, edit, and publish.
- Write details about what happened.
- Write complete sentences with correct capitalization, punctuation, grammar, and spelling.
- Circle two words that may be misspelled. Use a dictionary to check the spelling.

Transfer

Think of three more words that have the /**k**/ sound spelled **c, k,** and **ck**. Write the words in your Spelling Journal. Circle the letters that make the /**k**/ sound. Illustrate each word.

TEKS 2.23A Use phonological knowledge to match sounds to letters to construct unknown words.
2.23Bi Spell words with common orthographic patterns and rules: complex consonants. **2.23C** Spell high-frequency words from a commonly used list. **2.23F** Use resources to find correct spellings.

117

Word Study

back	kiss	sick	luck	cast
cat	cake	cave	bucket	dock
keep	lock	rock	carry	pike
cook	look	kick	peak	tackle

Pattern Power

1.

2.

3.

Word Building

4.

5.

6.

7.

8.

Meaning Mastery

9.

10.

Pattern Power

Use words from the list above to complete these exercises.

1–3. Write the one-syllable words with the spelling pattern **ock**.

Word Building

Add **c** or **k** to make a word from the list.

4. __ at

5. __ arry

6. pea __

7. __ ast

8. pi __ e

Meaning Mastery

Write the word from the list that matches each meaning.

9. a pail

10. to grab and throw to the ground

TEKS 2.23C Spell high-frequency words from a commonly used list.

Math

Word Hunt

Read the story below. Look for words with the /k/ sound spelled **c**, **k**, and **ck**.

Juan, Meg, and Mike go to Kids' Camp. Today they watched two men carry a new machine into the kitchen.

"Come over and have a look," said the cook. "This kind of machine has different flavors of cold fruit pops. Next to the machine I'll keep a cup of special coins you can use."

Mike was the first to pick a pop. He put in three coins and pushed button four. Out came twelve pops! Meg took four coins. She pressed button five. Out came twenty pops!

"We have enough for thirty-two campers," Juan said as they left.

"Don't forget to come back for more," the cook smiled.

1. _____

2. _____

3. _____

4. _____

5. _____

6. _____

7. _____

8. _____

WORD SORT

1–3. Write three words that rhyme with **book**.

4–6. Write the two-syllable words that start with **c** or **k**.

7–8. Write the two words that end with **ck**.

TEKS 2.23A Use phonological knowledge to match sounds to letters to construct unknown words. **2.23Bi** Spell words with common orthographic patterns and rules: complex consonants. **2.23C** Spell high-frequency words from a commonly used list.

Assess for Transfer

Unit 13

1.

2.

Unit 14

3.

4.

Unit 15

5.

6.

Unit 16

7.

8.

Unit 17

9.

10.

Units 13–17

Assessment

Write each assessment word under the unit number it fits.

Unit 13

1–2. The **long a** sound can be spelled in different ways: **a-consonant-e** in **save**, **ai** in **rain**, and **ay** in **day**.

Unit 14

3–4. The **long e** sound can be spelled in different ways: **ee** in **seen** and **ea** in **eat**.

Unit 15

5–6. The **long i** sound can be spelled in different ways: **y** in **sky** and **i-consonant-e** in **fine**.

Unit 16

7–8. The **long o** sound can be spelled in different ways: **o** in **old**, **oa** in **coat**, and **ow** in **low**.

Unit 17

9–10. The **/k/** sound can be spelled in different ways: **c** in **cave**, **k** in **look**, and **ck** in **sick**.

Words for Assessment

boat

sheet

sack

spy

tea

ray

mask

lime

gold

jail

Unit 13: Long a: a-Consonant-e, ai, ay

| may | rain | say | play | wait |

Write the spelling words by adding letters.

1. m ___ y   **3.** ___ ait

2. s ___ ___

Write the spelling word that completes each sentence.

4. We hope it will not _____ today.

5. Rodell wants to _____ at the park.

Unit 14: Long e: ee, ea

| eat | read | seem | week | need |

Write the spelling word that fits each clue.

6. This word starts like **nose** and ends like **seed**.

7. This word sounds like **reed**.

8. This word starts like **soap** and rhymes with **team**.

9. This word begins with the **long e** sound.

10. This word sounds like **weak**.

Unit 13

1. _____

2. _____

3. _____

4. _____

5. _____

Unit 14

6. _____

7. _____

8. _____

9. _____

10. _____

Unit 15

1.

2.

3.

4.

5.

Unit 16

6.

7.

8.

9.

10.

Unit 15: Long i: y, i-Consonant-e

my	try	nice	fine	by

1–2. Write the two spelling words in which the **long i** sound comes in the middle of the word.

3–5. Write the three spelling words in which the **long i** sound comes at the end of the word.

Unit 16: Long o: o, oa, ow

told	coat	own	know	old

6. Which word begins with the **long o** sound spelled **ow**?

7. Which word begins with the **long o** sound spelled **o**?

8. Which word uses the **oa** spelling?

9. Which word ends with the **long o** sound spelled **ow**?

10. Which word can be made by adding one letter to another word in the list?

Unit 17: /k/ Spelled c, k, ck

cook   kiss   lock   cake   look

1. Which word has **short i** followed by a double consonant?

2. Which word ends with two different letters that make one sound?

3–4. Which two words rhyme with **book**?

5. Which word has a long vowel sound?

Unit 17

1.

2.

3.

4.

5.

Spelling Study Strategy

Go Fish

Practice your spelling words with this game.

1. Make two sets of word cards so that you have two cards for every word.

2. Mix up the cards and give five cards to each person. Put the rest of the cards in a pile. If you have cards that match, put them down on the table.

3. Ask someone for a word that matches one in your hand. Spell the word out loud and say it. If your friend has the word, you take it. If your friend does not have the word, choose a card from the pile.

4. Take turns until all the cards are used.

Directions: Read the introduction and the passage that follows. Then read each question and fill in the space in front of the correct answer.

Jake wrote this story about a rainy day he spent with his grandfather. He learned a few things about weather and about his Grandpa Gus. Jake wants you to review his paper. As you read, think about ways Jake can make his story better.

Grandpa Saves the Day

(1) Rane was going to spoil my day outside with friends.

(2) "You can visit Grandpa Gus!" said Mom.

(3) "Grandpa will make the day lots of fun," I said.

(4) As soon as we arrived, Grandpa and I began to hike down the rowd to a field. (5) He toald me to look up at the sky. (6) "Clouds are mayd up of little drops of water, Jake. (7) It rains when these drops get too heavy to stay inside the clouds."

(8) That was the first of many neet things I learned that day. (9) On the way back, we talked about how every living thing neads water to grow. (10) Then we read a great book about a boy who found a cave when he was lost in a storm. (11) I now I was lucky to be inside, safe, and dry!

1 What change should be made in sentence 1?

- ⬭ Change *Rane* to **Rain**
- ⬭ Change *going* to **gong**
- ⬭ Change *my* to **mi**
- ⬭ Change *day* to **da**

2 What change, if any, should be made in sentence 3?

- ⬭ Change *make* to **macke**
- ⬭ Change *day* to **dae**
- ⬭ Change *said* to **sed**
- ⬭ Make no change

3 What change, if any, should be made in sentence 4?

- ⬭ Change *as* to **es**
- ⬭ Change *rowd* to **road**
- ⬭ Change *hike* to **hiek**
- ⬭ Make no change

4 What change, if any, should be made in sentence 5?

- ⬭ Change *toald* to **told**
- ⬭ Change *look* to **luk**
- ⬭ Change *sky* to **ski**
- ⬭ Make no change

5 What change, if any, should be made in sentence 6?

- ⬭ Change *mayd* to **made**
- ⬭ Change *little* to **littel**
- ⬭ Change *water* to **watre**
- ⬭ Make no change

6 What change, if any, should be made in sentence 7?

- ⬭ Change *rains* to **rayns**
- ⬭ Change *these* to **theas**
- ⬭ Change *stay* to **stey**
- ⬭ Make no change

7 What change should be made in sentence 8?

- ⬭ Change *That* to **Thet**
- ⬭ Change *many* to **meny**
- ⬭ Change *neet* to **neat**
- ⬭ Change *day* to **dae**

8 What change, if any, should be made in sentence 9?

- ⬭ Change *back* to **bak**
- ⬭ Change *neads* to **needs**
- ⬭ Change *grow* to **groa**
- ⬭ Make no change

9 What change, if any, should be made in sentence 10?

- ⬭ Change *book* to **buk**
- ⬭ Change *cave* to **caiv**
- ⬭ Change *lost* to **lawst**
- ⬭ Make no change

10 What change should be made in sentence 11?

- ⬭ Change *now* to **know**
- ⬭ Change *lucky* to **luky**
- ⬭ Change *safe* to **saif**
- ⬭ Change *dry* to **dri**

Grammar, Usage, and Mechanics
Commands and Exclamations

One kind of sentence gives a **command**. It usually ends with a period.

> Get a dictionary.

Another kind of sentence shows strong feeling. It is an **exclamation,** and it ends with an exclamation point.

> What an odd word!

Practice Activity

A. Which sentences below are commands? Write **command** if the sentence is a command. Write **no** if it is not a command.

  1. Is that your watch?

  2. Hold out your hand.

  3. Write me a nice letter.

  4. I like to eat beef.

B. Some of these sentences show strong feeling, and some do not. Write the mark you would use to end each sentence.

  5. Help me

  6. Stay with me for a while

  7. Go to the store

  8. Don't touch that

Practice Activity A

1.

2.

3.

4.

Practice Activity B

5.

6.

7.

8.

The Writing Process: Descriptive
Writing a Descriptive Paragraph

PREWRITING
Do you have a favorite toy? Choose a toy to describe. As you think about the toy, list words and phrases that describe it. Think about how the toy looks, sounds, and feels.

DRAFTING
Use your list to write a descriptive paragraph. Begin with a topic sentence that tells the main idea. Try to describe the toy by using the senses of sight, sound, and touch. Use as many spelling words as possible.

REVISING
Read your whole paragraph. Make sure that you included describing words. Now, write your final draft.

EDITING
Use the **Editing Checklist** to proofread your paragraph. Be sure to use proofreading marks. Circle two words that may be misspelled. Use a dictionary to check your spelling.

PUBLISHING
Make a copy of your descriptive paragraph. Add a drawing of the toy you wrote about, and share it with your readers.

EDITING CHECKLIST

Spelling
- ✓ Circle words that contain the spelling patterns and rules learned in Units 13–17.
- ✓ Check the circled words in your **Spelling Dictionary**.
- ✓ Check for other spelling errors.

Capital Letters
- ✓ Capitalize important words in the title.
- ✓ Capitalize the first word in each sentence.
- ✓ Capitalize proper nouns.

Punctuation
- ✓ End each sentence with the correct punctuation.
- ✓ Use commas, apostrophes, and quotation marks correctly.

 TEKS 2.23A Use phonological knowledge to match sounds to letters to construct unknown words.
2.23F Use resources to find correct spellings.

I consonant blend

1. _____

2. _____

3. _____

4. _____

5. _____

r consonant blend

6. _____

7. _____

8. _____

9. _____

10. _____

Connections to THINKING

Read the spelling words and sentences.

1. fly   Birds **fly** south in winter.
2. clean   Let's **clean** that dirty sink.
3. sleep   I **sleep** on that cot.
4. free   I got a **free** ride on the pony.
5. grade   Are you in second **grade**?
6. drive   José can **drive** a motorboat.
7. train   We ride the **train** to Portland.
8. tree   This **tree** has very deep roots.
9. please   Will you **please** sit down?
10. slow   My watch is **slow**.

Think & Sort the spelling words.

The words on the spelling list have consonant blends.

1–5. Write the words with an **l** consonant blend.

6–10. Write the words with an **r** consonant blend.

Remember

Consonant blends with **l** and **r** are heard at the beginning of the words **fly** and **free**.

TEKS 2.23A Use phonological knowledge to match sounds to letters to construct unknown words. **2.23Bi** Spell words with common orthographic patterns and rules: complex consonants. **2.23C** Spell high-frequency words from a commonly used list.

Segmentation

1. Write the spelling word that begins like **tree** and ends like **grain**.

2. Write the spelling word that begins like **trip** and ends like **see**.

3. Write the spelling word that begins like **drink** and ends like **hive**.

Word Structure

Replace the beginning sounds in each word below to write a spelling word.

4. throw

5. three

6. deep

7. blade

8. mean

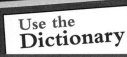
Use the Dictionary

The two words at the top of every dictionary page are called **guide words**. The guide words are the first and last words defined on that page. Write the spelling word that would be on the same page as each pair of guide words in a dictionary.

9. or • prance   **10.** fine • footstep

Segmentation
1.
2.
3.

Word Structure
4.
5.
6.
7.
8.

Use the Dictionary
9.
10.

 TEKS 2.23A Use phonological knowledge to match sounds to letters to construct unknown words. **2.23Bi** Spell words with common orthographic patterns and rules: complex consonants. **2.23C** Spell high-frequency words from a commonly used list.

Connections to READING

fly	clean	sleep	free	grade
drive	train	tree	please	slow

Use Analogies

Write a spelling word to complete each analogy.

1. **Morning** is to **wake** as **night** is to _____.
2. **Fading** is to **fade** as **grading** is to _____.
3. **Corn** is to **vegetable** as **oak** is to _____.
4. **Good-bye** is to **hello** as **thank you** is to _____.
5. **Road** is to **car** as **tracks** are to _____.

Use Context Clues

Replace each underlined word with a spelling word.

6. How <u>fast</u> was the turtle going when it raced the hare?
7. We will put <u>dirty</u> sheets on the bed.
8. Would you like to <u>swim</u> in an airplane?
9. Zena gave us <u>costly</u> tickets to the concert.
10. My aunt will <u>carry</u> her car to Houston.

Use Analogies

1. _____
2. _____
3. _____
4. _____
5. _____

Use Context Clues

6. _____
7. _____
8. _____
9. _____
10. _____

 TEKS 2.23C Spell high-frequency words from a commonly used list.

Connections to WRITING

Proofread an Interview

Find eight misspelled words in the interview below. Rewrite the interview using correct spellings. Make the corrections shown by the proofreading marks.

Question:	What ways do you travel?	
Answer:	we driv in a car. We also go by trane and plane.	
Question:	How was your first plane ride?	
Answer:	I was afraid to flie. After we got in the air, I was fine, felt feree.	
Question:	Pleeze tell me what you saw.	
Answer:	We were above every trea. the white clouds looked cleane. I felt so so calm, I went to sleap.	

Proofreading Marks

≡	Capital Letter
/	Small Letter
∧	Add
ℯ	Delete
⊙	Add a Period
¶	Indent

EXPOSITORY Writing Prompt

Write an Interview

Do you want to find out what another person knows or has done? You can ask this person questions. Write an interview. Use as many spelling words as you can.

- Use the writing process: prewrite, draft, revise, edit, and publish.
- Choose a person to interview. It can be a parent, a grandparent, or a friend.
- Write questions you want to ask.
- Ask the questions. Write what the person says.
- Write complete sentences with correct capitalization, punctuation, grammar, and spelling.
- Use a dictionary to check your spelling.

Transfer

Think of three more words that begin with an **l** or **r** consonant blend. Write the words in your Spelling Journal. Circle the letters that spell the consonant blend.

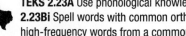

TEKS 2.23A Use phonological knowledge to match sounds to letters to construct unknown words. **2.23Bi** Spell words with common orthographic patterns and rules: complex consonants. **2.23C** Spell high-frequency words from a commonly used list. **2.23F** Use resources to find correct spellings.

Word Study

crash	tree	sleep	slowly
plum	please	free	braid
slip	slow	grade	grease
drive	fly	cloudy	pleat
train	clean	drugstore	sleeve

Rhyme Time

Choose a word from the list that rhymes with each word given. Write the word and underline the spelling that makes the long vowel sound.

1. paid

2. plane

3. cheese

4. sweep

5. cry

6. hive

7–8. Write the words that have **long o**. Circle the spelling that makes the **long o** sound.

Use Antonyms

Write the word that means the opposite of each word.

9. dirty _____

10. sunny _____

Rhyme Time

1. _____

2. _____

3. _____

4. _____

5. _____

6. _____

7. _____

8. _____

Use Antonyms

9. _____

10. _____

TEKS 2.23A Use phonological knowledge to match sounds to letters to construct unknown words. **2.23Biii** Spell words with common orthographic patterns and rules: long vowels. **2.23Biv** Spell words with common orthographic patterns and rules: vowel digraphs, diphthongs. **2.23C** Spell high-frequency words from a commonly used list.

Word Hunt

Read the paragraphs below. Look for words with **consonant blends** with **l** and **r**.

It is the Fourth of July. Slowly a parade passes by. The crowd cheers. Here comes the flag! Our flag is red, white, and blue with fifty stars. There is one star for each state. The number of stars changed as our country grew. There are thirteen red and white stripes. They stand for the first thirteen colonies.

The parade stops. The people make a pledge to the flag. The pledge is a promise to respect the flag. It is a promise to respect our country. Many people fly a flag in front of their home. This makes them feel proud. The flag reminds us all of the free country we share.

1. _____
2. _____
3. _____
4. _____
5. _____
6. _____
7. _____
8. _____

WORD SORT

1–3. Write the words that begin with the consonant blend **fr** or **gr**.

4–6. Write the words that begin with the consonant blend **fl** or **bl**.

7–8. Write the words that begin with the consonant blend **pr**.

TEKS 2.23Bi Spell words with common orthographic patterns and rules: complex consonants.
2.23C Spell high-frequency words from a commonly used list.

oi

1.

2.

3.

4.

5.

oy

6.

7.

8.

9.

10.

Connections to THINKING

Read the spelling words and sentences.

1. boy   The **boy** and the girl played a game.
2. toy   The baby played with her new **toy**.
3. joy   It was a **joy** to see Roy today.
4. coin   Our teacher showed us an old **coin**.
5. oil   The car runs on **oil** and gas.
6. soy   The farmer grows **soy** on her farm.
7. boil   Did you **boil** the water for eggs?
8. join   I want to **join** an art club.
9. toys   The child played with two **toys**.
10. coins   We found ten **coins** on the beach.

Think & Sort the spelling words.

1–5. Write the words that spell the /**oi**/ sound **oi**.

6–10. Write the words that spell the /**oi**/ sound **oy**.

Remember

The vowel sound you hear in **boil** is /**oi**/ spelled **oi**. The vowel sound you hear in **boy** is /**oi**/ spelled **oy**.

TEKS 2.23A Use phonological knowledge to match sounds to letters to construct unknown words.
2.23Biv Spell words with common orthographic patterns and rules: vowel digraphs, diphthongs.
2.23C Spell high-frequency words from a commonly used list.

Sound and Letter Patterns

Use **oi** or **oy** to finish each spelling word with the same vowel sound as in **boy**.

1. c __ __ n
2. t __ __ s
3. j __ __ n

Segment Sounds

Use **oi** or **oy** to make spelling words.
Write the words.

4. Change **at** in **bat**.
5. Change **ai** in **bail**.
6. Change **et** in **jet**.
7. Change **ip** in **sip**.
8. Change **ane** in **canes**.
9. Change **r** in **try**.

Use the Dictionary

Write the spelling word that would be on the same page as this pair of **guide words** in a dictionary.

10. off • only

Sound and Letter Patterns

1. _____
2. _____
3. _____

Segment Sounds

4. _____
5. _____
6. _____
7. _____
8. _____
9. _____

Use the Dictionary

10. _____

 TEKS 2.23A Use phonological knowledge to match sounds to letters to construct unknown words.
2.23Biv Spell words with common orthographic patterns and rules: vowel digraphs, diphthongs.
2.23C Spell high-frequency words from a commonly used list.

boy	joy	toy	boil	toys
oil	coin	soy	join	coins

Word Categorization

Write the spelling word that fits each group.

1. girl, man, _____

2. game, ball, _____

3. happiness, delight, _____

4. dime, penny, _____

5. cook, fry, _____

Use Context Clues

Write a spelling word to complete each sentence.

6. Farmers often grow _____ on the farm.

7. My mom put _____ in the pan before frying the meat.

8. A doll, small cars, and blocks are _____.

9. I want to _____ a 4-H Club.

10. Roy put three shiny _____ in his piggy bank.

Word Categorization

1. _____

2. _____

3. _____

4. _____

5. _____

Use Context Clues

6. _____

7. _____

8. _____

9. _____

10. _____

TEKS 2.23C Spell high-frequency words from a commonly used list.

Connections to WRITING

Proofread an Ad

Proofread the ad below for eight misspelled words. Then rewrite the ad. Write the spelling words correctly and make the corrections shown by the proofreading marks.

What's for Sale?

¶ What a joi! There are tois for sale cheap.

One girl had six cions. she got a game.

A boi had just one cone. He got a an oyl

truck. Call Victor at 555-4537. Joyn the

fun. Come and get a toi!

Proofreading Marks

☰	Capital Letter
/	Small Letter
∧	Add
ℒ	Delete
⊙	Add a Period
¶	Indent

PERSUASIVE Writing Prompt

Write an Ad

What might you sell? Write an ad that will make people want to buy it. Use as many spelling words as you can.

- Use the writing process: prewrite, draft, revise, edit, and publish.
- Tell what you are selling and how much it costs.
- Tell why someone would want to buy it.
- Give your name and how you can be reached.
- Write complete sentences with correct capitalization, punctuation, grammar, and spelling.
- Circle two words that may be misspelled. Use a dictionary to check the spelling.

Transfer

Think of three more words that contain the /oi/ sound that you hear in the word **toy**. These can be new words you used in your persuasive paragraph. Write the words in your **Spelling Journal**. Circle the spelling pattern **oy** or **oi** in each word.

TEKS 2.23A Use phonological knowledge to match sounds to letters to construct unknown words.
2.23Biv Spell words with common orthographic patterns and rules: vowel digraphs, diphthongs.
2.23C Spell high-frequency words from a commonly used list. **2.23F** Use resources to find correct spellings.

137

Word Study

boy	toy	toys	foil	soybean
oil	soy	coins	voice	noise
joy	boil	point	ahoy	
coin	join	soil		

Meaning Mastery

Write the word that matches each meaning.

1. something to play with
2. a feeling of happiness
3. to put together
4. dirt, earth
5. someone uses this to speak
6. a plant

Rhyming Words

Use words from the list above to complete these rhyming exercises. Circle the /**oi**/ spelling.

7–8. soil, oil, _____, _____

9. join, _____

10. toys _____

Meaning Mastery

1. _____
2. _____
3. _____
4. _____
5. _____
6. _____

Rhyming Words

7. _____
8. _____
9. _____
10. _____

TEKS 2.23A Use phonological knowledge to match sounds to letters to construct unknown words.
2.23Biv Spell words with common orthographic patterns and rules: vowel digraphs, diphthongs.
2.23C Spell high-frequency words from a commonly used list.

Math

Word Hunt

Read the paragraphs below. Look for words with /oi/ spelled **oy** or **oi**.

A boy named Jack felt no joy that day because his bank full of coins was missing.

Mrs. Simpson gave Jack a dollar to carry a box of toys to her car. Eight quarters went into the bank when he raked the soil in the garden. Jack also took Mr. Lee's tiny toy poodle for lots of walks. Mr. Lee had paid Jack ten dimes so far.

A noise made him look up. The voice of his friend, Roy, asked, "Can I join you?"

Jack said, "I lost some money and maybe you can help me find it."

WORD SORT

1–4. Write the words that have /oi/ spelled **oy**.

5–9. Write the words that have /oi/ spelled **oi**.

1. _____
2. _____
3. _____
4. _____
5. _____
6. _____
7. _____
8. _____
9. _____

TEKS 2.23A Use phonological knowledge to match sounds to letters to construct unknown words.
2.23Biv Spell words with common orthographic patterns and rules: vowel digraphs, diphthongs.
2.23C Spell high-frequency words from a commonly used list.

Add -s

1. _____
2. _____
3. _____
4. _____
5. _____

Add -es

6. _____
7. _____
8. _____
9. _____
10. _____

Connections to THINKING

Read the spelling words and sentences.

1. birds   The **birds** sing near my window.
2. boxes   We fill two **boxes** with books.
3. eggs   I fry two **eggs** for breakfast.
4. glasses   Pam wears **glasses**.
5. boats   Three **boats** are on the lake.
6. dishes   The **dishes** are not clean.
7. boys   Those **boys** are on my team.
8. foxes   I saw two **foxes** in the woods.
9. girls   The **girls** chat on the phone.
10. wishes   My mom sends her best **wishes**.

Think & Sort the spelling words.

1–5. Write the words that add **-s** to a base word.

6–10. Write the words that add **-es** to a base word.

Remember

Words that show "more than one" often end with **-s** (**boats**) or **-es** (**boxes**). These words are called **plurals**. They are formed by adding **-s** or **-es** to the base word.

 TEKS 2.23C Spell high-frequency words from a commonly used list. **2.23D** Spell base words with inflectional endings.

Make New Words

Replace the underlined vowel spelling to write a spelling word.

1. b<u>ea</u>ts

2. f<u>i</u>xes

3. d<u>a</u>shes

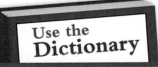

Plurals

Write spelling words by adding **-s** or **-es** to each word below. Circle the words you write that have two syllables.

4. egg

5. girl

6. glass

7. bird

8. wish

Use the Dictionary

9–10. A dictionary lists words in alphabetical order. Find **boy** and **box** in your **Spelling Dictionary**. Write the plural form of those spelling words in alphabetical order.

Make New Words

1. _____

2. _____

3. _____

Plurals

4. _____

5. _____

6. _____

7. _____

8. _____

Use the Dictionary

9. _____

10. _____

 TEKS 2.23C Spell high-frequency words from a commonly used list. **2.23D** Spell base words with inflectional endings.

141

| birds | boxes | eggs | glasses | boats |
| dishes | boys | foxes | girls | wishes |

Rhyme Time

Write pairs of words that rhyme in each silly sentence.

1–2. She _____ she hadn't broken the _____.

3–4. The sly _____ were sleeping in the _____.

Use Context Clues

Write more spelling words to finish these silly sentences.

5. In the nest were three _____ with no legs.

6–8. Big beaked _____ bullied _____ bouncing by in _____.

9–10. Giggling _____ in green dresses gave _____ to great grandmothers.

Rhyme Time

1.

2.

3.

4.

Use Context Clues

5.

6.

7.

8.

9.

10.

TEKS 2.23A Use phonological knowledge to match sounds to letters to construct unknown words.
2.23C Spell high-frequency words from a commonly used list.

Connections to WRITING

Proofread a Paragraph

Find eight misspelled words in the paragraph below. Rewrite the paragraph using correct spelling. Make the corrections shown by the proofreading marks.

My Wish

¶Today we hiked at Spring hill. The grils spotted eleven kinds of birdes. We found a Nest with three egges. The boyes saw fourteen kinds of trees. I saw two red foxs near some berry bushes. We ate lunch near a cold rocky stream. We were careful not to Pack dishs or glases that would break. If my wishs come true, I will go to Spring Hill again someday!

Proofreading Marks

≡	Capital Letter
/	Small Letter
∧	Add
℘	Delete
⊙	Add a Period
¶	Indent

DESCRIPTIVE Writing Prompt

Write a Descriptive Paragraph

Write about a place you have visited. Use as many spelling words as you can to create a picture of the place. Circle words that have **-s** or **-es** endings.

- Use the writing process: prewrite, draft, revise, edit, publish.
- Tell the name of the place and what you saw there.
- Use words that tell color, size, and shape.
- Use words to tell how things look, feel, sound, and smell.
- Write complete sentences with correct capitalization, punctuation, grammar, and spelling.
- Circle two words that may be misspelled. Use a dictionary to check the spelling.

Transfer

Think of two more words that end with **-s** and **-es**. Write the words in your Spelling Journal. Circle the letters that spell the plural ending. Draw a picture to go with each word.

 TEKS 2.23A Use phonological knowledge to match sounds to letters to construct unknown words.
2.23C Spell high-frequency words from a commonly used list. **2.23D** Spell base words with inflectional endings. **2.23F** Use resources to find correct spellings.

Word Study

bugs	boxes	eggs	wishes	guesses
cats	dishes	glasses	apples	radishes
pants	boys	boats	benches	sneakers
birds	girls	foxes	pies	trucks

Use words from the list above to complete these exercises.

Pattern Power

Write the plural form of each word and circle the **-s** or **-es** ending.

1. cat   **2.** box   **3.** guess

Word Categorization

Write the spelling word that belongs in each group.

4. ships, rafts, _____

5. cakes, cookies, _____

6. cars, vans, _____

7. beets, carrots, _____

Meaning Mastery

Write the spelling word that matches each meaning.

8. clothing you wear on your feet

9. long seats

10. red, yellow, or green fruits

Pattern Power

1.

2.

3.

Word Categorization

4.

5.

6.

7.

Meaning Mastery

8.

9.

10.

TEKS 2.23C Spell high-frequency words from a commonly used list. **2.23D** Spell base words with inflectional endings.

Art

Word Hunt

Read the paragraph below. Look for plurals that end with **-s** and **-es**.

Find your way south to Mexico. You will reach the state of Oaxaca (wa-HAH-ka). There are many small towns. In each town you will find artists. Some artists carve animals from wood. They carve frogs, rabbits, foxes, and more. An animal could be a few inches. Some are quite large. After an animal is carved it must dry. Then it is sanded. Often women paint the shape. Children might help. They use big and small brushes. After they put on one coat of paint, they add more color. They make a design. No two are alike.

1. _____

2. _____

3. _____

4. _____

5. _____

6. _____

7. _____

8. _____

WORD SORT

Circle the **-s** and **-es** endings on the words you write.

1–5. Write the words that end with **-s**.

6–8. Write the words that end with **-es**.

TEKS 2.23C Spell high-frequency words from a commonly used list.
2.23D Spell base words with inflectional endings.

End with -ed

1. _____

2. _____

3. _____

4. _____

5. _____

6. _____

End with -ing

7. _____

8. _____

9. _____

10. _____

Connections to THINKING

Read the spelling words and sentences.

1. walked   We **walked** around the park.
2. looking   I am **looking** at this book.
3. planted   Ron **planted** peas and beans.
4. asked   Jan **asked** a question.
5. jumping   Rachel likes **jumping** rope.
6. filled   I **filled** my glass to the top.
7. talking   We are **talking** on the phone.
8. needed   Pat **needed** to drink water.
9. spelling   This **spelling** test is easy.
10. played   Dan **played** checkers with me.

Think & Sort the spelling words.

1–6. Write the words that end with **-ed**.

7–10. Write the words that end with **-ing**.

Remember

Add **-ed** and **-ing** to verbs to make new words:
ask, asked, asking.

TEKS 2.23C Spell high-frequency words from a commonly used list.
2.23D Spell base words with inflectional endings.

Word Structure

Write the past tense or present participle form of each verb to complete the chart. Then circle the letters that spell the ending in each word.

Present	Past	Participle
need	**1.**	needing
walk	**2.**	walking
spell	spelled	**3.**
fill	**4.**	filling
jump	jumped	**5.**
look	looked	**6.**
play	**7.**	playing

Use the Dictionary

Find the following words in the **Spelling Dictionary**. Write the word that comes *before* it, adding the **-ed** or **-ing** ending to make a spelling word.

8. ate
9. plate
10. tall

Word Structure

1. _____
2. _____
3. _____
4. _____
5. _____
6. _____
7. _____

Use the Dictionary

8. _____
9. _____
10. _____

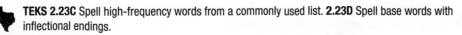 **TEKS 2.23C** Spell high-frequency words from a commonly used list. **2.23D** Spell base words with inflectional endings.

147

walked   looking   planted   asked   jumping
filled   talking   needed   spelling   played

Replace the Words

Replace the underlined word with a spelling word that makes more sense. Circle the **-ed** or **-ing** ending.

1. An almanac can tell you who holds the record for <u>digging</u> the highest.
2. A dictionary lets you check the <u>color</u> of a word.
3. Children's magazines can tell you how different games are <u>cooked</u>.
4. Nonfiction books can give you information on how flowers are <u>sailed</u>.

Use Context Clues

Write the spelling words that complete the paragraph.

Wanita went to the library to borrow a book. She __5.__ out a form to get a library card. Then she __6.__ through the library. She was __7.__ for her favorite book. It was very quiet. Everyone was reading. No one was __8.__. The librarian __9.__ Wanita if she __10.__ help. Wanita told her no. Soon she found her book.

Replace the Words

1.
2.
3.
4.

Use Context Clues

5.
6.
7.
8.
9.
10.

TEKS 2.23C Spell high-frequency words from a commonly used list.
2.23D Spell base words with inflectional endings.

Connections to WRITING

Proofread a Book Report

Find seven misspelled words in the book report below. Rewrite the report using correct spelling. Make the corrections shown by the proofreading marks.

¶ <u>Abe Lincoln's Hat</u> by Martha Brenner tells some tales of abe lincoln as a young /Lawyer. One tale is that Abe needded a tall black hat. Why? He filld it with important papers. Some boys were lokking at his hat and tallking about fooling Abe,⊙ They palyed a trick. They painted a high wire where Abe walkked by. Read the book to ̶t̶o̶ find out what happens.

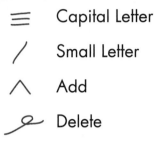

Proofreading Marks

☰	Capital Letter
/	Small Letter
∧	Add
℘	Delete
⊙	Add a Period
¶	Indent

PERSUASIVE Writing Prompt

Write a Book Report

One way to tell others about a good book you have read is to write a book report. The report tells about the characters, the setting, and some things that happen. Write a book report that will make your classmates want to read it. Use as many spelling words as you can.

- Use the writing process: prewrite, draft, revise, edit, and publish.
- Tell the title and author of the book you read. Underline the title.
- Tell about the characters and the main events, but don't tell the ending. Tell why you liked the book.
- Write complete sentences with correct capitalization, punctuation, grammar, and spelling.
- Circle two words that may be misspelled. Use a dictionary to check the spelling.

Transfer

Think of two more words that end with **-ing** and two more words that end with **-ed**. Write the words in your Spelling Journal. Circle the letters that spell the ending.

TEKS 2.23C Spell high-frequency words from a commonly used list. **2.23D** Spell base words with inflectional endings. **2.23F** Use resources to find correct spellings.

Word Study

packed	talking	jumping	sleeping
packing	needed	filled	cracking
picked	played	spelling	drifted
looking	walked	dashed	followed
asked	planted	fishing	pressed

Pattern Power

1. _____

2. _____

3. _____

Consonant Digraphs

4. _____

5. _____

6. _____

7. _____

8. _____

Meaning Mastery

9. _____

10. _____

Pattern Power

Add an ending to each word to show that something is happening right now.

1. talk   **2.** sleep   **3.** jump

Consonant Digraphs

Write words with two consonants together that make one sound to complete these sentences.

4. Have you _____ your suitcase for the trip?

5. Malia _____ to the store before it closed.

6. The squirrel had trouble _____ the nut.

7. I had trouble _____ that word.

8. Ciera likes _____ in the pond.

Meaning Mastery

Write the word that matches each meaning.

9. floated with the current

10. went after

 TEKS 2.23Bi Spell words with common orthographic patterns and rules: complex consonants. **2.23C** Spell high-frequency words from a commonly used list. **2.23D** Spell base words with inflectional endings.

Science

Word Hunt

Read the paragraphs below. Look for words that end with **-ed** and **-ing**.

A black bear came crashing through the brush. He had walked a long way through the forest looking for food. The bear picked some fruits, berries, and nuts. But this was only a snack for a bear of this size.

The bear followed the sound of water. It lead to a stream. For the bear, the stream was good for drinking and cooling off. It was also good for fishing. The bear dashed to the water and leaped toward a fish. It was a good catch!

After lunch the bear needed a nap, so he lay down in a pile of leaves. It was time for sleeping until the next meal.

1. _____

2. _____

3. _____

4. _____

5. _____

6. _____

7. _____

8. _____

WORD SORT

Circle the **-ed** and **-ing** ending on all of your answers.

1–4. Write four of the words that end with **-ing**.

5–8. Write four of the words that end with **-ed**.

TEKS 2.23C Spell high-frequency words from a commonly used list.
2.23D Spell base words with inflectional endings.

151

Connections to THINKING

Read the spelling words and sentences.

1. wood	The desk is made of **wood**.
2. took	Len **took** a bus to the game.
3. too	It is **too** cold for swimming.
4. noon	We eat lunch at **noon**.
5. good	I feel **good** after a nap.
6. root	A **root** grows underground.
7. book	This **book** tells about caves.
8. boot	That **boot** has a large heel.
9. wool	Is the vest made of **wool**?
10. food	We pack **food** for our trip.

Think & Sort the spelling words.

1–5. Write the words with the **long oo** sound you hear in **boot**.

6–10. Write the words with the **short oo** sound you hear in **wood**.

Remember

You can hear the **short oo** sound in **wood** and the **long oo** sound in **boot**. These sounds are often spelled **oo**.

Long oo sound

1. _____
2. _____
3. _____
4. _____
5. _____

Short oo sound

6. _____
7. _____
8. _____
9. _____
10. _____

TEKS 2.23A Use phonological knowledge to match sounds to letters to construct unknown words.
2.23Biv Spell words with common orthographic patterns and rules: vowel digraphs, diphthongs.
2.23C Spell high-frequency words from a commonly used list.

Word Analysis

Write the spelling word that fits each clue.

1. This word sounds the same as **two**.
2. This word sounds the same as **would**.
3. This word is the same spelled forward and backward.
4. This word rhymes with **cook** and begins like **top**.

Sound and Letter Patterns

Write the words that have the same vowel sound as **hoof**.

5. g __ __ d
6. w __ __ l
7. b __ __ k

Write the words that have the same vowel sound as **tooth**.

8. b __ __ t
9. f __ __ d

Use the Dictionary

10. There may be more than one entry for a word in the dictionary. Write the word that comes after **room** in your **Spelling Dictionary** and tell how many entries it has.

Word Analysis

1. _____

2. _____

3. _____

4. _____

Sound and Letter Patterns

5. _____

6. _____

7. _____

8. _____

9. _____

Use the Dictionary

10. _____

TEKS 2.23A Use phonological knowledge to match sounds to letters to construct unknown words.
2.23Biv Spell words with common orthographic patterns and rules: vowel digraphs, diphthongs.
2.23C Spell high-frequency words from a commonly used list.

wood	took	too	noon	good
root	book	boot	wool	food

Use Analogies

Write a spelling word to complete each analogy.

1. Breakfast is to **morning** as **lunch** is to _____.

2. Give is to **gave** as **take** is to _____.

Use Context Clues

Write the spelling words that complete the paragraphs.

Everything comes from something or somewhere. Trees give us many of the things we use. A **3.** is made from paper. Most paper is made from the **4.** of trees. Some tables and chairs are made from wood, **5.** .

Some important things come from animals. We use **6.** from sheep to make clothes, blankets, and rugs. A **7.** can be made from rubber, leather, or heavy cloth.

Did you know that some of our **8.** comes from the ground? A vegetable such as a carrot that grows in the ground is a **9.** . They are **10.** to eat. They give us some of what we need to grow and stay healthy.

Circle the **oo** spelling that makes the **long oo** sound in the words you wrote.

Use Analogies

1. _____

2. _____

Use Context Clues

3. _____

4. _____

5. _____

6. _____

7. _____

8. _____

9. _____

10. _____

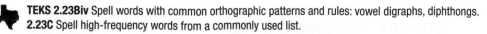

TEKS 2.23Biv Spell words with common orthographic patterns and rules: vowel digraphs, diphthongs. **2.23C** Spell high-frequency words from a commonly used list.

Connections to WRITING

Proofread a Letter

Find eight misspelled words in the letter below. Rewrite the letter using correct spelling. Make the corrections shown by the proofreading marks.

April 15, 2010

dear Grace,

¶ A bus tuke our class to pine Farm. The woode from the trees there is used to make paper. We saw wull cut from sheep. We learned about rout Vegetables and other crops we eat as fuud. We had a gud time.

were
We back by nune. I wish you had been there two.

Your pal,

Sean

Proofreading Marks

≡	Capital Letter
/	Small Letter
∧	Add
℘	Delete
⊙	Add a Period
¶	Indent

NARRATIVE Writing Prompt
Write a Letter

A letter is a way to share news and feelings. Write a letter to a friend about something fun you did. As you write your letter, use as many spelling words as you can.

- Use the writing process: prewrite, draft, revise, edit, and publish.
- Your greeting is *Dear* and the person's name.
- The body of the letter tells about your activities in a logical order.
- End with a closing such as *Your friend* followed by a comma. Then sign your name.
- Write complete sentences with correct capitalization, punctuation, grammar, and spelling.

Transfer

Think of two more words with the **short oo** in **book** and two words with the **long oo** sound in **boot**. Write the words in your Spelling Journal. Circle the letters that spell the vowel sound.

TEKS 2.23A Use phonological knowledge to match sounds to letters to construct unknown words.
2.23Biv Spell words with common orthographic patterns and rules: vowel digraphs, diphthongs.
2.23C Spell high-frequency words from a commonly used list.

Extend & Transfer

Word Study

moon	too	wood	wool	moose
room	noon	root	barefoot	scooter
soon	good	book	choose	stood
took	food	boot	goose	woodpecker

Rhyming Words

1. _____

2. _____

3. _____

Categorizing Words

4. _____

5. _____

6. _____

7. _____

8. _____

Meaning Mastery

9. _____

10. _____

Use words from the list above to complete these exercises. Circle the **long oo** spellings.

Rhyming Words

Write the word or words that rhyme with each word pair.

1. took, shook, _____

2–3. hood, wood, _____, _____

Categorizing Words

Write the word that belongs to each group.

4. bear, elk, _____

5. shoe, flip-flop, _____

6. bike, skateboard, _____

7–8. robin, bluebird, _____, _____

Meaning Mastery

Write the word that matches each meaning.

9. without shoes or socks

10. before long

TEKS 2.23A Use phonological knowledge to match sounds to letters to construct unknown words.
2.23Biv Spell words with common orthographic patterns and rules: vowel digraphs, diphthongs.
2.23C Spell high-frequency words from a commonly used list.

Word Hunt

Read the paragraph below. Look for words with **short oo** and **long oo**.

You need to read a book for school. How do you choose one? You can ask a friend, or you can do a search on the computer. Use a website that tells about books for children. When the site opens, type in a topic. Maybe you want to learn about the moon. This is your topic. Look at the list of books about the moon. Click on a title such as *The Moon Book*. You can click on a link to find it in your library. You can click on a link to buy the book, too. The next time you are in the mood for a good book, try using a website for suggestions.

1. _____

2. _____

3. _____

4. _____

5. _____

6. _____

7. _____

8. _____

WORD SORT

Circle the **long oo** and **short oo** spellings for the words you write.

1–3. Write the words that have the **short oo** sound.

4–8. Write the words that have the **long oo** sound.

TEKS 2.23A Use phonological knowledge to match sounds to letters to construct unknown words.
2.23Biv Spell words with common orthographic patterns and rules: vowel digraphs, diphthongs.
2.23C Spell high-frequency words from a commonly used list.

Unit 19

1.

2.

Unit 20

3.

4.

Unit 21

5.

6.

Unit 22

7.

8.

Unit 23

9.

10.

Units 19–23

Assessment

Write each assessment word under the unit number it fits.

Unit 19

1–2. Consonant blends with **l** and **r** are heard at the beginning of the words **fly** and **free**.

Unit 20

3–4. The vowel sound you hear in **boil** and **boy** can be spelled **oi** and **oy**.

Unit 21

5–6. Words that show "more than one" often end with **-s** or **-es: boats, boxes**. These words are called **plurals**.

Unit 22

7–8. You can add **-ed** and **-ing** to verbs to make new words: **ask, asked, asking**.

Unit 23

9–10. You can hear the **short oo** sound in **wood** and the **long oo** sound in **boot**.

Words for Assessment

joyful

looked

days

sly

hood

being

weeks

frame

void

stoop

Review

Unit 19: Consonant Blends: l and r

slow	train	please	drive	tree

Write a spelling word by adding a letter before each word.

1. rain   **2.** low

Write the spelling word that rhymes with each word.

3. strive   **5.** free

4. sneeze

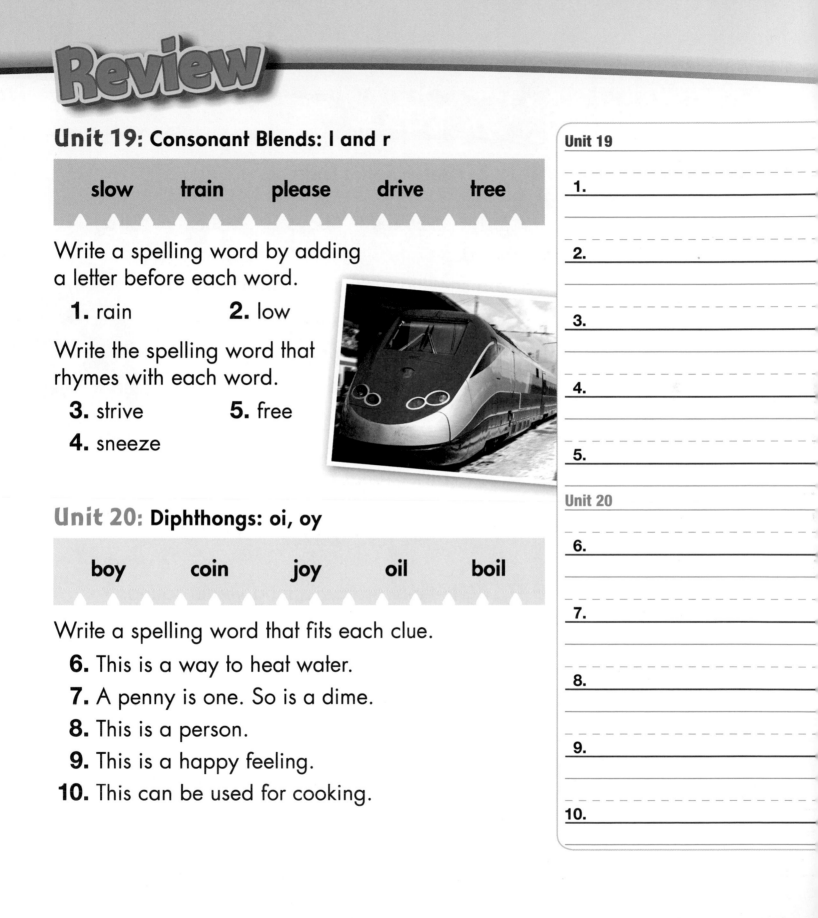

Unit 20: Diphthongs: oi, oy

boy	coin	joy	oil	boil

Write a spelling word that fits each clue.

6. This is a way to heat water.

7. A penny is one. So is a dime.

8. This is a person.

9. This is a happy feeling.

10. This can be used for cooking.

Unit 19

1. _____

2. _____

3. _____

4. _____

5. _____

Unit 20

6. _____

7. _____

8. _____

9. _____

10. _____

Review

1.

2.

3.

4.

5.

6.

7.

8.

9.

10.

Unit 21: Inflectional Endings: -s, -es

| girls | boxes | boys | dishes | birds |

Write a spelling word by adding **-s** or **-es**.

1. dish   **2.** box   **3.** boy

Replace the underlined letters to write a spelling word.

4. g<u>ull</u>s   **5.** b<u>ea</u>ds

Unit 22: Inflectional Endings: -ed, -ing

| asked | needed | played | looking | talking |

6–7. Write the words with long vowel sounds.

Write the word that rhymes with each word below.

8. masked

9. walking

10. cooking

Unit 23: Long and Short oo

good	too	took	noon	food

Write the spelling word that completes each sentence. The spelling word will rhyme with the underlined word.

1. <u>Soon</u> it will be _____.

2. I am in the <u>mood</u> for some tasty _____.

3. Did you happen to find any _____, dry <u>wood</u>?

4. Jamie just _____ the big fish off the <u>hook</u>.

5. Is this what <u>you</u> want, _____?

Spelling Study Strategy

Sorting by Sounds

Here is a way to practice spelling words by placing them into groups.

1. Make three columns on a piece of paper. Label one column *Short Vowels*. Label the next column *Long Vowels* and the last column *Other*.

2. With a partner, take turns finding spelling words to write in each column. Write the words.

3. Say the words aloud and check the spelling of each word.

Directions: Read the introduction and the passage that follows. Then read each question and fill in the space in front of the correct answer.

Olga wrote this story about a girl selling eggs on her family's farm in Texas many years ago. One day the girl has to make a hard decision. Olga wants you to review her paper. As you read, think about ways she can make her story better.

Eggs on Sale!

(1) Before nune, Fran gathered all the eggs from the hen house. (2) She filled two boxs with the eggs. (3) She wisht that finding friends out here in the country was that easy! (4) Then she plantd herself by the road. (5) She needed to sell every egg, but sales were slow.

(6) Fran finally saw a boi walking up the road. (7) "I need six eggs, pleese," he said, "but I can only pay for five. (8) I lost a coin."

(9) Fran felt sorry for the boy, but if she gave him a frea egg, she would lose money. (10) If she did not, he might get in trouble.

(11) "Eggs are on sale today," said Fran with joi. (12) As the boy began to smile, Fran felt she had made a gud friend.

1 What change, if any, should be made in sentence 1?
- ⬭ Change *nune* to **noon**
- ⬭ Change *from* to **frum**
- ⬭ Change *house* to **howse**
- ⬭ Make no change

2 What change, if any, should be made in sentence 2?
- ⬭ Change *filled* to **felled**
- ⬭ Change *boxs* to **boxes**
- ⬭ Change *eggs* to **egges**
- ⬭ Make no change

3 What change should be made in sentence 3?
- ⬭ Change *wisht* to **wished**
- ⬭ Change *here* to **heer**
- ⬭ Change *country* to **countree**
- ⬭ Change *easy* to **eazy**

4 What change, if any, should be made in sentence 4?
- ⬭ Change *Then* to **Than**
- ⬭ Change *plantd* to **planted**
- ⬭ Change *road* to **rood**
- ⬭ Make no change

5 What change, if any, should be made in sentence 5?
- ⬭ Change *needed* to **neaded**
- ⬭ Change *sell* to **cell**
- ⬭ Change *slow* to **sloa**
- ⬭ Make no change

6 What change, if any, should be made in sentence 6?
- ⬭ Change *saw* to **was**
- ⬭ Change *boi* to **boy**
- ⬭ Change *walking* to **waking**
- ⬭ Make no change

7 What change should be made in sentence 7?
- ⬭ Change *six* to **sax**
- ⬭ Change *pleese* to **please**
- ⬭ Change *pay* to **pai**
- ⬭ Change *five* to **fiv**

8 What change, if any, should be made in sentence 9?
- ⬭ Change *felt* to **falt**
- ⬭ Change *gave* to **gaiv**
- ⬭ Change *frea* to **free**
- ⬭ Make no change

9 What change, if any, should be made in sentence 11?
- ⬭ Change *eggs* to **egges**
- ⬭ Change *sale* to **sail**
- ⬭ Change *joi* to **joy**
- ⬭ Make no change

10 What change should be made in sentence 12?
- ⬭ Change *smile* to **smil**
- ⬭ Change *felt* to **flet**
- ⬭ Change *made* to **maide**
- ⬭ Change *gud* to **good**

163

Grammar, Usage, and Mechanics
Nouns

A **noun** names a person, place, or thing. A **common noun** names any person, place, or thing.

The **student** went to that **state** and saw a **fort**.

A **proper noun** names a certain person, place, or thing. Proper nouns begin with a capital letter.

Sally went to **Texas** and saw the **Alamo**.

A. Write **P** if the word is a proper noun.
Write **C** if the word is a common noun.
Write **no** if the underlined word is not a noun.

1. Juan walked <u>here</u>.   **2.** I took the <u>train</u>.

3. Did <u>Tina</u> go slow?   **4.** Let's go to <u>Rome</u>.

5. I like <u>yellow</u> flowers.

B. Complete each sentence with a noun from the box. Write the word.

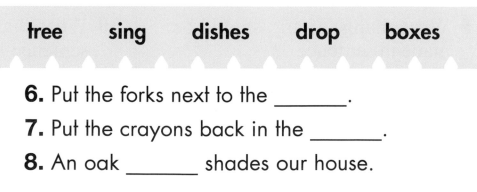

| tree | sing | dishes | drop | boxes |

6. Put the forks next to the _____.

7. Put the crayons back in the _____.

8. An oak _____ shades our house.

Practice Activity A

1. _____

2. _____

3. _____

4. _____

5. _____

Practice Activity B

6. _____

7. _____

8. _____

The Writing Process: Descriptive
Writing a Character Sketch

PREWRITING
Think about a character in one of your favorite books. Write down ideas about what the character does, says, and thinks. Include how he or she looks. Ask an adult to help you look on the Internet for model character sketches.

DRAFTING
Use your ideas to write a character sketch. Use as many spelling words as possible.

REVISING
When you have finished writing, read your sketch. Check to see if you have included all of your ideas. Now write your final draft.

EDITING
Use the **Editing Checklist** to proofread your character sketch. Be sure to use proofreading marks.

PUBLISHING
Make a copy of your character sketch. Draw a portrait of your character and share it with your readers.

EDITING CHECKLIST

Spelling
- ✓ Circle words that contain the spelling patterns and rules learned in Units 19–23.
- ✓ Check the circled words in your **Spelling Dictionary**.
- ✓ Check for other spelling errors.

Capital Letters
- ✓ Capitalize important words in the title.
- ✓ Capitalize the first word in each sentence.
- ✓ Capitalize proper nouns.

Punctuation
- ✓ End each sentence with the correct punctuation.
- ✓ Use commas, apostrophes, and quotation marks correctly.

 TEKS 2.23A Use phonological knowledge to match sounds to letters to construct unknown words.
2.23F Use resources to find correct spellings.

165

Connections to THINKING

Read the spelling words and sentences.

1.	put	I **put** the key in the lock.
2.	want	Do you **want** a new bike?
3.	many	Paul asked **many** questions.
4.	out	The sign says, "Keep **out**."
5.	saw	I **saw** a deer cross the road.
6.	who	Ed is the one **who** read last.
7.	off	Please stay **off** the roof.
8.	any	Do you have **any** money left?
9.	from	This letter is **from** Sylvia.
10.	her	Amanda lost **her** book.

Think & Sort the spelling words.

1–8. Write the words with one syllable.

9–10. Write the words with two syllables.

Remember

It is important to correctly spell words that you use often in writing.

One syllable

1.
2.
3.
4.
5.
6.
7.
8.

Two syllables

9.
10.

TEKS 2.23C Spell high-frequency words from a commonly used list.

Word Analysis

Write a spelling word that matches each clue.

1. It begins with a **short e** sound spelled **a**.
2. It has the vowel sound in **ball** and a double consonant.
3. It rhymes with **to**.
4. It has a **short u** sound spelled with **o**.
5. It has a **short o** sound spelled with **a**.
6. It rhymes with **shout**.

PLEASE KEEP OFF THE GRASS

Sound and Letter Patterns

Write the spelling word that fits each clue.

7. This word begins like **help** and rhymes with **fur**.
8. This word begins like **pup** and rhymes with **foot**.
9. This word begins like **made** and rhymes with **penny**.

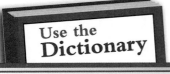

Use the Dictionary

10. Write one spelling word that has both of these meanings.
    - a tool or machine used for cutting
    - the past tense of **see**

Dictionary Check Check the meanings in your **Spelling Dictionary**. Write the page where you find the word.

Word Analysis

1. _____
2. _____
3. _____
4. _____
5. _____
6. _____

Sound and Letter Patterns

7. _____
8. _____
9. _____

Use the Dictionary

10. _____

TEKS 2.23A Use phonological knowledge to match sounds to letters to construct unknown words.
2.23C Spell high-frequency words from a commonly used list.

167

put	want	many	out	saw
who	off	any	from	her

Complete the Analogies

Write a spelling word to complete each analogy.

1. Food is to **bread** as **tool** is to _____.

2. Sometimes is to **some** as **anymore** is to _____.

3. Help is to **aid** as **wish** is to _____.

4. He is to **his** as **she** is to _____.

5. Send is to **receive** as **to** is to _____.

Use Context Clues

Write spelling words that complete the paragraph.

The Story of Earmuffs

Do you know **6.** invented earmuffs? Chester Greenwood invented them in 1873. He was fifteen years old. First he made loops **7.** of wire. His grandmother **8.** fur and velvet on them. Then Chester hooked the loops to his cap. Today, you see **9.** people wearing earmuffs to keep their ears warm. "Hats **10.** " to Chester Greenwood!

Complete the Analogies

1. _____
2. _____
3. _____
4. _____
5. _____

Use Context Clues

6. _____
7. _____
8. _____
9. _____
10. _____

Connections to WRITING

Proofread a Poster

Find eight misspelled words in the poster below. Rewrite the poster using correct spelling. Make the corrections shown by the proofreading marks.

Used Toy Sale

Saturday, june 4, 10 A.M. to noon

Tammy DiLuca's house, 10 Maple Street

Do you wont more toys? I will have meny toys for Sale. I don't want there to be anny toys left when the sale is over. Choose frum dolls, games, balls, and kites. My sister will sell some of herr toys, too. Be there at 10 when I putt them owt! I will give a Free toy to the first five people whoo come.

Proofreading Marks

≡	Capital Letter
/	Small Letter
∧	Add
℘	Delete
⊙	Add a Period
¶	Indent

PERSUASIVE Writing Prompt
Poster

A poster is a kind of ad that tells about an event coming up. It tries to get people to come. Write a poster for a yard sale or another event that will make people want to come. Use as many spelling words as you can.

- Use the writing process: prewrite, draft, revise, edit, and publish.
- Tell what the event is. Give the date, time, and place.
- Give information about the event.
- Give reasons why people should come.
- Write complete sentences with correct capitalization, punctuation, grammar, and spelling.
- Use a dictionary to check your spelling.

Transfer
Think of three more words that you think writers use. Write the words in your Spelling Journal. Write each word in a sentence.

TEKS 2.23A Use phonological knowledge to match sounds to letters to construct unknown words.
2.23C Spell high-frequency words from a commonly used list. **2.23F** Use resources to find correct spellings.

Word Study

name	many	put	from	full
was	saw	out	away	move
we	off	who	busy	pull
want	her	any	real	says

Use words from the list to complete these exercises.

Word Building

Add **a** or **e** to make a spelling word.

1. w ___

2. s ___ w

3. aw ___ y

4. m ___ ny

5. s ___ ys

Use Antonyms

Write the word that means the opposite.

6. the opposite of **on**

7. the opposite of **push**

8. the opposite of **made up**

9. the opposite of **to**

10. the opposite of **empty**

Word Building

1.

2.

3.

4.

5.

Use Antonyms

6.

7.

8.

9.

10.

TEKS 2.23C Spell high-frequency words from a commonly used list.

Social Studies

Read the paragraph below. Look for words that writers use.

Tomás Rivera was born in Texas. His parents moved from farm to farm to pick crops. The work was hard, and they were busy. Tomás helped when he could. At the end of a long day, his grandpa told stories. Tomás wanted to tell stories, too. He read many books. Books helped him write. Tomás had a lot of ideas. He wrote stories and poems. Some were about farm work. When Tomás grew up, he got a job in a school as a teacher. People saw the good work he did. They wanted to thank him. They put his name on a library. Some schools have his name, too.

WORD SORT

1–4. Write the words with the same vowel sound as **stood**.

5–9. Write the words with the same vowel sound as **boot**.

1. _____
2. _____
3. _____
4. _____
5. _____
6. _____
7. _____
8. _____
9. _____

TEKS 2.23A Use phonological knowledge to match sounds to letters to construct unknown words.
2.23C Spell high-frequency words from a commonly used list.

Connections to THINKING

Read the spelling words and sentences.

1.	how	I know **how** to ride a bike.
2.	count	I need to **count** all my books.
3.	cow	A **cow** gives milk.
4.	clown	The **clown** makes us laugh.
5.	house	The **house** has many rooms.
6.	town	Our **town** has one post office.
7.	loud	The birds are very **loud**.
8.	now	We must leave the room **now**.
9.	ouch	I said, "**Ouch!**" when I fell.
10.	down	Go **down** the stairs.

Think & Sort the spelling words.

1–6. Write the words with the /**ou**/ sound spelled **ow**.

7–10. Write the words with the /**ou**/ sound spelled **ou**.

Remember

The vowel sound you hear in **cow** is /**ou**/ spelled **ow**. The vowel sound you hear in **loud** is /**ou**/ spelled **ou**.

/ou/ spelled ow

1. _____
2. _____
3. _____
4. _____
5. _____
6. _____

/ou/ spelled ou

7. _____
8. _____
9. _____
10. _____

TEKS 2.23A Use phonological knowledge to match sounds to letters to construct unknown words.
2.23Biv Spell words with common orthographic patterns and rules: vowel digraphs, diphthongs.
2.23C Spell high-frequency words from a commonly used list.

Sound and Letter Patterns

Use **ou** or **ow** to finish each spelling word.

1. h __ __ se

2. d __ __ n

3. t __ __ n

4. l __ __ d

Match Sounds

Use **ou** or **ow** to make spelling words. Circle the vowel spellings in your answers.

5. Write the word that starts like **cat** and ends like **mount**.

6. Write the word that rhymes with **couch**.

7. Write the word that starts like **hen** and ends like **cow**.

8–9. Write the spelling words that rhyme with your answer to 7.

Use the Dictionary

10. Look in your **Spelling Dictionary**. Find a spelling word that names a person who acts funny to make us laugh. It sounds like **kloun,** but the first letter is not **k,** and the vowel spelling is different. Write the word and the dictionary page number where you find it.

Sound and Letter Patterns

1. _____

2. _____

3. _____

4. _____

Match Sounds

5. _____

6. _____

7. _____

8. _____

9. _____

Use the Dictionary

10. _____

TEKS 2.23A Use phonological knowledge to match sounds to letters to construct unknown words.
2.23Biv Spell words with common orthographic patterns and rules: vowel digraphs, diphthongs.
2.23C Spell high-frequency words from a commonly used list. **2.23F** Use resources to find correct spellings.

how	now	down	clown	town
count	ouch	cow	house	loud

Use Synonyms

Write the spelling word that means the same.

1. village
2. at this time

Complete the Analogies

Write a spelling word to complete each analogy.

3. **School** is to **teacher** as **circus** is to _____.
4. **High** is to **low** as **up** is to _____.
5. **Forest** is to **deer** as **farm** is to _____.
6. **Small** is to **big** as **quiet** is to _____.
7. **Page** is to **book** as **room** is to _____.

Use Context Clues

Write a spelling word to complete each sentence.

8. I could _____ to ten when I was four years old.
9. Do you know _____ old she is?
10. She said, "_____!" when she bumped her toe.

Use Synonyms

1.

2.

Complete the Analogies

3.

4.

5.

6.

7.

Use Context Clues

8.

9.

10.

 TEKS 2.23C Spell high-frequency words from a commonly used list.

Connections to WRITING

Proofread a Realistic Story

Find eight misspelled words in the realistic story below. Rewrite the story using correct spelling. Make the corrections shown by the proofreading marks.

A Brand New Pouncer

¶One day Pouncer hurt his leg. Kate did not know howe he did it. Maybe he fell doawn. Maybe he jumped off the roof of the howse when he heard a lowed noise⊙ Maybe he got stepped on by a coww on Kate's farm. Owch! That would hurt! Kate took him to the vet in her toun. The vet put pouncer's leg in in a splint. nou he is all better.

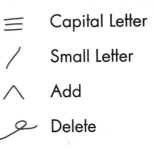

Proofreading Marks

≡	Capital Letter
/	Small Letter
∧	Add
ℯ	Delete
⊙	Add a Period
¶	Indent

NARRATIVE Writing Prompt
Realistic Story

A realistic story has characters that could be real and events that could happen. Write a realistic story about friends or a pet. Use as many spelling words as you can.

- Use the writing process: prewrite, draft, revise, edit, and publish.
- Tell story events in order.
- Make sure your story has a beginning, a middle, and an ending.
- Write complete sentences with correct capitalization, punctuation, grammar, and spelling.
- Circle two words that might be misspelled. Use a dictionary to check the spelling.

Transfer

Think of two more words with /ou/ spelled **ow** and two with /ou/ spelled **ou**. Write the words in your Spelling Journal. Circle the letters that spell the vowel sound in each word.

TEKS 2.23A Use phonological knowledge to match sounds to letters to construct unknown words.
2.23Biv Spell words with common orthographic patterns and rules: vowel digraphs, diphthongs. **2.23C** Spell high-frequency words from a commonly used list. **2.23F** Use resources to find correct spellings.

Extend & Transfer

Word Study

how	down	town	towns	towel
count	cow	loud	frown	about
now	clown	cloud	sound	
ouch	house	found		

Use words from the list to complete these exercises.

Word Building

Change the underlined letters in each word to make a spelling word.

1. cl<u>ea</u>n
2. st<u>a</u>nd
3. ch<u>a</u>nt
4. t<u>ee</u>ns
5. <u>i</u>nch

Rhyme Time

Write a word from the list that rhymes with the word in dark type in each sentence. Circle the vowel spelling in the words you write.

6. I _____ a dime on the **ground**.
7. Do you know _____ to milk a **cow**?
8. The _____ is dark and the storm is **loud**.
9. There is a **mouse** in the _____.
10. He looked **down** with a _____.

Word Building

1.

2.

3.

4.

5.

Rhyme Time

6.

7.

8.

9.

10.

 TEKS 2.23A Use phonological knowledge to match sounds to letters to construct unknown words.
2.23Biv Spell words with common orthographic patterns and rules: vowel digraphs, diphthongs.
2.23C Spell high-frequency words from a commonly used list.

Science

Word Hunt

Read the paragraph below. Look for words with /**ou**/ spelled **ow** and **ou**.

Around noon, a black cloud rolled across the sky. Lulu was outside in the garden. When she saw a flash of lightning, she began to count slowly. She got to five before she heard a powerful clap of thunder. Her teacher said you always see the lightning before you hear the thunder. Soon raindrops were coming down hard and Lulu was wet. She went into her house and dried off with a towel.

"The rain smells wonderful, Dad," she said. "I think it will help my flowers, too."

A loud boom of thunder made her jump. "That was a big one!" she cried.

1. _____

2. _____

3. _____

4. _____

5. _____

6. _____

7. _____

8. _____

1–4. Write the words with the /**ou**/ sound spelled the same as in the word **cow**.

5–8. Write the one-syllable words with the /**ou**/ sound spelled the same as in the word **ouch**.

TEKS 2.23A Use phonological knowledge to match sounds to letters to construct unknown words.
2.23Biv Spell words with common orthographic patterns and rules: vowel digraphs, diphthongs.
2.23C Spell high-frequency words from a commonly used list.

Connections to THINKING

Read the spelling words and sentences.

1. he's — Tell Manuel **he's** next at bat.
2. what's — I do not know **what's** happening.
3. don't — I **don't** have your e-mail address.
4. I'm — **I'm** walking to school.
5. that's — Tell me **that's** your best work.
6. doesn't — A lion **doesn't** have stripes.
7. there's — **There's** our new neighbor.
8. she's — **She's** coming to the party.
9. isn't — That joke **isn't** funny.
10. here's — **Here's** the pen I lost.

Think & Sort the spelling words.

1. Write the contraction that uses **is** and shortens **not**.
2. Write the contraction that uses **am**.
3–8. Write the contractions that use **is**.
9–10. Write the contractions that use **not**.

Remember

Remember that a **contraction** combines two words into one shorter word: **I am, I'm**. The apostrophe (') takes the place of a letter or letters.

Uses is and not

1. _____

Contraction with am

2. _____

Contractions with is

3. _____

4. _____

5. _____

6. _____

7. _____

8. _____

Contractions with not

9. _____

10. _____

TEKS **2.23C** Spell high-frequency words from a commonly used list. **2.23E** Spell simple contractions.

Word Structure

Follow the directions to write a spelling word. Be sure to add an apostrophe in the place where a letter was taken out.

1. here + is – i = _____

2. what + is – i = _____

3. I + am – a = _____

4. do + not – o = _____

5. does + not – o = _____

Vowel Sounds

6–7. Write the words with the **long e** sound. Draw a line under the vowel spelling.

8. Write the word with the **short i** sound. Draw a line under the vowel spelling.

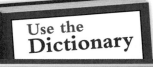
Use the Dictionary

9–10. Write the two spelling words that begin with **th** in a-b-c order. Remember that since both words begin with the same two letters, you must look to the third letter to decide which word comes first. Then check the order in your **Spelling Dictionary**. Write the page where you find it.

Word Structure

1. _____

2. _____

3. _____

4. _____

5. _____

Vowel Sounds

6. _____

7. _____

8. _____

Use the Dictionary

9. _____

10. _____

TEKS 2.23A Use phonological knowledge to match sounds to letters to construct unknown words.
2.23Biii Spell words with common orthographic patterns and rules: long vowels. **2.23C** Spell high-frequency words from a commonly used list. **2.23E** Spell simple contractions.

179

he's	what's	don't	I'm	that's
doesn't	there's	she's	isn't	here's

Complete the Sentences

1.

2.

3.

4.

5.

6.

Complete the Analogies

7.

8.

9.

10.

Complete the Sentences

Write the spelling word that completes each sentence. Use a contraction of the words at the end of each sentence.

1. Today _____ going to help Dad. (I am)

2. I know _____ a lot of work. (that is)

3. I would like to find out _____ in that box. (what is)

4. I think _____ a bird's nest up in the tree. (there is)

5. Do you think _____ going to help us? (he is)

6. Sal _____ want to go to the park. (does not)

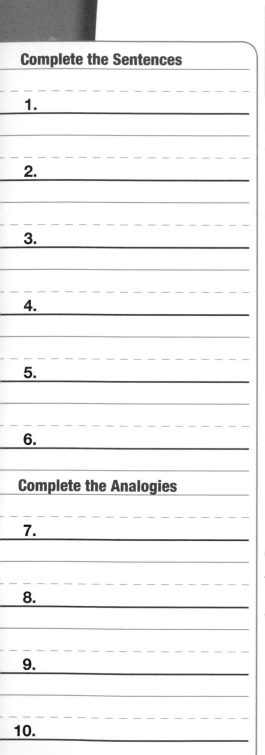

Complete the Analogies

Write the spelling word that completes each analogy.

7. Far is to **near** as **there's** is to _____.

8. Does is to **doesn't** as **do** is to _____.

9. Find is to **lose** as **is** is to _____.

10. He is to **he's** as **she** is to _____.

TEKS 2.23C Spell high-frequency words from a commonly used list. **2.23E** Spell simple contractions.

Connections to WRITING

Proofread a Post Card

Find eight misspelled words in the post card below. Rewrite the post card using correct spelling. Make the corrections shown by the proofreading marks.

dear Mark,

¶Whats' new with you? Im having fun. Thats our hotel on the front of this card⊙Ther'es a pool and a place to play games. I met a boy from Ohio, too. Hees here with his family. The beach isnt crowded. The waves are are small but fun. Dosen't it sound great? Dont you wish you were here? I will see you soon⊙

        Your friend,

        sean

Mark Sm
12345 Pi
Columbus

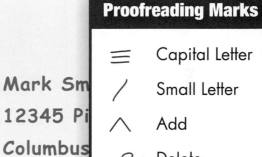

Proofreading Marks

≡	Capital Letter
/	Small Letter
∧	Add
ℯ	Delete
⊙	Add a Period
¶	Indent

DESCRIPTIVE Writing Prompt
Write a Post Card

Write a post card to tell a friend about a place you have visited. Give brief details. Use as many spelling words as you can.

- Use the writing process: prewrite, draft, revise, edit, and publish.
- Use a capital letter in your greeting and closing and a comma after each.
- Indent your message, your closing, and your signature.
- Put your ideas in logical order.
- Use a dictionary to check your spelling.

Transfer
Write two more contractions you know. Then write the two words that mean the same in your Spelling Journal.

TEKS 2.23A Use phonological knowledge to match sounds to letters to construct unknown words.
2.23C Spell high-frequency words from a commonly used list. **2.23E** Spell simple contractions.
2.23F Use resources to find correct spellings.

Word Study

didn't	I'm	there's	who's	wasn't
can't	that's	she's	aren't	couldn't
he's	what's	isn't	hasn't	weren't
don't	doesn't	here's	where's	

Pattern Power

Pattern Power

_1._
_2._
_3._
_4._
_5._
_6._

Word Meaning

Word Meaning

_7._
_8._
_9._
_10._

Pattern Power

Make a contraction using **not** with each of these words. Write the contractions.

1. does
2. are
3. has
4. was
5. could
6. were

Word Meaning

Write the contraction for each underlined pair of words. Check each answer in your **Spelling Dictionary**. Write the page number where you find each word.

7. I <u>did not</u> know that Rico wanted to go with us.

8. Anya said <u>she is</u> riding with us.

9. <u>Here is</u> the paint you were looking for.

10. Do you know <u>who is</u> going to the concert?

 TEKS 2.23C Spell high-frequency words from a commonly used list. **2.23E** Spell simple contractions. **2.23F** Use resources to find correct spellings.

Math

Word Hunt

Read the story below and look for words that are **contractions**.

Trong looked at his old shoes and said to his mom, "Mom, I'm going to need new sneakers. I can't wear these anymore. There's a pair in the store for eighty dollars."

Trong's Mom couldn't agree with the price. "I'll give you thirty dollars toward the shoes but you'll have to earn the rest," she said.

Trong did extra jobs by helping a neighbor. He managed to earn thirty dollars. Trong showed his mother the sixty dollars. "I haven't earned all the money, but how's this price?"

He showed his mom an ad for sixty-dollar shoes.

"When's the sale?" Mom asked.

"It's today," said Trong. "Let's go!"

1. _____

2. _____

3. _____

4. _____

5. _____

6. _____

7. _____

8. _____

WORD SORT

1. I am _____

2. have not _____

3. could not _____

4. can not _____

5. there is _____

6. when is _____

7. how is _____

8. it is _____

TEKS 2.23C Spell high-frequency words from a commonly used list. 2.23E Spell simple contractions.

183

Rhyme with bar

1. _____

2. _____

3. _____

Rhyme with harm

4. _____

5. _____

Rhyme with cart

6. _____

7. _____

Rhyme with bark

8. _____

9. _____

Rhyme with yard

10. _____

Connections to THINKING

Read the spelling words and sentences.

1. far — My house is not **far** from here.
2. farm — We saw cows at the **farm**.
3. art — I draw and paint in **art** class.
4. park — Mom can **park** the van here.
5. car — His **car** had a flat tire.
6. part — A switch is **part** of a light.
7. dark — I cannot see you in the **dark**.
8. star — Look at that **star** in the sky.
9. hard — Old bread gets stale and **hard**.
10. arm — My **arm** is tired from throwing.

Think & Sort the spelling words.

1–3. Write the words that rhyme with **bar**.

4–5. Write the words that rhyme with **harm**.

6–7. Write the words that rhyme with **cart**.

8–9. Write the words that rhyme with **bark**.

10. Write the word that rhymes with **yard**.

Remember

The /är/ sound you hear in **car** can be spelled **ar**.

TEKS 2.23A Use phonological knowledge to match sounds to letters to construct unknown words. **2.23Bii** Spell words with common orthographic patterns and rules: r-controlled vowels. **2.23C** Spell high-frequency words from a commonly used list.

Circle the vowel spellings in the words you write.

Word Structure

Replace the underlined letter or letters to write a spelling word.

1. f<u>u</u>r

2. pa<u>c</u>k

3. s<u>t</u>ep

4. p<u>in</u>t

Word Analysis

Write the spelling word that fits each clue.

5. This word rhymes with **card**.

6. This word contains the smaller word **arm**.

7. Remove the **p** in **part** and this word is left.

8. This word rhymes with **park** and has one more letter than **ark**.

Use the **Dictionary**

9–10. Write the two spelling words you have not used on this page. One begins with /är/ and one ends with /är/. Write the page numbers where you find them in your **Spelling Dictionary**.

Word Structure

1. _____

2. _____

3. _____

4. _____

Word Analysis

5. _____

6. _____

7. _____

8. _____

Use the Dictionary

9. _____

10. _____

 TEKS 2.23A Use phonological knowledge to match sounds to letters to construct unknown words.
2.23Bii Spell words with common orthographic patterns and rules: r-controlled vowels. **2.23C** Spell high-frequency words from a commonly used list.

far	farm	art	park	car
part	dark	star	hard	arm

Complete the Analogies

Write a spelling word to complete each analogy.
Circle the letters that spell the vowel sound.

1. Pilot is to **plane** as **driver** is to _____.

2. Foot is to **leg** as **hand** is to _____.

3. Shine is to **sun** as **twinkle** is to _____.

4. Plane is to **land** as **car** is to _____.

5. Day is to **night** as **light** is to _____.

Use Context Clues

Write the spelling words to complete the paragraph.

Anna Mary Robertson, known as Grandma Moses, was a famous painter. Grandma Moses was born on a **6.** . As a child, she worked **7.** . She also spent **8.** of her time picking wildflowers. Most of her paintings were done after she was seventy years old. Many of her paintings show pictures of life in the country. In 1940, her paintings were seen at an **9.** show. Soon Grandma Moses became very famous. Her paintings were admired by thousands. Today people come from near and **10.** to see her work.

Complete the Analogies

1. _____
2. _____
3. _____
4. _____
5. _____

Use Context Clues

6. _____
7. _____
8. _____
9. _____
10. _____

 TEKS 2.23Bii Spell words with common orthographic patterns and rules: r-controlled vowels. **2.23C** Spell high-frequency words from a commonly used list.

Connections to WRITING

Proofread a Poem

Find eight misspelled words in the poem below. Rewrite the poem using correct spelling. Make the corrections shown by the proofreading marks.

A Shooting Star

Our family got in the carr and drove to a paark.

We got there just as it was turning darke.

We put down a blanket and sat on the ground.

I leaned on my arme and gazed all around.

the sky looked like artt with each twinkling star.

The lights were so tiny and seemed so faar.

One paart of the sky suddenly caught my ~~my~~ eye.

I saw a Shooting starr go by!

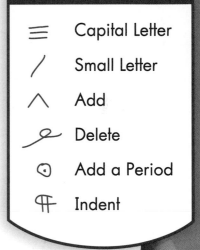
DESCRIPTIVE Writing Prompt
Write a Poem

Use spelling words to write a rhyming poem. Include words that appeal to the senses.

- Use the writing process: prewrite, draft, revise, edit, and publish.
- Choose a topic. Make a list of rhyming words.
- Choose a rhyme pattern, such as every two lines together or every other line.
- Read your poem aloud. How does it sound?
- Write complete sentences with correct capitalization, punctuation, grammar, and spelling.
- Use a dictionary to check your spelling.

Transfer

Think of four more words with **ar**. Write the words in your Spelling Journal. Circle the letters that spell the vowel sound in each word.

TEKS 2.23A Use phonological knowledge to match sounds to letters to construct unknown words. **2.23Bii** Spell words with common orthographic patterns and rules: r-controlled vowels. **2.23C** Spell high-frequency words from a commonly used list. **2.23F** Use resources to find correct spellings.

Word Study

are	park	far	arm	parka
card	car	art	starfish	party
cards	part	dark	shark	scarf
farm	hard	star	faraway	start

Use words from the list above to complete these exercises. Circle the **ar** spellings.

Word Building

Replace the underlined letter in each word to make a word from the list.

1. c<u>o</u>rd   **2.** h<u>e</u>rd   **3.** f<u>i</u>rm

Word Categorization

Write the words that belong to each group.

4–5. hat, mittens, _____, _____

6. guests, gifts, cake, _____

7. e-mails, letters, _____

Use Antonyms

Write the word that means the opposite of each word.

8. nearby _____   **10.** whole _____

9. finish _____

Word Building

1. _____

2. _____

3. _____

Word Categorization

4. _____

5. _____

6. _____

7. _____

Use Antonyms

8. _____

9. _____

10. _____

TEKS 2.23A Use phonological knowledge to match sounds to letters to construct unknown words.
2.23Bii Spell words with common orthographic patterns and rules: r-controlled vowels. **2.23C** Spell high-frequency words from a commonly used list.

Art

Word Hunt

Read the paragraph below. Look for words with ar.

Have you seen a whale up close? Robert Wyland has. He swims with them! Wyland is known for his art. He makes paintings and sculptures of sea life. He dives in the oceans. He swims with dolphins and whales. Then he paints what he sees.

Wyland became an artist at age three. He started by painting dinosaurs. Now he paints whales, sharks, and seals. His art can be small or large. He can make a small starfish charm. He can paint a large mural. All his art has a message. It tells us to do our part to protect sea life.

1. _____

2. _____

3. _____

4. _____

5. _____

6. _____

7. _____

8. _____

WORD SORT

Circle the **ar** spellings.

1–5. Write the words with **ar** with one syllable.

6–8. Write the words with **ar** with two syllables.

 TEKS 2.23Bii Spell words with common orthographic patterns and rules: r-controlled vowels.
2.23C Spell high-frequency words from a commonly used list.

189

Connections to THINKING

Read the spelling words and sentences.

1. chop — We **chop** onions for the stew.
2. each — I gave one bag to **each** child.
3. when — Six o'clock is **when** we eat.
4. chin — The **chin** is part of the face.
5. what — Please find out **what** Jeff wants.
6. such — This is **such** windy weather.
7. why — I don't know **why** Sam did that.
8. much — How **much** does that hat cost?
9. while — I water **while** Raven weeds.
10. which — **Which** one is mine?

Think & Sort the spelling words.

1. Write the word that is spelled with both **wh** and **ch**.

2–5. Write the words that are spelled with **wh**.

6–10. Write the words that are spelled with **ch**.

Remember

The sound you hear at the beginning of **which** is spelled **wh**. The sound you hear at the end of **which** is spelled **ch**.

wh and ch

1. _____

wh

2. _____

3. _____

4. _____

5. _____

ch

6. _____

7. _____

8. _____

9. _____

10. _____

TEKS 2.23A Use phonological knowledge to match sounds to letters to construct unknown words.
2.23Bi Spell words with common orthographic patterns and rules: complex consonants. **2.23C** Spell high-frequency words from a commonly used list.

Sound and Letter Patterns

Write a spelling word to fit each clue.

1. This word has the **long i** sound spelled **i-consonant-e**. It rhymes with **mile**.

2. This word begins with the **long e** sound spelled **ea**. It rhymes with **beach**.

3. This word has the **long i** sound spelled **y**. It rhymes with **fly**.

Word Structure

Replace the underlined letters to write a spelling word.

4. <u>sh</u>in

5. m<u>a</u>th

6. su<u>ng</u>

7. s<u>hi</u>p

Use the Dictionary

The words in a dictionary are in a-b-c order.

8–10. Write these words in a-b-c order and write the page in your Spelling Dictionary where you found them.

| which | when | what |

Dictionary Check Check the a-b-c order of the words in your **Spelling Dictionary**.

Sound and Letter Patterns
1.
2.
3.

Word Structure
4.
5.
6.
7.

Use the Dictionary
8.
9.
10.

 TEKS 2.23A Use phonological knowledge to match sounds to letters to construct unknown words. **2.23Bi** Spell words with common orthographic patterns and rules: complex consonants. **2.23Biii** Spell words with common orthographic patterns and rules: long vowels. **2.23C** Spell high-frequency words from a commonly used list.

chop	each	when	chin	what
such	why	much	while	which

Use Synonyms

Write the spelling word that could best take the place of the underlined word or words.

1. It can be sad to see people <u>cut</u> down trees.
2. Do you know <u>at what time</u> Ava will come to the meeting?
3. I did not learn <u>for what reason</u> we could not go to the park.

Use Context Clues

Write the word that completes each sentence.

4. The forest ranger said hello to _____ one of us.
5. He had a smile on his face and a big beard on his _____.
6. Some rangers meet with groups like ours, _____ others stay in the forest.
7. He spoke to us about _____ forest rangers do to protect the trees and animals.
8. They must be on the lookout for fires, _____ are not always easy to find.
9. There is so _____ work in the forest that rangers are always busy.
10. There are books about forest rangers, _____ as <u>What Does a Forest Ranger Do?</u>

Use Synonyms

1. _____
2. _____
3. _____

Use Context Clues

4. _____
5. _____
6. _____
7. _____
8. _____
9. _____
10. _____

TEKS 2.23C Spell high-frequency words from a commonly used list.

Connections to WRITING

Proofread Interview Questions

Find eight misspelled words in the interview below. Rewrite the interview using correct spelling. Make the corrections shown by the proofreading marks.

1. Hwat is your ~~J~~ob?

2. Wich part of your job do **you** ∧ like best?

3. Wen did you know you wanted that job∧**?**

4. Whi did you choose that kind of work?

5. How does it feel to have suche an important job?

6. how musch time do you spend at work eatch day?

7. Do you take extra ~~C~~lasses wile you work?

Proofreading Marks

≡	Capital Letter
/	Small Letter
∧	Add
ℓ	Delete
⊙	Add a Period
⫓	Indent

EXPOSITORY Writing Prompt
Interview Questions

In an interview you learn about a person or topic by asking questions. Some of the spelling words ask questions: **when, what, which,** and **why**.

- Use the writing process: prewrite, draft, revise, edit, and publish.
- Choose a person who interests you and who you would like to interview.
- Use spelling words to write questions you plan to ask this person.
- Begin each question with a question word and end with a question mark.
- Write complete sentences with correct capitalization, punctuation, grammar, and spelling.
- Use a dictionary to check your spelling.

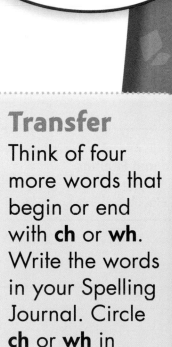

Transfer

Think of four more words that begin or end with **ch** or **wh**. Write the words in your Spelling Journal. Circle **ch** or **wh** in each word.

TEKS 2.23A Use phonological knowledge to match sounds to letters to construct unknown words.
2.23Bi Spell words with common orthographic patterns and rules: complex consonants. **2.23C** Spell high-frequency words from a commonly used list.

Word Study

cheek	each	chin	while	bench
chips	when	such	chain	chatter
wheel	what	why	lunch	whisper
chop	which	much	whale	wrench

Word Building

1.

2.

3.

4.

Long Vowels

5.

6.

Inflectional Endings

7.

8.

9.

10.

Use the word list above to complete these exercises.

Word Building

Add the consonant digraph **ch** or **wh** to make a spelling word.

1. __ eek   3. __ in
2. __ ale   4. __ isper

Long Vowels

5–6. Write the words that have **long a**.

Inflectional Endings

Write the base form of each word. Circle the consonant digraph in each.

7. chattering   9. chopped
8. lunches   10. benches

TEKS 2.23A Use phonological knowledge to match sounds to letters to construct unknown words. **2.23Bi** Spell words with common orthographic patterns and rules: complex consonants. **2.23Biii** Spell words with common orthographic patterns and rules: long vowels. **2.23C** Spell high-frequency words from a commonly used list. **2.23D** Spell base words with inflectional endings.

Technology

 Word Hunt

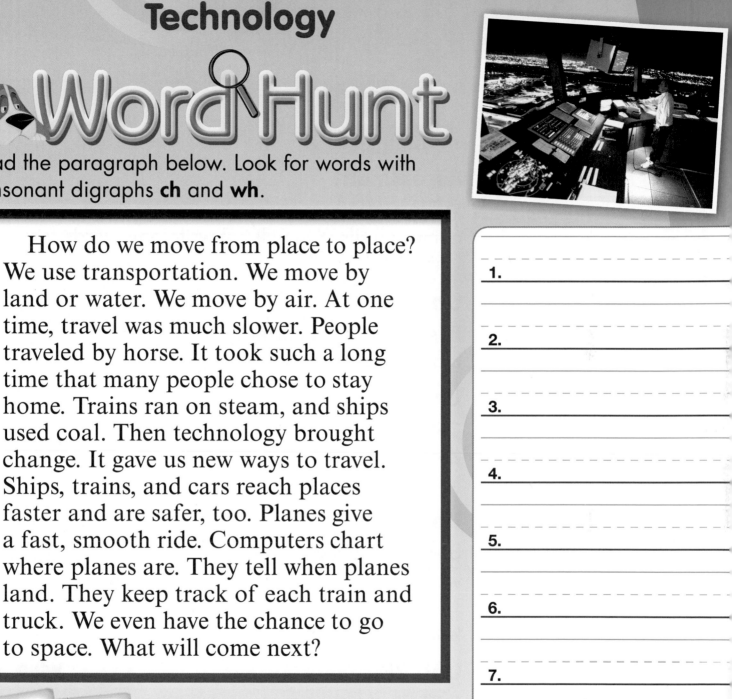

Read the paragraph below. Look for words with consonant digraphs **ch** and **wh**.

How do we move from place to place? We use transportation. We move by land or water. We move by air. At one time, travel was much slower. People traveled by horse. It took such a long time that many people chose to stay home. Trains ran on steam, and ships used coal. Then technology brought change. It gave us new ways to travel. Ships, trains, and cars reach places faster and are safer, too. Planes give a fast, smooth ride. Computers chart where planes are. They tell when planes land. They keep track of each train and truck. We even have the chance to go to space. What will come next?

1. _____

2. _____

3. _____

4. _____

5. _____

6. _____

7. _____

8. _____

WORD SORT

1–3. Write three of the words that begin with **ch**.

4–6. Write the words that begin with **wh**.

7–8. Write two of the words that end with **ch**.

Circle the **wh** or **ch** in each word you wrote.

 TEKS 2.23Bi Spell words with common orthographic patterns and rules: complex consonants. **2.23C** Spell high-frequency words from a commonly used list.

195

Unit 26

1. _____

2. _____

Unit 27

3. _____

4. _____

Unit 28

5. _____

6. _____

7. _____

Unit 29

8. _____

9. _____

10. _____

Units 25–29

Assessment

Write each assessment word under the unit number it fits. You will not write any words for Unit 25.

Unit 25

It is important to correctly spell words that you use often in writing.

Unit 26

1–2. The sound you hear in **loud** is /**ou**/ spelled **ou**. The sound you hear in **cow** is /**ou**/ spelled **ow**.

Unit 27

3–4. A **contraction** combines two words into one shorter word: **I am, I'm**. The **apostrophe** (') takes the place of a letter or letters.

Unit 28

5–7. The /**är**/ sound you hear in **car** can be spelled **ar**.

Unit 29

8–10. The digraph you hear at the beginning of **which** is spelled **wh**. The digraph you hear at the end of **which** is spelled **ch**.

Words for Assessment

bark

rich

gown

round

jar

chat

whip

how's

card

hadn't

Review

Unit 25: Words Writers Use

| want | many | off | saw | her |

Write the word that

1. starts like **see** and ends like **draw**.
2. starts like **moon** and rhymes with **penny**.
3. starts like **hand** and rhymes with **were**.
4. begins with a vowel.
5. starts like **win** and rhymes with **front**.

Unit 26: Diphthongs: ow, ou

| house | loud | down | now | how |

Replace the underlined letter or letters to make a spelling word.

6. ho<u>r</u>se
7. l<u>ea</u>d
8. n<u>e</u>w
9. ho<u>t</u>
10. do<u>ck</u>

Unit 25

1. _____
2. _____
3. _____
4. _____
5. _____

Unit 26

6. _____
7. _____
8. _____
9. _____
10. _____

Unit 27

1.

2.

3.

4.

5.

Unit 28

6.

7.

8.

9.

10.

Unit 27: Contractions

| he's | don't | I'm | that's | what's |

Write the contraction that

1. has a **short a**.

2. has a **long e**.

3. has a **long i**.

4. has a **long o**.

5. rhymes with **nuts**.

Unit 28: r-Controlled Vowel: /är/

| car | farm | hard | park | part |

Replace the underlined letter or letters to make a spelling word.

6. yard

7. cab

8. foam

9. post

10. pack

Unit 29: Digraphs: ch, wh

chop	which	when	what	each

Write a spelling word by adding the missing letters.

1. ea ___ ___

2. ___ ___ op

3. ___ ___ en

4. ___ ___ at

5. whi ___ ___

Spelling Study Strategy

Word Swap

Here's a spelling game you can try with a friend.

1. Swap spelling lists with a partner.

2. Ask your partner to read the first word on your list. Write the word.

3. Ask your partner to check your spelling. If you spelled the word correctly, your partner should say the next word on your list. If you did not spell the word correctly, ask your partner to spell the word out loud for you. Write the correct spelling.

4. Keep going until you have practiced five words. Then trade jobs. Keep going until you and your partner have practiced all the words on your lists.

Unit 29

1.

2.

3.

4.

5.

Directions: Read the introduction and the passage that follows. Then read each question and fill in the space in front of the correct answer.

Jamie wrote this paper about an object he had to bring to class and how he learned something new about his family. He wants you to review his paper. As you read, think about ways Jamie can make his story better.

A Lucky Day at an Art Show

(1) Last Monday I had to bring something to class that told about my family's history. (2) I had a hard time finding any old item in our howse that seemed like it was from our history.

(3) On Sunday I went to my mom's art show in the parck. (4) I helped herr carry some paintings from the car. (5) "Here's my favorite," I said, holding up her painting of a cou. (6) "That's Lucky, my best friend on our farm," she said.

(7) "What farm?" I said.

(8) "Didn't you know your grandparents had a farm down south?"

(9) Thats how I figured out what to bring to class. (10) I took my mom's painting and talked about Lucky and meny other animals. (11) I told how my grandparents had to shop wood and what they grew. (12) My class learned about whats on a farm, and I learned a lot, too!

1 What change should be made in sentence 2?

- ○ Change *howse* to **house**
- ○ Change *hard* to **harrd**
- ○ Change *any* to **eny**
- ○ Change *from* to **frum**

2 What change, if any, should be made in sentence 3?

- ○ Change *art* to **ort**
- ○ Change *show* to **sho**
- ○ Change *parck* to **park**
- ○ Make no change

3 What change should be made in sentence 4?

- ○ Change *helped* to **helpt**
- ○ Change *herr* to **her**
- ○ Change *some* to **sum**
- ○ Change *car* to **care**

4 What change, if any, should be made in sentence 5?

- ○ Change *Here's* to **Heres**
- ○ Change *her* to **hir**
- ○ Change *cou* to **cow**
- ○ Make no change

5 What change, if any, should be made in sentence 6?

- ○ Change *That's* to **Thats**
- ○ Change *best* to **beste**
- ○ Change *our* to **are**
- ○ Make no change

6 What change, if any, should be made in sentence 8?

- ○ Change *Didn't* to **Didnt'**
- ○ Change *farm* to **form**
- ○ Change *down* to **don**
- ○ Make no change

7 What change, if any, should be made in sentence 9?

- ○ Change *Thats* to **That's**
- ○ Change *how* to **haw**
- ○ Change *what* to **wat**
- ○ Make no change

8 What change should be made in sentence 10?

- ○ Change *took* to **tuke**
- ○ Change *talked* to **talkt**
- ○ Change *about* to **abuot**
- ○ Change *meny* to **many**

9 What change, if any, should be made in sentence 11?

- ○ Change *how* to **haw**
- ○ Change *shop* to **chop**
- ○ Change *grew* to **gru**
- ○ Make no change

10 What change, if any, should be made in sentence 12?

- ○ Change *class* to **classe**
- ○ Change *whats* to **what's**
- ○ Change *farm* to **farme**
- ○ Make no change

Grammar, Usage, and Mechanics
Verbs

A **verb** can tell what the subject of a sentence does or did.

> The cow **jumped** over the moon.

A verb can also tell what the subject of a sentence is, was, or will be.

> That cow **is** not real.

Practice Activity

A. Find the verb in each sentence. Write the verb.

1. Ramon fixed my notebook.

2. Someone answered the blue phone.

3. The dark living room was empty.

4. My pet mouse sleeps a lot.

B. Complete each sentence with a verb from the box.

hard	count	want	chop	down	saw

5. Let's _____ how many inches I've grown.

6. Yes, I _____ that red bird.

7. Ruth and I _____ more water.

8. We _____ wood every fall.

Practice Activity A

1. _____

2. _____

3. _____

4. _____

Practice Activity B

5. _____

6. _____

7. _____

8. _____

The Writing Process: Persuasive
Writing a Persuasive Paragraph

PREWRITING

How can you persuade others to try your favorite game? One good way is to give your reasons for playing. You can read about games at the library. An adult can help you find games on the Internet. As you think about the game, write down the reasons others should try it.

DRAFTING

Use your reasons to write a persuasive paragraph. Use as many spelling words as possible.

REVISING

When you have finished writing your first draft, read your whole paragraph. Check to see if you have included all of your reasons. Then write your final draft.

EDITING

Use the **Editing Checklist** to proofread your paragraph. Use proofreading marks when you make corrections. Circle two words that might be misspelled. Use a dictionary to check your spelling.

PUBLISHING

Make a copy of your persuasive paragraph and share it with your readers.

 TEKS 2.23A Use phonological knowledge to match sounds to letters to construct unknown words.
2.23F Use resources to find correct spellings.

Connections to THINKING

Read the spelling words and sentences.

1. for — What did you eat **for** lunch?
2. more — There are no **more** apples left.
3. corn — The **corn** grows in that field.
4. or — Jen **or** I will meet you there.
5. door — Shut the **door** when you leave.
6. fork — You need a **fork** to eat that.
7. horse — Tom will ride the small **horse**.
8. torn — Will you sew the **torn** pocket?
9. store — We buy bread at the **store**.
10. born — The baby was **born** yesterday.

Think & Sort the spelling words.

1–7. Write the words that spell the /ôr/ sound **or**.

8–9. Write the words that spell the /ôr/ sound **ore**.

10. Write the word that spells the /ôr/ sound **oor**.

Remember

The /ôr/ sound can be spelled **or** as in **for**, **ore** as in **more**, and **oor** as in **door**.

or

1.

2.

3.

4.

5.

6.

7.

ore

8.

9.

oor

10.

TEKS 2.23A Use phonological knowledge to match sounds to letters to construct unknown words.
2.23Bii Spell words with common orthographic patterns and rules: r-controlled vowels. **2.23C** Spell high-frequency words from a commonly used list.

Word Structure

Take one letter away from each word to make a spelling word. Write each spelling word.

1. four   **2.** ore   **3.** hoarse

Word Analysis

Write the spelling word that fits each clue.

4. It rhymes with **horn** and begins like **coat**.

5. It contains the words **do** and **or**.

6. It begins like **toad** and rhymes with **corn**.

7. It has four letters and contains another spelling word with three letters.

8. It begins like **made** and ends with **ore**.

9. It begins like **boy** and rhymes with **torn**.

Use the
Thesaurus

A **thesaurus** lists words and their synonyms. Write the spelling word found in the **Writing Thesaurus** that means:

10. a place where items are sold.

Synonyms are **drugstore, market, shop,** and **supermarket**.

Word Structure
1.
2.
3.

Word Analysis
4.
5.
6.
7.
8.
9.

Use the Thesaurus
10.

TEKS 2.23A Use phonological knowledge to match sounds to letters to construct unknown words. **2.23Bii** Spell words with common orthographic patterns and rules: r-controlled vowels. **2.23C** Spell high-frequency words from a commonly used list.

| for | more | corn | or | door |
| fork | horse | torn | store | born |

Word Categorization

1.

2.

3.

4.

5.

Word Categorization

Write the spelling word that belongs in each group.

Circle the /ôr/ sound in each word.

1. spoon, knife, _____

2. peas, carrots, _____

3. donkey, zebra, _____

4. stairs, window, roof, _____

5. ripped, split, _____

Use Context Clues

6.

7.

8.

9.

10.

Use Context Clues

Write spelling words to complete the paragraph.

My new cousin was __6.__ on March 13. Everyone was so happy to get the news. I wanted to get a special present __7.__ her. The question was what to get. I went to the __8.__ with my mom. There we saw many things. In the end, I did not know whether to get her a rattle __9.__ a bib. Mom laughed and said, "Don't worry. You will get her __10.__ presents later!"

 TEKS 2.23Bii Spell words with common orthographic patterns and rules: r-controlled vowels. **2.23C** Spell high-frequency words from a commonly used list.

Connections to WRITING

Proofread a Book Report

Proofread the book report below for eight misspelled words. Then rewrite the book report. Write the spelling words correctly and make the corrections shown by the proofreading marks.

I read <u>Mama and Papa Have a Store</u>. It is by Amelia Lau Carling. It tells about ^her^ parents. They were borne in China. They moved to ~~to~~ Guatemala <u>c</u>ity and opened a store⊙Fabric was fore sale. Shoppers came through the dore. Their clothes may have been worn or torne. They bought new silk orr thread. The family lived behind the stoar. They cooked /lunch on a wok. They ate corrn tortillas, too⊙Find out moor. Read this book!

Proofreading Marks

≡	Capital Letter
/	Small Letter
∧	Add
ℰ	Delete
⊙	Add a Period
⁋	Indent

PERSUASIVE Writing Prompt

Write a Book Report

Have you read a good book lately? Tell your classmates about it. Give some details that will make them want to read the book. Use as many spelling words as you can.

- Use the writing process: prewrite, draft, revise, edit, and publish.
- Tell the title and author of the book. Underline the title.
- Tell about the characters, setting, and main events, but don't tell the ending.
- Write complete sentences with correct capitalization, punctuation, grammar, and spelling.
- Circle two words that might be misspelled. Use a dictionary to check the spelling.

Transfer
Think of four more words that have **or, oor,** or **ore**. Write the words in your Spelling Journal. Circle **or, oor,** or **ore** in each word.

TEKS 2.23A Use phonological knowledge to match sounds to letters to construct unknown words.
2.23Bii Spell words with common orthographic patterns and rules: r-controlled vowels. **2.23C** Spell high-frequency words from a commonly used list. **2.23F** Use resources to find correct spellings.

Word Study

for	born	fork	storm	porch
door	more	torn	acorn	stork
horse	corn	explore	hornet	
store	or	morning		

Pattern Power

1.

2.

Word Building

3.

4.

5.

6.

Word Categorization

7.

8.

9.

10.

Use the word list above to complete these exercises.

Pattern Power

1–2. Write four-letter words that rhyme with **corn**.

Word Building

Change the underlined letter or letters in these words to make a spelling word.

3. fo<u>o</u>t

5. <u>c</u>ourse

4. explo<u>d</u>e

6. p<u>ea</u>ch

Word Categorization

Write the word that belongs in each group. Circle the **or** spelling in the words you write

7. afternoon, evening, _____

8. pelican, flamingo, _____

9. bee, wasp, _____

10. walnut, pecan, _____

208

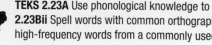 **TEKS 2.23A** Use phonological knowledge to match sounds to letters to construct unknown words. **2.23Bii** Spell words with common orthographic patterns and rules: r-controlled vowels. **2.23C** Spell high-frequency words from a commonly used list.

Technology

Word Hunt

Read the story below. Look for words with **or, oor,** and **ore**.

Kim ran back from the corner store. She stood on her porch. She saw dark clouds form.

"Come inside and close the door. A storm is coming," called Dad.

Dad was watching television. The weather map told the story.

"How can we know the weather before it happens?" asked Kim.

"Weather people measure rain or wind speed. They know how fast clouds are moving. Radar tells more. It shows where rain is falling and it tells how much. People who report the weather use computers. They show weather for the next few days."

"I use my eyes and ears. I see dark clouds and hear thunder. I know a storm is here!"

1. _____

2. _____

3. _____

4. _____

5. _____

6. _____

7. _____

WORD SORT

1–5. Write the one-syllable words with **or**.

6. Write the word with **oor**.

7. Write the two-syllable word with **ore**.

TEKS 2.23Bii Spell words with common orthographic patterns and rules: r-controlled vowels.
2.23C Spell high-frequency words from a commonly used list.

Connections to THINKING

Read the spelling words and sentences.

1.	shine	The sun might **shine** later.
2.	rush	People **rush** to catch the bus.
3.	shoe	That **shoe** fits my foot.
4.	cash	Ten dollars is a lot of **cash**!
5.	short	One block is a **short** distance.
6.	dash	They **dash** to the finish line.
7.	bush	This **bush** has small leaves.
8.	shore	We find shells at the **shore**.
9.	wash	Please **wash** with soap.
10.	shout	I must **shout** so Liz can hear.

Think & Sort the spelling words.

1–5. Write the words that begin with **sh**.

6–10. Write the words that end with **sh**.

Remember

The /**sh**/ sound you hear in **shoe** and **bush** can be spelled **sh**.

Words that begin with sh

1. _____

2. _____

3. _____

4. _____

5. _____

Words that end with sh

6. _____

7. _____

8. _____

9. _____

10. _____

TEKS 2.23A Use phonological knowledge to match sounds to letters to construct unknown words. **2.23Bi** Spell words with common orthographic patterns and rules: complex consonants. **2.23C** Spell high-frequency words from a commonly used list.

Word Analysis

Write the **sh** spelling word that fits each clue.

1. This word rhymes with **or**.
2. This word contains the smaller word **out**.
3. This word begins like **cat** and contains the smaller word **ash**.
4. This word rhymes with **sort**. It has one more letter than **sort**.

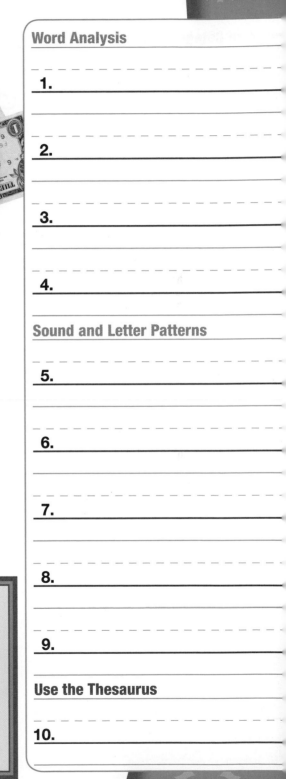

Sound and Letter Patterns

Write spelling words by adding the missing letters.

5. wa __ __
6. ru __ __
7. b __ __ h
8. __ __ oe
9. da __ __

Use the Thesaurus

A **thesaurus** lists words and their synonyms. Find and write the **long i** spelling word in the **Writing Thesaurus** that means:

10. to give off light

Next to the word, write the number of synonyms the word has.

Word Analysis
1.
2.
3.
4.
Sound and Letter Patterns
5.
6.
7.
8.
9.
Use the Thesaurus
10.

 TEKS 2.23A Use phonological knowledge to match sounds to letters to construct unknown words. **2.23Bi** Spell words with common orthographic patterns and rules: complex consonants. **2.23Biii** Spell words with common orthographic patterns and rules: long vowels. **2.23C** Spell high-frequency words from a commonly used list.

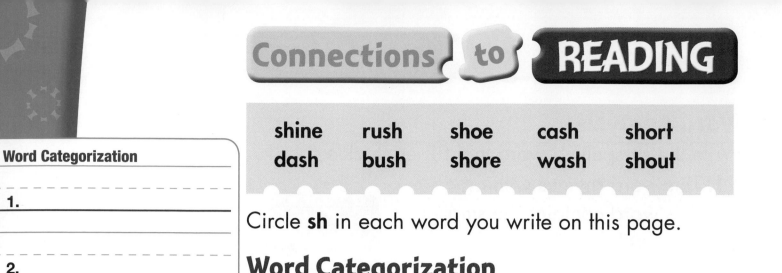

| shine | rush | shoe | cash | short |
| dash | bush | shore | wash | shout |

Circle **sh** in each word you write on this page.

Word Categorization

Write the spelling word that belongs in each group.

1. sneaker, sandal, _____

2. race, broad jump, high jump, _____

3. hurry, speed, _____

4. small, low, _____

Name the Category

Write the spelling word that
names each group of words.

5. dollars, coins, money

6. Hey! Stop! Hurray!

Use Context Clues

Write the spelling word that completes each sentence.

7. The sun does not _____ brightly on a
cloudy day.

8. I saw a seal resting in the sun on the sandy
_____.

9. I will use soap to _____ this dirty cup.

10. The leaves on that _____ turn bright red in
the fall.

Sidebar

Word Categorization

1. _____

2. _____

3. _____

4. _____

Name the Category

5. _____

6. _____

Use Context Clues

7. _____

8. _____

9. _____

10. _____

TEKS 2.23Bi Spell words with common orthographic patterns and rules: complex consonants. **2.23C** Spell
high-frequency words from a commonly used list.

Connections to WRITING

Proofread a Paragraph

Proofread the paragraph below for eight misspelled words. Then rewrite the paragraph. Write the spelling words correctly and make the corrections shown by the proofreading marks.

¶ After a drive to the shor, our car was Dirty. We were in a big russ to get it clean. We decided to dashe out to the car wassh. In a very shorrt time, it came out so clean! It even seemed to chine! My dad was so pleased with it. the car looked better than it had had in a long time. I thought Dad would showt for joy! he said it was worth every bit of cashe it cost to have the car washed⊙

Proofreading Marks

≡	Capital Letter
/	Small Letter
∧	Add
℘	Delete
⊙	Add a Period
¶	Indent

NARRATIVE Writing Prompt

Write a Narrative Paragraph

Stories about real people are fun to read. Write a narrative paragraph to tell about an event in your life. Use as many spelling words as you can.

- Use the writing process: prewrite, draft, revise, edit, and publish.
- Tell what happened, where it happened, and who was there.
- Tell about your event in the same order that things happened.
- Write complete sentences with correct capitalization, punctuation, grammar, and spelling.
- Use a dictionary to check your spelling.

Transfer
Think of four more words that begin or end with **sh**. Write the words in your Spelling Journal. Circle **sh** in each word.

TEKS 2.23A Use phonological knowledge to match sounds to letters to construct unknown words. **2.23Bi** Spell words with common orthographic patterns and rules: complex consonants. **2.23C** Spell high-frequency words from a commonly used list.

hush	short	shine	shout	brush
she	bush	rush	bushel	marsh
shop	shore	cash	fresh	shift
shoe	wash	dash	shaggy	shiny

Pattern Power

1.

2.

3.

4.

5.

6.

Use Antonyms

7.

8.

9.

10.

Use the word list above to complete these exercises.

Pattern Power

1–2. One spelling word begins another word. Write the two words.

3–4. One spelling word ends another word. Write the two words.

5. Write the word that rhymes with **lift**.

6. Write the word that ends with two vowels.

Use Antonyms

Write the word that means the opposite of each word.

7. rotten _____

8. dull _____

9. whisper _____

10. tall _____

 TEKS 2.23A Use phonological knowledge to match sounds to letters to construct unknown words.
2.23C Spell high-frequency words from a commonly used list.

Social Studies

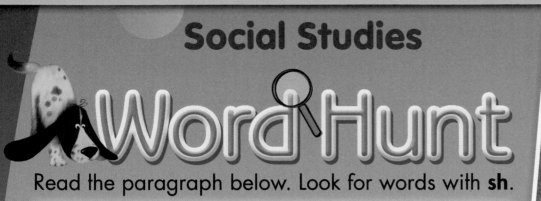 Word Hunt

Read the paragraph below. Look for words with **sh**.

It's time to shop for a wool sweater. How does a sweater get from a shaggy sheep to you? A sheep's wool coat keeps it warm. It is not needed in hotter months. So the wool is cut short. Workers clip the wool. This is like having your hair cut. The cut wool is called fleece. Shearing sheep is like getting a hair cut. Workers wash and brush the wool. Some is dyed in colors. Workers use machines to spin the wool. When they finish, it becomes thread or yarn. One pound of wool can make ten miles of yarn! Workers weave the yarn into cloth. People can make warm clothing and blankets from wool. Wool sweaters keep people warm in winter. The sheep grow new coats, too!

1. _____

2. _____

3. _____

4. _____

5. _____

6. _____

7. _____

8. _____

WORD SORT

1–5. Write the words that begin with **sh**.

6–8. Write the words that end with **sh**.

TEKS 2.23Bi Spell words with common orthographic patterns and rules: complex consonants.
2.23C Spell high-frequency words from a commonly used list.

Connections to THINKING

Read the spelling words and sentences.

1. they — Are **they** the boys you saw?
2. teeth — I brush my **teeth** often.
3. those — We like **those** pants in the window.
4. than — Steve is taller **than** Carlos.
5. tooth — My front **tooth** is loose.
6. these — I made **these** cards myself.
7. moth — The **moth** flies into the light.
8. them — I had toys, but I lost **them**.
9. both — I like **both** Jada and Brad.
10. thank — Did you **thank** Jed for helping us?

Think & Sort the spelling words.

1–6. Write the words that begin with **th**.

7–10. Write the words that end with **th**.

Remember

The **th** digraph you hear at the beginning
of **these** and at the end of **teeth** is spelled **th**.

Words that begin with th

1. _____
2. _____
3. _____
4. _____
5. _____
6. _____

Words that end with th

7. _____
8. _____
9. _____
10. _____

TEKS 2.23A Use phonological knowledge to match sounds to letters to construct unknown words.
2.23Bi Spell words with common orthographic patterns and rules: complex consonants. **2.23C** Spell
high-frequency words from a commonly used list.

Sound and Letter Patterns

1–2. Write the words with the **long o** sound.

3–4. Write the words with the **long e** sound.

5. Write the word with the **long a** sound.

Missing Letters

Write spelling words by adding the missing letters.

6. too __ __

7. __ __ an

8. mo __ __

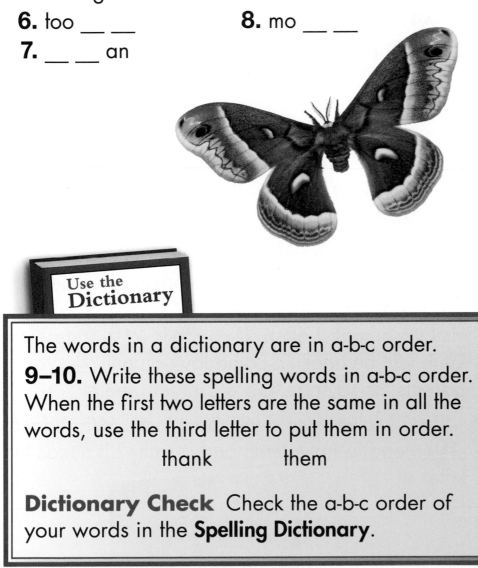

Use the Dictionary

The words in a dictionary are in a-b-c order.

9–10. Write these spelling words in a-b-c order. When the first two letters are the same in all the words, use the third letter to put them in order.

thank them

Dictionary Check Check the a-b-c order of your words in the **Spelling Dictionary**.

Sound and Letter Patterns

1. _____

2. _____

3. _____

4. _____

5. _____

Missing Letters

6. _____

7. _____

8. _____

Use the Dictionary

9. _____

10. _____

 TEKS 2.23A Use phonological knowledge to match sounds to letters to construct unknown words. **2.23Bi** Spell words with common orthographic patterns and rules: complex consonants. **2.23Biii** Spell words with common orthographic patterns and rules: long vowels. **2.23C** Spell high-frequency words from a commonly used list.

| they | teeth | those | than | tooth |
| these | moth | them | both | thank |

Use Context Clues

Use Context Clues

Write the spelling words to complete the paragraphs. Use each word once and circle the digraph **th** in each word.

When was the last time you lost a **1.** ? Did you know that your first **2.** are called primary teeth? You probably know that **3.** are also called baby teeth.

There are ten primary teeth in **4.** the upper and lower jaws. When **5.** teeth fall out, there is room for the second set of teeth. There are more teeth in the second set **6.** there are in the first set.

Your teeth are very important. You should take good care of **7.** . You should brush after meals, try not to eat too many sweets, floss once a day, and visit your dentist often. If you follow **8.** rules, your teeth will be healthy. Someday you will **9.** your parents for saying, "Go brush your teeth!"

Try to solve this riddle about teeth. What does a **10.** need to have teeth and a smile? It needs the letter **u**!

1. _____
2. _____
3. _____
4. _____
5. _____
6. _____
7. _____
8. _____
9. _____
10. _____

 TEKS 2.23Bi Spell words with common orthographic patterns and rules: complex consonants.
2.23C Spell high-frequency words from a commonly used list.

Connections to WRITING

Proofread a Thank-You Note

Find eight misspelled words in the thank-you note below. Rewrite the note using correct spelling. Make the corrections shown by the proofreading marks.

April 14, 2012

Dear Grandpa,

Thanke you for thos toys you sent. I really like themm.

I play that board game more thin any any other game.

I also like the spaceship and launch pad. I think thay

are boath cool! Thanks for the apples, too. Mom says

I shouldn't eat too much Sugar. It's bad for my teethe.

Theze apples taste good and are good for me!

love,

Jimmy

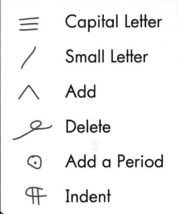
EXPOSITORY Writing Prompt
Write a Thank-You Note

Has someone done something nice for you? Show them how you feel by writing a thank-you note. Use as many spelling words as you can.

- Use the writing process: prewrite, draft, revise, edit, and publish.
- Begin with **Dear,** the person's name, and a comma.
- Tell the person why you are thanking him or her.
- Use a comma after your closing and sign your name.
- Write complete sentences with correct capitalization, punctuation, grammar, and spelling.
- Use a dictionary to check your spelling.

Transfer

Think of four more words that begin or end with **th**. Write the words in your Spelling Journal. Circle **th** in each word.

TEKS 2.23A Use phonological knowledge to match sounds to letters to construct unknown words. **2.23Bi** Spell words with common orthographic patterns and rules: complex consonants. **2.23C** Spell high-frequency words from a commonly used list. **2.23F** Use resources to find correct spellings.

Extend & Transfer

Word Study

the	than	teeth	thank	birth
then	these	those	father	thimble
with	them	tooth	smooth	thread
they	both	moth	thumb	health

Use the word list above to complete these exercises. Circle the vowel digraphs.

Pattern Power

Write the spelling word you see inside each word.

1. birthday

2. grandfather

3. healthy

4. smoothly

5. within

6. thankful

Meaning Mastery

Write the word that matches each meaning. Check your **Spelling Dictionary** if you are not sure.

7. a fine strand used for sewing

8. one of the hard, white bony objects in the mouth, used for chewing

9. an insect that is like a butterfly and flies at night

10. a cap worn on the finger to push a sewing needle

Pattern Power

1. _____

2. _____

3. _____

4. _____

5. _____

6. _____

Meaning Mastery

7. _____

8. _____

9. _____

10. _____

TEKS 2.23Biv Spell words with common orthographic patterns and rules: vowel digraphs, diphthongs.
2.23C Spell high-frequency words from a commonly used list.

Word Hunt

Read the paragraphs below. Look for words with **th**.

Can animals be friends? What do you think? The plover is a small bird. The crocodile is its friend. The croc lies with its mouth open. The bird flies inside. Then it picks food from each tooth.

Have you seen zebras on television? Were there ostriches nearby? The zebra hears and smells very well. It warns the ostrich if danger is near. The zebra can see well and so can the ostrich. The ostrich is a lookout for both of them.

The rhino and tickbird are a pair. The bird sits on the rhino's back. It picks off bugs that get in the rhino's thick skin. You help your friends. Other animals do, too!

1. _____

2. _____

3. _____

4. _____

5. _____

6. _____

7. _____

8. _____

WORD SORT

1–3. Write the five-letter words that begin with **th**.

4–6. Write the four-letter words that begin with **th**.

7–8. Write the five-letter words that end with **th**.

TEKS 2.23Bi Spell words with common orthographic patterns and rules: complex consonants. **2.23C** Spell high-frequency words from a commonly used list.

Connections to THINKING

Read the spelling words and sentences.

1.	deer	The **deer** lives in the woods.
2.	here	Please be **here** by noon.
3.	meet	I will **meet** you at the store.
4.	tale	She told a funny **tale**.
5.	hour	We will be ready in an **hour**.
6.	tail	The dog wagged its **tail**.
7.	hear	Did you **hear** a bell ring?
8.	dear	He is a very **dear** friend.
9.	our	We will show you **our** pictures.
10.	meat	Dad likes mustard on his **meat**.

Think & Sort the spelling words.

1–10. Write each homophone and its partner. Think about the meanings of the homophones in each pair.

Remember

Homophones are words that sound the same but have different spellings and meanings. **Hear** and **here** are homophones.

Think & Sort

1. _____

2. _____

3. _____

4. _____

5. _____

6. _____

7. _____

8. _____

9. _____

10. _____

TEKS 2.23Bii Spell words with common orthographic patterns and rules: r-controlled vowels. **2.23Biii** Spell words with common orthographic patterns and rules: long vowels. **2.23Biv** Spell words with common orthographic patterns and rules: vowel digraphs, diphthongs. **2.23C** Spell high-frequency words from a commonly used list.

Connections to PHONICS

Word Analysis

1. Write the word that has four letters and begins with the /**ou**/ sound.
2. Write the word that spells the **long a** sound **ai**.
3. Write the word that begins like **dog** and ends with **ear**.
4. Write the word made by changing one letter in **hare**.

Rhyming Words

Write the spelling word that rhymes with the underlined word to complete the sentence.

5. I <u>fear</u> the _____ ran across the road.
6. We will <u>meet</u> Mom at the _____ store.
7. The story of the <u>whale</u> is a really good _____.
8. It's very <u>clear</u>. I can _____ you well.
9. I will clean _____ <u>shower</u>.

Use the **Writing Thesaurus** to find the homophone for the word **meat** that means:

10. to come face to face with; to come together

Write the word. Next to the word, write the number of synonyms it has.

Word Analysis

1. _____

2. _____

3. _____

4. _____

Rhyming Words

5. _____

6. _____

7. _____

8. _____

9. _____

Use the Thesaurus

10. _____

 TEKS 2.23A Use phonological knowledge to match sounds to letters to construct unknown words. **2.23Biii** Spell words with common orthographic patterns and rules: long vowels. **2.23Biv** Spell words with common orthographic patterns and rules: vowel digraphs, diphthongs. **2.23C** Spell high-frequency words from a commonly used list.

| deer | here | meet | tale | hour |
| tail | hear | dear | our | meat |

Word Categorization

Write the spelling word that fits in each group.

1. ears, paws, nose, _____

2. see, taste, touch, smell, _____

3. moose, elk, _____

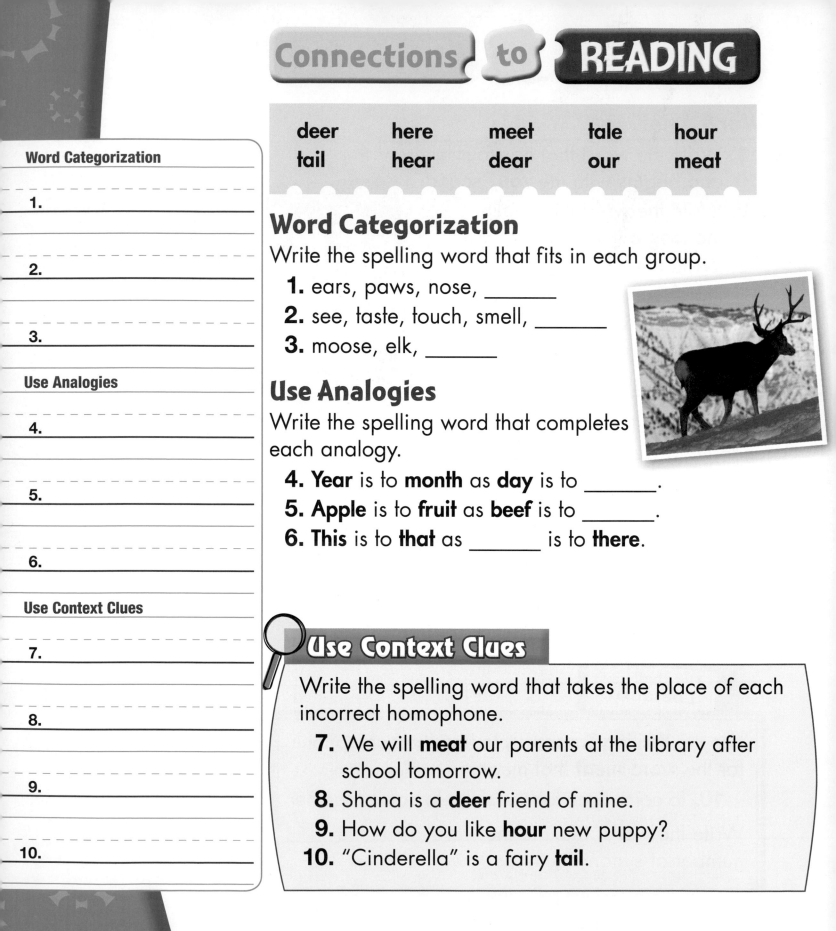

Use Analogies

Write the spelling word that completes each analogy.

4. Year is to **month** as **day** is to _____.

5. Apple is to **fruit** as **beef** is to _____.

6. This is to **that** as _____ is to **there**.

Use Context Clues

Write the spelling word that takes the place of each incorrect homophone.

7. We will **meat** our parents at the library after school tomorrow.

8. Shana is a **deer** friend of mine.

9. How do you like **hour** new puppy?

10. "Cinderella" is a fairy **tail**.

Word Categorization

1. _____
2. _____
3. _____

Use Analogies

4. _____
5. _____
6. _____

Use Context Clues

7. _____
8. _____
9. _____
10. _____

TEKS 2.23C Spell high-frequency words from a commonly used list.

Connections to WRITING

Proofread a Diary Entry

Find eight misspelled words in the diary entry below. Rewrite the note using correct spelling. Make the corrections shown by the proofreading marks.

Deare Diary,   june 13

¶ We are hear! It's the top of Bald Mountain. Mom and I had a great hike We traveled along a cold, clear stream for the first our. we could heare fish jumping in the water. Then we saw a dear! It ran right across hour path. It had soft brown fur and a big white tale. I'll have a talle to tell my friends when i get home.

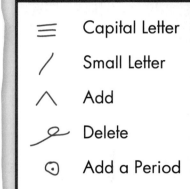

Proofreading Marks

≡	Capital Letter
/	Small Letter
∧	Add
ℒ	Delete
⊙	Add a Period
¶	Indent

DESCRIPTIVE Writing Prompt
Write a Diary Entry

Have you seen or done something special? One way to remember something special is to write about it in a diary. As you write, use as many spelling words as you can.

- Use the writing process: prewrite, draft, revise, edit, and publish.
- Write details to describe what you did, saw, heard, smelled, and felt.
- Tell what made what you saw or did special.
- Write complete sentences with correct capitalization, punctuation, grammar, and spelling.
- Circle two words that might be misspelled. Use a dictionary to check the spelling.

Transfer

The words **hair, tow, aunt,** and **weak** have homophones. Write these words in your Spelling Journal. Write the homophone next to each word.

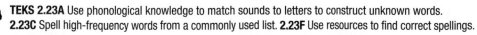

TEKS 2.23A Use phonological knowledge to match sounds to letters to construct unknown words.
2.23C Spell high-frequency words from a commonly used list. **2.23F** Use resources to find correct spellings.

225

Word Study

be	here	deer	dear	ant
bee	hour	tail	meat	aunt
son	hear	meet	grate	toe
sun	our	tale	great	tow

Use the word list above to complete these exercises. Circle the vowel digraphs.

Pattern Power

1–4. Write the words with the **long a** sound.

5–6. Write the **long e** words that end with **t**.

Meaning Mastery

Write the word that matches each homophone and meaning.

7. a homophone for **ant** that names my mother's sister

8. a homophone for **toe** that means "to tug or pull something"

9. a homophone for **hear** that means "in this place"

10. a homophone for **our** that means "sixty minutes"

Pattern Power

1.

2.

3.

4.

5.

6.

Meaning Mastery

7.

8.

9.

10.

TEKS 2.23A Use phonological knowledge to match sounds to letters to construct unknown words. **2.23Biii** Spell words with common orthographic patterns and rules: long vowels. **2.23Biv** Spell words with common orthographic patterns and rules: vowel digraphs, diphthongs. **2.23C** Spell high-frequency words from a commonly used list.

Art

Word Hunt

Read the paragraphs below. Look for words that are **homophones**.

Some Native Americans live in the Northwest. Totem poles are one of their art forms. A totem pole is carved from wood. Some tell family history. Others tell a tale. The people lived in clans or groups. Small poles were part of a house.

Each part of the pole is carved. They often show an eagle, a bear, a wolf, or a raven. Some have human shapes, too. After the pole was finished, men dug a hole for it. They used ropes to put it in place. People would meet there to dance and sing. This form of art is still made today. The artists are proud of their great work.

1. _____

2. _____

3. _____

4. _____

5. _____

6. _____

7. _____

8. _____

Find a homophone for each of the following words.

1. would   **4.** whole   **7.** sum

2. grate   **5.** there   **8.** won

3. bare   **6.** two

TEKS 2.23C Spell high-frequency words from a commonly used list.

227

Connections to THINKING

Read the spelling words and sentences.

1. inside   The dog is **inside** the fence.
2. myself   I made **myself** a sandwich.
3. bedroom   I sleep in this **bedroom**.
4. football   Who threw that **football**?
5. birthday   I will be ten on my **birthday**.
6. downtown   We shop **downtown**.
7. baseball   I like the game of **baseball**.
8. cannot   Len can dive, but I **cannot**.
9. outside   The dog can go **outside** now.
10. into   I pour water **into** my glass.

Think & Sort the spelling words.

Write a compound word that is built from each word below.

1–3. town, to, foot

4–7. in, not, my, base

8–10. day, out, room

Remember

A **compound word** is two or more words joined to make a new word: **can + not = cannot**.

town, to, foot

1. _____
2. _____
3. _____

in, not, my, base

4. _____
5. _____
6. _____
7. _____

day, out, room

8. _____
9. _____
10. _____

 TEKS 2.23C Spell high-frequency words from a commonly used list.

Connections to PHONICS

Vowel Sounds

1. Write the word that has two /**ou**/ diphthongs.

2–4. Write three words with the **long i** sound.

5–6. Write the two words with the **long a** sound.

7. Write the word that has one vowel digraph and one consonant digraph.

8. Write the word with a **short e** in the first syllable.

Use the Dictionary

9. Write the spelling word that comes before **isn't** in your **Spelling Dictionary**.

10. Write the spelling word that comes before **can't** in your **Spelling Dictionary**.

Vowel Sounds
1.
2.
3.
4.
5.
6.
7.
8.

Use the Dictionary
9.
10.

TEKS 2.23A Use phonological knowledge to match sounds to letters to construct unknown words. **2.23Bi** Spell words with common orthographic patterns and rules: complex consonants. **2.23Biii** Spell words with common orthographic patterns and rules: long vowels. **2.23Biv** Spell words with common orthographic patterns and rules: vowel digraphs, diphthongs. **2.23C** Spell high-frequency words from a commonly used list..

inside	myself	bedroom	football
birthday	downtown	baseball	cannot
outside	into		

Word Categorization

Write the spelling word that belongs in each group.

1. indoors, in the house, _____

2. yourself, herself, _____

3. does not, did not, _____

Replace the Words

Write the spelling word that could take the place of the underlined words in each sentence.

4. I have pictures of my favorite basketball players on the walls of my <u>room with a bed</u>.

5. This year my parents gave me a new winter coat on my <u>day of birth</u>.

Use Context Clues

Write the spelling word that best completes each sentence.

6. It is a beautiful day, so we should go _____ to play!

7. He kicked the _____ forty yards.

8. Many big city buildings are being built _____.

9. Sandy hit a home run at the _____ game.

10. The girl dove _____ the deep end of the pool.

Word Categorization

1. _____

2. _____

3. _____

Replace the Words

4. _____

5. _____

Use Context Clues

6. _____

7. _____

8. _____

9. _____

10. _____

TEKS. 2.23C Spell high-frequency words from a commonly used list.

Proofread an E-Mail

Proofread the e-mail below for eight misspelled words. Then rewrite the e-mail. Write the spelling words correctly and make the corrections shown.

Send   Save as a Draft   Cancel   Attach Files

From: BillyJones@mymail.com

To: JakeMendez@yourmail.com

Subject: Birthday Party

---

dear Jake,

I hope you are coming to my birtday party. I helped plan it myselff. We will play basebal and futball outsside. Then we will go insied to eat eat cake. We will Play in my beddroom, too. We will have a lot of fun. If you canot come, you will miss a great party.

Your friend,

Billy

Proofreading Marks

≡	Capital Letter
/	Small Letter
∧	Add
ℓ	Delete
⊙	Add a Period
⊩	Indent

PERSUASIVE Writing Prompt

Write an E-Mail

Do you want to talk a friend into doing something with you? Write an e-mail to tell him or her about it. Use as many spelling words as you can.

- Use the writing process.
- Use the correct e-mail address for your friend.
- Give reasons why your friend should join you.
- Write complete sentences with correct capitalization, punctuation, grammar, and spelling.

Transfer

Write four more **compound words** you know in your Spelling Journal. Draw a line between the two words in each compound word.

TEKS. 2.23A Use phonological knowledge to match sounds to letters to construct unknown words. **2.23C** Spell high-frequency words from a commonly used list.

231

Word Study

inside	myself	beeswax	dragonfly
birthday	bedroom	foghorn	notebook
cannot	football	rowboat	shoelace
outside	downtown	flagpole	
into	baseball		

Word Building

1.

2.

3.

4.

5.

6.

7.

Meaning Mastery

8.

9.

10.

Use the word list above to complete these exercises.

Word Building

1–3. Write the three words that have the **long o** sound.

4. Which three-syllable word has a **long i** sound?

What compound words are formed with these words?

5. down   **6–7.** in

Meaning Mastery

Write the compound that matches each clue.

8. One-half of this word is a musical instrument.

9. One-half of this word can be part of something you wear on your foot.

10. This word has a diphthong and is an antonym for **inside**.

TEKS 2.23A Use phonological knowledge to match sounds to letters to construct unknown words. **2.23Biii** Spell words with common orthographic patterns and rules: long vowels. **2.23Biv** Spell words with common orthographic patterns and rules: vowel digraphs, diphthongs. **2.23C** Spell high-frequency words from a commonly used list.

Math

Word Hunt

Read the paragraph below. Look for words that are **compound** words.

You use math each time you get into a game. In baseball, you score one for each run. In football, you earn six points for each touchdown. You add to the score by six. Are you on a basketball team? You get two or three points for each basket! If you don't play a team sport, a sidewalk game is something you might like. Try hopscotch. Use chalk to draw the game. Put in the numbers. Hop from one to ten to play. Maybe you like playing board games with someone. You keep score. The best part of games is having fun.

WORD SORT

1–3. Write three compound words that have the word **ball**.

4–5. Write two compound words that have the word **some**.

Write the compound word that includes these words.

6. a **short i** word + to   **7.** a **long a** word + be

8. two **short o** words

1. _____
2. _____
3. _____
4. _____
5. _____
6. _____
7. _____
8. _____

TEKS 2.23A Use phonological knowledge to match sounds to letters to construct unknown words. **2.23Biii** Spell words with common orthographic patterns and rules: long vowels. **2.23C** Spell high-frequency words from a commonly used list.

Unit 36

Assess for Transfer

Unit 31

1. _____

2. _____

3. _____

Unit 32

4. _____

5. _____

Unit 33

6. _____

7. _____

Unit 34

8. _____

9. _____

Unit 35

10. _____

Units 31–35

Assessment

Write each assessment word under the unit number it fits. Use each word once.

Unit 31

1–3. The /ôr/ sound can be spelled **or** as in **for, ore** as in **more,** and **oor** as in **door.**

Unit 32

4–5. The /sh/ sound you hear in **shoe** and **bush** can be spelled **sh.**

Unit 33

6–7. The **th** digraph you hear at the beginning of **these** and at the end of **teeth** is spelled **th.**

Unit 34

8–9. Homophones are words that sound the same but have different spellings and meanings. **Hear** and **here** are homophones.

Unit 35

10. A **compound word** is two or more words joined to make a new word: **can + not = cannot.**

Words for Assessment

sail

cloth

horn

chore

crush

doorstep

thing

pancake

shack

sale

Review

Unit 31: r-Controlled Vowel /ôr/: or, ore, oor

born	horse	store	door	for

Write the spelling word that

1. starts like **fine** and ends like **nor**

2. starts like **deer** and ends like **floor**

3. starts like **bake** and ends like **torn**

4. starts like **hand** and rhymes with **force**

5. starts like **stem** and ends like **core**

Unit 32: Digraph: sh

shoe	wash	short	bush	shore

Write a spelling word that rhymes with the underlined word and fits the sentence.

6. We stood on the <u>core</u> to watch the waves.

7. This pencil is too <u>sport</u>.

8. The bird sat on the <u>push</u>.

Replace one letter in each word below to create a spelling word.

9. wish

10. shot

Unit 31

1. _____

2. _____

3. _____

4. _____

5. _____

Unit 32

6. _____

7. _____

8. _____

9. _____

10. _____

Unit 33

1.

2.

3.

4.

5.

Unit 34

6.

7.

8.

9.

10.

Unit 33: Digraph: th

| than | them | they | both | these |

Write the **th** digraph words with the following sounds.

1. short a

2. long a

3. long o

4. long e

5. short e

Unit 34: Homophones

| hear | our | here | hour | tail |

Write the spelling word that best fits with the others.

6. second, minute, _____

7. _____, there, everywhere

8. head, paws, _____

9. my, your, _____

10. see, taste, _____

Unit 35: Compound Words

into   birthday   outside   cannot   inside

Match one word from each column to make a spelling word. Write the word.

1. in   not

2. out   side

3. in   day

4. can   to

5. birth   side

Unit 35

1.

2.

3.

4.

5.

Spelling Study Strategy

Sorting by Spelling Patterns

Here is a good way to practice your spelling words. Place the words into groups by their spelling patterns.

1. Make three columns on a large piece of paper or on the chalkboard.

2. Write one spelling pattern at the top of each column:

(1) **or, ore, oor**   (2) **sh**   (3) **th**

3. Have a partner say a spelling word from Unit 31, 32, or 33.

4. Write the spelling word in the column that shows the spelling pattern.

Directions: Read the introduction and the passage that follows. Then read each question and fill in the space in front of the correct answer.

Selma wrote this story about a girl who almost lets a few lost teeth ruin her birthday. She wants you to review her story. As you read, think about ways Selma can make her story better.

A Birthday Surprise

(1) Annie sat inside her bedrome all alone. (2) Today was her birthday, and her mom was taking her to the zoo in downtown Dallas. (3) They were going with Annie's friend Casey and her mom.

(4) Now she didn't want to go. (5) She'd lost one front toth Monday and another last night. (6) She thought she looked silly and couldn't even talk right.

(7) "Please wach your face now so we don't have to rush, dear," said her mom. (8) An hour later, Annie heard a knock on her dore and opened it. (9) "I'm here to say happy birtday, Annie!" shouted Casey, with a big smile.

(10) Annie could not believe her eyes. (11) Bothe Casey's front teeth were missing!

(12) "Meat your twin!" said Annie, grinning back. (13) "I cannot ask for a better present then this one!"

1 What change, if any, should be made in sentence 1?

- ⬭ Change *inside* to **enside**
- ⬭ Change *her* to **hir**
- ⬭ Change *bedrome* to **bedroom**
- ⬭ Make no change

2 What change, if any, should be made in sentence 2?

- ⬭ Change *Today* to **Todae**
- ⬭ Change *birthday* to **birtday**
- ⬭ Change *downtown* to **dountoun**
- ⬭ Make no change

3 What change, if any, should be made in sentence 3?

- ⬭ Change *They* to **Thay**
- ⬭ Change *going* to **goin**
- ⬭ Change *friend* to **frend**
- ⬭ Make no change

4 What change should be made in sentence 5?

- ⬭ Change *lost* to **laust**
- ⬭ Change *front* to **frunt**
- ⬭ Change *toth* to **tooth**
- ⬭ Change *last* to **lasst**

5 What change, if any, should be made in sentence 7?

- ⬭ Change *wach* to **wash**
- ⬭ Change *rush* to **ruch**
- ⬭ Change *dear* to **deer**
- ⬭ Make no change

6 What change, if any, should be made in sentence 8?

- ⬭ Change *An* to **And**
- ⬭ Change *hour* to **our**
- ⬭ Change *dore* to **door**
- ⬭ Make no change

7 What change, if any, should be made in sentence 9?

- ⬭ Change *shouted* to **souted**
- ⬭ Change *hear* to **here**
- ⬭ Change *birtday* to **birthday**
- ⬭ Make no change

8 What change, if any, should be made in sentence 11?

- ⬭ Change *Bothe* to **Both**
- ⬭ Change *front* to **frunt**
- ⬭ Change *were* to **wear**
- ⬭ Make no change

9 What change should be made in sentence 12?

- ⬭ Change *Meat* to **Meet**
- ⬭ Change *your* to **yor**
- ⬭ Change *said* to **sed**
- ⬭ Change *back* to **bak**

10 What change should be made in sentence 13?

- ⬭ Change *cannot* to **canot**
- ⬭ Change *better* to **beter**
- ⬭ Change *then* to **than**
- ⬭ Change *one* to **won**

Enrichment

Grammar, Usage, and Mechanics
Adjectives

An **adjective** describes, or tells about, a noun. It can tell what kind, how much, or how many.

I like your **red** sweater.

Molly made a **small** salad.

Many trees have flowers.

Practice Activity

A. Write the adjective in each sentence.

   1. Chris has a new pair of shoes.

   2. A black dog trotted into the yard.

   3. I gave flowers to my dear friend.

   4. The menu has several sandwiches.

B. Complete each sentence with an adjective from the box.

white	short	both	slow

   5. You may have _____ apples.

   6. Jim wore a _____ shirt and tan pants.

   7. The rope was too _____ to make a swing.

   8. This is a very _____ bus ride!

Practice Activity A

1. _____

2. _____

3. _____

4. _____

Practice Activity B

5. _____

6. _____

7. _____

8. _____

The Writing Process: Expository
Writing a How-to Essay

PREWRITING

Do you know how to make a craft? Choose something you know how to do. Describe the steps in a how-to essay. Write the steps in order. Look for how-to ideas at the library. Have an adult help you check out Internet sites.

DRAFTING

Use your steps to write a how-to essay. Begin with a topic sentence. Follow your steps as you write sentences. Use as many spelling words as possible.

REVISING

When you have finished writing, read your essay from beginning to end. Check to see if you have included all of the steps. Now, write your final draft.

EDITING

Use the **Editing Checklist** to proofread your essay. Be sure to use proofreading marks when you make corrections. Circle two words that might be misspelled. Use a dictionary to check your spelling.

PUBLISHING

Make a copy of your how-to essay and share it with your readers.

EDITING CHECKLIST

Spelling
- ✓ Circle words that contain the spelling patterns and rules learned in Units 31–35.
- ✓ Check the circled words in your **Spelling Dictionary**.
- ✓ Check for other spelling errors.

Capital Letters
- ✓ Capitalize important words in the title.
- ✓ Capitalize the first word in each sentence.
- ✓ Capitalize proper nouns.

Punctuation
- ✓ End each sentence with the correct punctuation.
- ✓ Use commas, apostrophes, and quotation marks correctly.

 TEKS 2.23A Use phonological knowledge to match sounds to letters to construct unknown words.
2.23F Use resources to find correct spellings.

Spelling and the Writing Process

When you write anything—a friendly letter, a paper for school—you should follow the writing process. The writing process has five steps. It might look like this:

Part of the writing process forms a loop. That is because not every writing task is the same. It is also because writers often jump back and forth between the steps as they change their minds and think of new ideas.

Here is what you do in each step:

PREWRITING Think about your audience and your purpose for writing. Brainstorm ideas for writing. Use a graphic organizer to record your ideas.

DRAFTING Get your ideas down on paper. Try to spell correctly, but if you don't know a spelling, make your best guess. You can fix any mistakes later.

REVISING Improve your draft. Rewrite, change, and add words to make your message clear and descriptive.

EDITING Proofread your paper for spelling, grammar, and punctuation errors. Be sure to use a print or online dictionary to check your spelling.

PUBLISHING Make a copy of your writing and share it with your readers. Put your writing in a form that your readers will enjoy.

Confident spellers are better writers. Confident writers understand the writing process better. Know how these five steps best fit the way you write.

Spelling and
Writing Ideas

Being a good speller can help make you a more confident writer. Writing often can make you a better writer. Here are descriptions of each type of writing and some ideas to get you started.

Descriptive writing describes something.

You might...

- describe how your pet sees you and your family.
- describe your most prized possession.

Narrative writing tells a story.

You might...

- write a fantasy story with make-believe characters.
- write a story about a bad day or a good day playing your favorite sport.

Persuasive writing tries to persuade the reader to think or do something.

You might...

- try to persuade your classmates to read a book you like.
- try to persuade your parents to let you have a pet.
- try to persuade your friends to play a new game.

Expository writing explains something.

You might...

- write instructions on how to prepare your favorite food dish.
- write directions from your home to a favorite place such as a park or a friend's home.
- inform your classmates about recycling efforts in your neighborhood.

Handwriting Models

A B C D E
F G H I J K
L M N O P
Q R S T U
V W X Y Z

a b c d e f
g h i j k
l m n o p q
r s t u v
w x y z

1 2 3 4 5
6 7 8 9 10

? ! . , " " '

High Frequency Writing Words

A

a
about
afraid
after
again
air
all
almost
also
always
am
America
an
and
animal
animals
another
any
anything
are
around
as
ask
asked
at
ate
away

B

baby
back
bad
ball
balloons
baseball
basketball
be
bear
beautiful
because
become
bed
been
before
being
believe
best
better
big
bike
black
boat
book
books
both
boy

boys
bring
broke
brother
build
bus
but
buy
by

C

call
called
came
can
candy
can't
car
care
cars
cat
catch
caught
change
charge
children
Christmas
circus
city

class
clean
clothes
come
comes
coming
could
couldn't
country
cut

D

Dad
day
days
decided
did
didn't
died
different
dinner
do
does
doesn't
dog
dogs
doing
done
don't

door
down
dream

E

each
earth
eat
eighth
else
end
enough
even
every
everybody
everyone
everything
except
eyes

F

family
fast
father
favorite
feel
feet
fell
few

field
fight
finally
find
fire
first
fish
five
fix
food
football
for
found
four
free
Friday
friend
friends
from
front
fun
funny
future

G

game
games
gas
gave

get
gets
getting
girl
girls
give
go
God
goes
going
good
got
grade
grader
great
ground
grow

H

had
hair
half
happened
happy
hard
has
have
having
he

head
heard
help
her
here
he's
high
hill
him
his
hit
home
homework
hope
horse
horses
hot
hour
house
how
hurt

I

I
I'd
if
I'm
important
in

into
is
it
its
it's

J

job
jump
just

K

keep
kept
kids
killed
kind
knew
know

L

lady
land
last
later
learn
leave
left
let

let's
life
like
liked
likes
little
live
lived
lives
long
look
looked
looking
lost
lot
lots
love
lunch

M

mad
made
make
making
man
many
math
may
maybe

me
mean
men
might
miss
Mom
money
more
morning
most
mother
mouse
move
Mr.
Mrs.
much
music
must
my
myself

N

name
named
need
never
new
next
nice
night

no
not
nothing
now

O

of
off
oh
OK
old
on
once
one
only
or
other
our
out
outside
over
own

P

parents
park
party
people
person
pick

place
planet
play
played
playing
police
president
pretty
probably
problem
put

R

ran
read
ready
real
really
reason
red
responsibilities
rest
ride
riding
right
room
rules
run
running

S

said
same
saw
say
scared
school
schools
sea
second
see
seen
set
seventh
she
ship
shot
should
show
sick
since
sister
sit
sleep
small
snow
so
some
someone

something
sometimes
soon
space
sport
sports
start
started
states
stay
still
stop
stopped
store
story
street
stuff
such
sudden
suddenly
summer
sure
swimming

T

take
talk
talking
teach
teacher

teachers
team
tell
than
Thanksgiving
that
that's
the
their
them
then
there
these
they
they're
thing
things
think
this
thought
three
through
throw
time
times
to
today
together

told
too
took
top
tree
trees
tried
trip
trouble
try
trying
turn
turned
TV
two

U

united
until
up
upon
us
use
used

V

very

W

walk
walked
walking
want
wanted
war
was
wasn't
watch
water
way
we
week
weeks
well
went
were
what
when
where
which
while
white
who
whole
why
will

win
winter
wish
with
without
woke
won
won't
work
world
would
wouldn't

Y

yard
year
years
yes
you
your
you're

Guide Words

The **guide words** at the top of each dictionary page can help you find the word you want quickly. The first guide word tells you the first word on that page. The second guide word tells you the last word on that page. The entries on the page fall in alphabetical order between these two guide words.

Entries

Words in the dictionary are called **entries**. Entries provide a lot of information besides the correct spelling. Look at the sample entry below.

Tips for Finding a Word in a Dictionary

- Practice using guide words in a dictionary. Think of words to spell. Then use the guide words to find each word's entry. Do this again and again until you can use guide words easily.

- Some spellings are listed with the base word. To find **easiest,** you would look up **easy.** To find **remaining,** you would look up **remain.** To find **histories,** you would look up **history.**

- If you do not know how to spell a word, guess the spelling before looking it up. Try to find the first three letters of the word. (If you use just the first letter, it will probably take too long to find the word.)

- If you can't find a word, think of how else it might be spelled. For example, if a word starts with the /**k**/ sound, the spelling might begin with **k, c,** or even **ch.**

entry the correct spelling, sometimes broken into syllables

other spellings other word forms, including plurals that change the spelling of the base word

pronunciation

fox /fŏks/ *n.* (**fox•es** *pl.*) a wild animal like a dog but with a bushy tail. *A fox may live in a den.*

definition to be sure you have the correct entry word

sample sentence to make the definition clearer

a•bout[1] /ə bout′/ *prep.* relating to. *This book is about insects.*

a•bout[2] /ə bout′/ *adv.* nearly, almost. *The cereal is about gone.*

a•corn /ā′ kôrn′/ or /ā′ kərn/ *n.* the nut of an oak tree. *An acorn fell from the branch.*

a•go /ə gō′/ *adv.* and *adj.* past; gone. *We met two days ago.*

a•hoy /ə hoi′/ *interj.* term used to attract the attention of a ship or a person. *The captain called, "Ahoy."*

a•like[1] /ə līk′/ *adj.* similar; without a difference. *The twin sisters look alike.*

a•like[2] /ə līk′/ *adv.* in the same way. *You can't treat all children alike.*

all[1] /ôl/ *adj.* each one of. *All the books are here.*

all[2] /ôl/ *adv.* entirely. *Our milk is all gone.*

al•most /ôl′ mōst′/ or /ôl mōst′/ *adv.* nearly; just about. *That bus is almost on time; it is only two minutes late.*

al•ways /ôl′ wāz/ or /ôl′ wēz/ *adv.* all the time; constantly. *At the North Pole, it is always cold.*

and /ănd/ *conj.* **a.** with; together with; besides. *She likes to sing and dance.* **b.** added to. *In math, 4 and 5 are 9.*

ant /ănt/ *n.* a social insect. *We watched the ant crawl across the porch.*

➤ **Ant** sounds like **aunt**.

an•y /ĕn′ ē/ *adj.* **a.** one out of a group. *Read any book you like.* **b.** some. *Would you like any orange juice?*

ape /āp/ *n.* an animal like a monkey except it has long arms and no tail. *An ape can walk on two feet.*

ap•ple /ăp′ əl/ *n.* (**ap•ples** *pl.*) a fruit for eating that grows on a tree. *An apple may be red, green, or yellow.*

are /är/ *v.* the form of the verb **be** used with you, we, and they. *You are next. They are last.*

aren't /ärnt/ are not. *We aren't going to the park.*

arm /ärm/ *n.* the part of the body between the shoulder and the hand. *To raise your hand, you must lift your arm.*

art /ärt/ *n.* writing, painting, music, and so on. *We are drawing pictures for our art show.*

as /ăz/ *adv.* to the same degree; equally. *Tom can run as fast as I can.*

ask /ăsk/ *v.* (**asks, asked, ask•ing**) to try to find out or get by using words. *Let's ask Mr. Fulton how to get there.*

ate /āt/ *v.* past tense of **eat**. *She ate a banana.*

aunt /ănt/ or /änt/ *n.* the sister of your father or mother; the wife of your uncle. *My aunt Linda is my mom's sister.*

➤ **Aunt** sounds like **ant**.

a•way /ə wā′/ *adv.* **a.** from a place; to a different place. *Our dog ran away last week.* **b.** aside; out of the way. *He put the dishes away after supper.*

back[1] /băk/ *n.* **a.** the part of the body on the other side from the chest. *Give her a pat on the back.* **b.** the part farthest from the front. *Meet us in the back of the house.*

back[2] /băk/ *adj.* farthest from the front. *We are going to paint the back porch.*

bake /bāk/ *v.* (**bakes, baked, bak•ing**) to cook in an oven. *We like to bake bread.*

ball /bôl/ *n.* **a.** a toy for throwing or kicking. *Catch the ball!* **b.** something round. *The cat loves to play with a ball of yarn.*

bank /băngk/ *n.* **a.** the ground at the edge of a lake or river. *Can you swim to the bank?* **b.** a place where people may keep or borrow money. *Do you have an account at the bank?*

bank

bare•foot /bâr′ foŏt′/ *adv.* and *adj.* without shoes or socks. *The barefoot boy played in the sand.*

Pronunciation Key

ă	pat	ŏ	pot	th	**th**in
ā	pay	ō	toe	*th*	**th**is
âr	care	ô	paw, for	hw	**wh**ich
ä	father	oi	n**oi**se	zh	vi**s**ion
ĕ	pet	ou	**ou**t	ə	**a**bout,
ē	be	ŏŏ	t**oo**k		it**e**m,
ĭ	pit	ōō	b**oo**t		penc**i**l,
ī	pie	ŭ	c**u**t		gall**o**p,
îr	p**ier**	ûr	**ur**ge		circ**u**s

---

base /bās/ *n.* **a.** a starting or resting place. *Robert ran around the field, then back to the base.* **b.** the lowest part. *The base of the jar was blue.*

base•ball /bās′ bôl/ *n.* a game played with a bat and a ball by two teams of nine players each. *Debbie wants to play baseball.*

bas•ket /băs′ kĭt/ *n.* a container woven together with wood, straw, or heavy threads. *We keep fruit in the basket.*

bat[1] /băt/ *n.* a heavy stick used to hit a ball. *Mike showed me how to hold the bat.*

bat[2] /băt/ *v.* (**bats, bat•ted, bat•ting**) to hit. *She batted the ball out of the park for a home run.*

be /bē/ *v.* (**am, are, is, was, were, been, be•ing**) **a.** to equal. *I want to be a hero.* **b.** to happen. *When is the game going to be?*

➤ **Be** sounds like **bee**.

bea•ver /bē′ vər/ *n.* a furry animal with strong, sharp teeth, a broad, flat tail, and webbed hind feet. *Beavers are noted for building dams.*

beaver

be•come /bĭ kŭm′/ *v.* (**be•comes, be•came, be•come, be•com•ing**) to develop into; to come or grow to be. *A caterpillar may become a butterfly or a moth.*

bed•room /bĕd′ rōōm′/ *n.* a room used for sleeping. *We have bunk beds in our bedroom.*

bee /bē/ *n.* a stinging insect with wings. *We watched the bee fly from its hive.*
➤ **Bee** sounds like **be**.

beef /bēf/ *n.* the meat of a cow or steer. *We had beef, carrots, and peas for supper.*

been /bĭn/ *v.* a form of **be**. *She has been a teacher for twenty years.*

bees•wax /bēz′ wăks′/ *n.* the wax made by bees. *Beeswax is used for making candles.*

beet /bēt/ *n.* a plant grown for its juicy root. *He ate the red beet with his supper.*

bell /bĕl/ *n.* a hollow piece of metal that makes a ringing sound when struck. *The bell in the tower rings every hour.*

be•long /bĭ lông′/ or /bĭ lŏng′/ *v.* **a.** to have a proper place. *Pots and pans belong in the kitchen.* **b.** to be the property of someone. *The bike belongs to Anita.*

be•low /bĭ lō′/ *prep.* in a lower place than; to a lower place than. *Put the towels on the shelf below the blankets.*

bench /bĕnch/ *n.* (**bench•es** *pl.*) a long seat. *Dad sits on the bench at the park.*

bend•ing /bĕnd′ ĭng/ *v.* (**bend, bent, bend•ing**) **a.** to make something curve. *Help me bend this wire.* **b.** to stoop or lean over. *Can you bend and touch your toes?*

best /bĕst/ *adj.* better than all others. *That was the best lunch I ever had.*

big /bĭg/ *adj.* (**big•ger, big•gest**) large. *Our dog is big.*

bike /bīk/ *n.* a bicycle. *Juan rides his bike.*

bill /bĭl/ *n.* **a.** a statement of money owed. *The doctor sent a bill for my shots.* **b.** a piece of paper money. *I found a dollar bill.* **c.** the beak of a bird. *Ducks have wide, flat bills.*

bird /bûrd/ *n.* (**birds** *pl.*) an animal that has feathers and wings. *Almost all birds can fly.*

birth /bûrth/ *n.* the act of being born. *The dog gave birth to three puppies.*

birth•day /**bûrth′** dā′/ *n.* the day one was born, or the same date in another year. *Rosa and I have the same birthday.*

bit /bĭt/ *v.* (**bites, bit•ten** or **bit, bit•ing**) grabbed, held, or cut with teeth. *The dog bit and nibbled the bone.*

blew /blо̄о̄/ *v.* past tense of blow. *I blew out the candle.*

➤ **Blew** sounds like **blue.**

blink /blĭngk/ *v.* to close and open the eyes quickly. *The sun may make you blink your eyes.*

block /blŏk/ *n.* **a.** a solid piece of wood, stone, metal, etc. *Children play with blocks.* **b.** a part of a town or city surrounded by four streets. *The new shopping center covers a city block.*

boat /bōt/ *n.* (**boats** *pl.*) a small vessel for traveling on water. *The boat sailed across the lake.*

bod•y /**bŏd′** ē/ *n.* (**bod•ies** *pl.*) all the parts that make up a person or an animal. *Take good care of your body.*

boil /boil/ *v.* to heat something to the boiling point. *Boil the pasta for four minutes.*

bone /bōn/ *n.* a hard part inside the body; a part of the skeleton. *Your longest bone is in your leg.*

bon•net /**bŏn′** ĭt/ *n.* a kind of hat; a cloth or straw hat tied under the chin. *Jill wore a yellow bonnet.*

book /bо̆о̆k/ *n.* written or printed sheets of paper put together inside a cover. *That book has a red jacket.*

Pronunciation Key

ă	pat	ŏ	pot	th	**th**in
ā	pay	ō	toe	*th*	**th**is
âr	care	ô	paw, for	hw	**wh**ich
ä	father	oi	noise	zh	vi**s**ion
ĕ	pet	ou	out	ə	about,
ē	be	о̄о̄	took		item,
ĭ	pit	о̄о̄	boot		pencil,
ī	pie	ŭ	cut		gallop,
îr	pier	ûr	urge		circus

boot /bо̄о̄t/ *n.* a cover for the foot and leg. *Sean and I have rubber boots.*

born /bôrn/ *v.* brought into life. *A new baby was born next door.*

both /bōth/ *adj.* the two. *Tell me both ways to get to school.*

box /bŏks/ *n.* (**box•es** *pl.*) a case for holding things. *Please put the tools back in the box.*

box

boy /boi/ *n.* (**boys** *pl.*) a male child. *We have only one boy in our family.*

braid¹ /brād/ *v.* (**braids, braid•ed, braid•ing**) to weave three or more strands of hair or cloth into a braid. *Will you braid my hair?*

braid² /brād/ *n.* three or more strands of hair or cloth woven together. *Marie's braid is ten inches long.*

bring /brĭng/ *v.* (**brings, brought, bring•ing**) to carry from somewhere else. *Please bring my book with you.*

broke /brōk/ *v.* (**breaks, broke, brok•en, break•ing**) **a.** came apart; separated into pieces. *The pie plate dropped and broke.* **b.** failed to keep or carry out. *He broke his promise.* **c.** went beyond; did better than. *He broke the school's track records.*

broke

broom /bro͞om/ or /broŏm/ *n.* a brush with a long handle, used for sweeping. *You can use the broom to sweep the walk.*

brush¹ /brŭsh/ *n.* (**brush•es** *pl.*) a tool for painting or cleaning. *He used a brush to paint the door.*

brush² /brŭsh/ *v.* (**brush•es, brushed, brush•ing**) to paint or clean by moving a brush back and forth. *Did you brush your teeth yet?*

buck•et /bŭk' ĭt/ *n.* a pail; a container for carrying liquids, sand, or other substances. *Please put the mop in the bucket.*

bug /bŭg/ *n.* (**bugs** *pl.*) an insect, usually one that crawls. *Even a small bug can crawl fast.*

bump¹ /bŭmp/ *v.* to knock or hit against something. *Try not to bump into the wall.*

bump² /bŭmp/ *n.* a raised place. *The bump in the road makes the car bounce.*

bush /boŏsh/ *n.* (**bush•es** *pl.*) a small tree; a shrub. *A rose grows on a bush.*

bush•el /boŏsh' əl/ *n.* a unit of measure for dry goods such as grains, fruits, and vegetables. *The farmer gave us a bushel of apples.*

bus•y /bĭz' ē/ *adj.* (**bus•i•er, bus•i•est; bus•i•ly** *adv.*) **a.** at work; active. *We will be busy until dark cleaning up the backyard.* **b.** full of work or activity. *The first day of school is always busy.*

by /bī/ *prep.* **a.** near. *Stay by her.* **b.** along. *We came home by the old road.* **c.** through the effort of. *The project was done by the second grade class.*

cab•in /kăb′ ĭn/ *n.* a small house, often built of logs. *Abraham Lincoln lived in a cabin.*

cake /kāk/ *n.* a sweet, breadlike food made from batter. *The cake is mixed and ready to bake.*

call[1] /kôl/ *v.* to shout; to cry out. *Did Lani hear you call her?*

call[2] /kôl/ *n.* a cry. *That bird's call sounds like a whistle.*

can[1] /kăn/ or /kĕn/ *v.* (**could**) to know how or to be able to. *He can play the piano.*

can[2] /kăn/ or /kĕn/ *n.* a metal container. *Here is a can of peas.*

can•not /kăn′ ŏt/ or /kə nŏt′/ *v.* is or are not able to. *They cannot come with us.*

can't /kănt/ cannot. *I can't lift this heavy box.*

cap /kăp/ *n.* a small hat that fits closely on the head. *How do you like my baseball cap?*

car /kär/ *n.* an automobile. *We went for a ride in the car.*

card /kärd/ *n.* (**cards** *pl.*) a small piece of stiff paper. *We wrote each letter on a separate card.*

car•ry /kăr′ ē/ *v.* (**car•ries, car•ried, car•ry•ing**) to take from one place to another. *Will you carry this package home?*

cash[1] /kăsh/ *n.* money in coins and bills. *I have two dollars in cash.*

Pronunciation Key

ă	pat	ŏ	pot	th	**th**in
ā	pay	ō	toe	*th*	**th**is
âr	care	ô	paw, for	hw	**wh**ich
ä	father	oi	n**oi**se	zh	vi**s**ion
ĕ	pet	ou	**ou**t	ə	**a**bout,
ē	be	ŏŏ	t**oo**k		it**e**m,
ĭ	pit	ōō	b**oo**t		penc**i**l,
ī	pie	ŭ	cut		gall**o**p,
îr	p**ier**	ûr	**ur**ge		circ**u**s

cash[2] /kăsh/ *v.* (**cash•es, cashed, cash•ing**) to exchange for money. *The bank will cash this check.*

cash

cast[1] /kăst/ *v.* (**casts, cast, cast•ing**)
a. threw or tossed a line or net. *The fisherman cast his net into the sea.*
b. gave roles in a movie or play to actors. *My teacher cast me as the queen in the school play.*

cast² /kăst/ *n.* **a.** a throw of a line or net. *His cast went past the pier.* **b.** all of the people who act in a movie or play. *The movie's cast is very talented.*

cat /kăt/ *n.* (**cats** *pl.*) **a.** a small furry animal that can purr. *Our cat loves to sit on my lap.* **b.** any larger animal that is also a part of the cat family. *A lion is a cat.*

cave /kāv/ *n.* a hollow space that goes into the earth. *They found a fossil inside the cave.*

cel•er•y /sĕl′ ə rē/ *n.* (**cel•er•ies** *pl.*) a green vegetable with a long, crunchy stalk. *Mom puts cream cheese on celery.*

chain /chān/ *n.* **a.** a number of links or rings fastened together. *She strung the beads on a gold chain.* **b.** a series of things that are connected or joined. *The Rockies are a chain of mountains.*

chalk /chôk/ *n.* a soft mineral used for writing or drawing. *It's fun to use colored chalk on the board.*

chat•ter /chăt′ ər/ *v.* **a.** to talk fast and nonstop. *Does Jack always chatter about soccer?* **b.** to click your teeth together fast and nonstop. *My teeth chatter when I'm cold.* **c.** to give a fast series of speechlike sounds. *We could hear the monkeys chatter at the zoo.*

cheek /chēk/ *n.* the side of the face below the eye. *She had a little smudge on her cheek.*

chin /chĭn/ *n.* the part of the face beneath the bottom lip. *You move your chin when you chew.*

chips /chĭps/ *n.* (**chip** *sing.*) small pieces broken or cut off something. *Where did these chips of paint come from?*

choose /chōōz/ *v.* (**choos•es, chose, chos•en, choos•ing**) **a.** to pick out. *Choose the kind of candy you want.* **b.** to prefer. *I do not choose to tell you my age.*

chop /chŏp/ *v.* (**chops, chopped, chop•ping**) to cut by hitting with a sharp tool such as an ax. *We need to chop wood for our campfire.*

chute /shōōt/ *n.* a slide or tube used to send things down. *The laundry went down the chute.*

clap¹ /klăp/ *v.* (**claps, clapped, clap•ping**) to strike the hands together. *After the play we all began to clap.*

clap² /klăp/ *n.* a sudden loud noise or crash. *I heard a clap of thunder.*

class /klăs/ *n.* (**class•es** *pl.*) a group of students learning together. *There are more boys than girls in my class.*

clean¹ /klēn/ *adj.* free from dirt. *Put on clean clothes for the party.*

clean² /klēn/ *v.* to make clean. *Dad made me clean my room.*

cliff /klĭf/ *n.* a high, steep rock with a side that goes almost straight up. *Cliffs are difficult to climb.*

cloud /kloud/ *n.* very small water droplets collected in the air. *There is one large cloud in the sky.*

cloud•y /klou′ dē/ *adj.* (**cloud•i•er, cloud•i•est; cloud•i•ly** *adv.*) full of clouds. *The sky was gray and cloudy.*

clown /kloun/ *n.* a person who dresses up and acts funny to make us laugh. *The clown drove a tiny car in the parade.*

clown

club /klŭb/ *n.* **a.** a heavy stick used in playing games. *She hit the golf ball with her club.* **b.** a group of people meeting together. *I want to join the stamp club.*

cluck[1] /klŭk/ *n.* a sound made by a chicken. *When a hen calls her chicks, it sounds like "cluck, cluck."*

cluck[2] /klŭk/ *v.* to make a sound like a hen. *Hens will cluck at their chicks.*

coach /kōch/ *n.* (**coach•es** *pl.*) **a.** a carriage pulled by horses. *We rode in a coach to the castle.* **b.** a person who trains athletes or teams. *Our coach showed us how to stretch before practice.*

coat /kōt/ *n.* an outer garment with sleeves. *In winter I wear a heavy coat over my other clothes.*

coin /koin/ *n.* (**coins** *pl.*) a piece of metal money. *Pennies, nickels, dimes, and quarters are coins.*

cold[1] /kōld/ *adj.* having a low temperature; not warm. *January is a cold month.*

cold[2] /kōld/ *n.* a common illness. *Drink lots of orange juice when you have a cold.*

come /kŭm/ *v.* (**comes, came, come, com•ing**) **a.** to move toward. *Come over to my house.* **b.** to happen. *Your birthday comes once a year.*

cook¹ /kŏŏk/ *v.* to prepare food for eating by using heat. *Broiling is one way to cook food.*

cook² /kŏŏk/ *n.* a person who prepares food. *Everybody likes the cook at our school.*

corn /kôrn/ *n.* a grain that grows in kernels or seeds on large ears. *We ate corn and peas for dinner.*

cot /kŏt/ *n.* a light bed that can be folded up. *Many cots are made of canvas on a metal or wood frame.*

could•n't /kŏŏd' nt/ could not. *I couldn't see the Big Dipper in the night sky.*

count /kount/ *v.* **a.** to name the numbers in order. *Our baby is learning to count already.* **b.** to add to find the total. *He counted the quarters in his bank.* **c.** depend. *You can count on Alex to be on time.*

cow /kou/ *n.* a large farm animal that gives milk. *Our cow just had a calf.*

crack•ing /krăk' ĭng/ *v.* present participle of crack; breaking or splitting apart. *The sidewalk is cracking.*

crank•y /krăng' kē/ *adj.* (**crank•i•er, crank•i•est**) angry or grumpy. *My uncle is cranky in very hot weather.*

crash /krăsh/ *n.* (**crash•es** *pl.*) the very loud noise of something falling, breaking, or hitting. *The tree fell with a loud crash.*

crate /krāt/ *n.* a wooden box. *The oranges were mailed in a crate.*

crawl /krôl/ *v.* **a.** to move slowly along the ground by pulling the body. *Worms and caterpillars crawl.* **b.** to move on hands and knees. *Babies crawl before they walk.* **c.** to move slowly. *The traffic crawled along the crowded highway.*

crisp¹ /krĭsp/ *adj.* (**crisp•er, crisp•est**) fresh and crunchy. *Crisp potato chips taste good.*

crisp² /krĭsp/ *n.* a baked dessert with fruit. *Grandma bakes the best apple crisp!*

cross•walk /krôs′ wôk′/ or /krŏs′ wôk′/ *n.* an area marked off for persons to use when crossing a street. *Always cross at a crosswalk.*

cry¹ /krī/ *v.* (**cries, cried, cry•ing**) to weep; to shed tears. *We heard the baby cry.*

cry

cry[2] /krī/ *n.* (**cries** *pl.*) the sound made by an animal. *We woke up to the cry of the bird.*

cup /kŭp/ *n.* a small, hollow container used for drinking. *Pour some milk into my cup, please.*

cute /kyōōt/ *adj.* (**cut•er, cut•est**) pretty; attractive. *We saw a cute puppy at the pet shop.*

dad /dăd/ *n.* short word for father. *My dad took us for a walk.*

dai • sy /dā′ zē/ *n.* (**dai•sies** *pl.*) a flower with white or pink petals and a yellow center. *The pink daisy is so pretty.*

dark[1] /därk/ *adj.* not light; having little or no light. *I like to look at stars on a clear, dark night.*

dark[2] /därk/ *n.* darkness; nightfall. *You must return before dark.*

dash[1] /dăsh/ *v.* (**dash•es, dashed, dash•ing**) to rush quickly. *We dashed to the store, but it had closed.*

dash[2] /dăsh/ *n.* (**dash•es** *pl.*) **a.** a mark (—) used to show a break or pause. *A dash causes a complete stop—like this.* **b.** a small amount. *Add a dash of pepper.*

dashed /dăsht/ *v.* past tense of dash. *We dashed out in the rain to the car.*

Pronunciation Key

ă	pat	ŏ	pot	th	**th**in
ā	pay	ō	toe	*th*	**th**is
âr	care	ô	paw, for	hw	**wh**ich
ä	father	oi	n**oi**se	zh	vi**si**on
ĕ	pet	ou	**ou**t	ə	**a**bout,
ē	be	ŏŏ	t**oo**k		it**e**m,
ĭ	pit	ōō	b**oo**t		penc**i**l,
ī	pie	ŭ	cut		gall**o**p,
îr	pier	ûr	**ur**ge		circ**u**s

day /dā/ *n.* **a.** the time between sunrise and sunset. *We traveled during the day and slept at night.* **b.** a period of twenty-four hours. *A week has seven days.*

dear /dîr/ *adj.* greatly loved. *She gave the book to a dear friend.*

➤ **Dear** sounds like **deer**.

deep /dēp/ *adj.* (**deep•er, deep•est**) going far down or back. *Big fish swim in deep water.*

deer /dîr/ *n.* (**deer** *pl.*) a graceful animal with hooves. *The male deer has antlers.*

➤ **Deer** sounds like **dear**.

did • n′t /dĭd′ nt/ did not. *I didn't know you were moving to a new house.*

dime /dīm/ *n.* a silver coin used as money by the United States and Canada. *A dime is worth ten cents.*

dish[1] /dĭsh/ *n.* (**dish•es** *pl.*) a container for holding food. *Put the peas in a big dish.*

dish[2] /dĭsh/ v. to put food into a serving dish. *Todd, please dish up the applesauce.*

dock[1] /dŏk/ n. a landing area for ships and boats; a pier. *Our ship got to the dock safely.*

dock[2] /dŏk/ v. to steer a boat to a resting place. *Dad likes to dock his boat by 8 P.M.*

does /dŭz/ v. a form of do. *Tim does neat work.*

does•n't /dŭz' ənt/ does not. *It doesn't look like rain today.*

dog /dôg/ or /dŏg/ n. a four-legged animal that makes a good pet. *Some dogs watch houses or tend sheep.*

do•ing /doo' ĭng/ v. present tense of do. *What are you doing tonight after school?*

doll /dŏl/ n. a toy that looks like a person. *The doll I like best has a lot of different clothes.*

done /dŭn/ v. a form of do. *Have you done your math homework yet?*

don't /dōnt/ do not. *I don't know what time we are leaving.*

door /dôr/ or /dōr/ n. a movable part that can be opened and closed to form an entrance. *Open the door and go in.*

down[1] /doun/ adv. from a high place or position to a lower one. *The airplane came down for a landing.*

down[2] /doun/ n. soft feathers. *The baby birds were covered with down.*

down•town /doun' toun'/ adv. in or toward the main business part of a city. *We all went downtown to shop.*

drag•on•fly /drăg' ən flī'/ n. (**drag•on•flies** pl.) a flying insect with four big wings. *The dragonfly flew over the lake.*

dress[1] /drĕs/ n. (**dress•es** pl.) an outer garment with a skirt. *Judy has a plaid dress.*

dress[2] /drĕs/ v. (**dress•es, dressed, dress•ing**) to put clothes on. *Can you dress in five minutes?*

drift•ed /drĭf' tĕd/ v. past tense of **drift**. floated; moved by winds or waves. *The boat drifted to shore.*

drink[1] /drĭngk/ v. (**drinks, drank, drunk, drink•ing**) to take a liquid into the mouth and swallow it. *Do you drink much milk?*

drink[2] /drĭngk/ n. liquid that is swallowed. *May I have a drink of water?*

drive[1] /drīv/ v. (**drives, drove, driv•en, driv•ing**) to make a car, vehicle, or working animal go. *Who is going to drive me home?*

drive[2] /drīv/ n. a trip in a car. *We took a drive last Sunday.*

drug•store /drŭg' stôr'/ or /drŭg' stōr'/ n. a store where medicines and other items are sold. *You can buy toothpaste at the drugstore.*

drum /drŭm/ *n.* a musical instrument that makes a sound when beaten. *The marchers kept time to the beat of a drum.*

drum

dry[1] /drī/ *adj.* (**dri•er, dri•est**) not wet or moist. *The ground was dry before the rain came.*

dry[2] /drī/ *v.* (**dries, dried, dry•ing**) to make or become dry. *Please dry the dishes.*

dust[1] /dŭst/ *n.* a light powder of dirt. *I could see the dust on the old table.*

dust[2] /dŭst/ *v.* to remove dust by wiping. *He will dust the books in the bookcase.*

each /ēch/ *adj.* every one in a larger group. *Each child wore a nametag.*

ea•sel /ē′ zəl/ *n.* a stand to hold an artist's canvas. *Most oil painters use an easel.*

eas•y /ē′ zē/ *adj.* (**eas•i•er, eas•i•est**) not hard to get or do. *A toy on wheels is easy to pull.*

eat /ēt/ *v.* (**eats, ate, eat•en, eat•ing**) **a.** to take food into the mouth, chew it, and swallow it. *We eat beans for lunch.* **b.** to have a meal. *Did you eat yet?*

egg /ĕg/ *n.* (**eggs** *pl.*) the rounded container in which a baby bird grows. *Our hens lay many eggs.*

el•e•phant /ĕl′ ə fənt/ *n.* a large, gray four-footed animal that has long white tusks and a long trunk with which it can grasp or carry objects. *Elephants are found in Africa and in India.*

end[1] /ĕnd/ *n.* the point at which something either begins or stops. *A piece of string has two ends.*

end[2] /ĕnd/ *v.* to finish. *I didn't want the story to end.*

ex•plore /ĭk splôr′/ or /ĭk splōr′/ *v.* (**ex•plores, ex•plored, ex•plor•ing**) to travel in unknown lands; to journey in a strange place with hopes of discovery. *Many people explored America before the country was settled.*

face /fās/ *n.* the front part of the head; that part of the head on which the eyes, nose, and mouth are located. *Her face was covered by a funny mask.*

fall¹ /fôl/ *v.* (**falls, fell, fall•en, fall•ing**) to drop from a higher place. *Leaves fall from trees.*

fall² /fôl/ *n.* the season that follows summer; autumn. *Thanksgiving is in the fall.*

fan¹ /făn/ *n.* anything used to move the air. *When it got hot, I turned on the fan.*

fan² /făn/ *v.* (**fans, fanned, fan•ning**) to stir up air. *I used a paper to fan myself.*

fan•cy /făn′ sē/ *adj.* (**fan•ci•er, fan•ci•est; fan•ci•ly** *adv.*) decorated or ornamented; not plain. *Sue wore a fancy dress to the dance.*

far /fär/ *adj.* a long way off; distant. *The school is far from my house, so I leave very early.*

far•a•way /fär′ ə wā′/ *adj.* distant. *Movies show scenes of faraway places.*

farm /färm/ *n.* the land used for growing crops or for raising animals. *My uncle raises wheat on his farm in Kansas.*

fat¹ /făt/ *n.* a greasy substance in animals and plants. *I trim the fat from my meat.*

fat² /făt/ *adj.* having much flesh; plump. *Those cows are fat.*

fa•ther /fä′ thər/ *n.* the male parent. *My father is a very kind man.*

fell /fĕl/ *v.* past tense of fall. *Brad fell and scraped his knee.*

fill /fĭl/ *v.* (**fills, filled, fill•ing**) to put as much as you can into; to make full. *Mom is filling the goldfish bowl.*

fine¹ /fīn/ *adj.* good; excellent. *Today is a fine day for a picnic.*

fine² /fīn/ *n.* money paid for breaking a rule. *I paid a fine because my library book was overdue.*

fin•ger /fĭng′ gər/ *n.* one of the five digits of the hand. *Don't put your finger in the pie!*

fire /fīr/ *n.* flame; heat and light caused by burning. *The campers made a fire at night.*

fire

fish[1] /fĭsh/ *n.* (**fish** or **fish•es** *pl.*) an animal that lives in water, has fins, and breathes through gills. *Most fish have scales covering their bodies.*

fish[2] /fĭsh/ *v.* (**fish•es, fished, fish•ing**) to try to catch fish. *Tracy and her father go to the lake each summer to fish.*

fish•ing /fĭsh′ ĭng/ *v.* present tense of fish. *We are fishing for bass.*

fit[1] /fĭt/ *v.* (**fits, fit** or **fit•ted, fit•ting**) to be right for. *My new shoes fit my feet.*

fit[2] /fĭt/ *adj.* in good condition. *My sister is running to get fit.*

fix /fĭks/ *v.* (**fix•es, fixed, fix•ing**) to repair or mend. *Grandpa can fix that broken toy.*

flag•pole /flăg′ pōl′/ *n.* a pole for raising and flying a flag. *Our flagpole is very tall.*

flat /flăt/ *adj.* (**flat•ter, flat•test**) level and even. *The tabletop is flat.*

fluff•y /flŭf′ ē/ *adj.* (**fluff•i•er, fluff•i•est**) light and soft. *I like fluffy pillows.*

fly[1] /flī/ *v.* (**flies, flew, fly•ing**) **a.** to move through the air by using wings. *Birds fly.* **b.** to travel by air. *This summer we will fly to Dallas.*

fly[2] /flī/ *n.* (**flies** *pl.*) an insect with two wings. *Can you swat that fly?*

foam /fōm/ *n.* a quantity of small bubbles. *The big waves of the ocean have foam on top.*

fog /fôg/ or /fŏg/ *n.* a cloud near the surface of the land; heavy mist. *Fog is made of tiny drops of water.*

Pronunciation Key

ă	pat	ŏ	pot	th	thin
ā	pay	ō	toe	*th*	this
âr	care	ô	paw, for	hw	which
ä	father	oi	noise	zh	vision
ĕ	pet	ou	out	ə	about,
ē	be	ŏŏ	took		item,
ĭ	pit	ōō	boot		pencil,
ī	pie	ŭ	cut		gallop,
îr	pier	ûr	urge		circus

fog•horn /fôg′ hôrn′/ or /fŏg′ hôrn′/ *n.* a loud horn used to warn ships of danger, especially during a dense fog. *Ships sound their foghorns to let other ships know they are coming.*

foil /foil/ *n.* a very thin sheet of metal. *Wrap your sandwich in foil, and put it into your lunch bag.*

fol•low /fŏl′ ō/ *v.* (**fol•lows, fol•lowed, fol•low•ing**) **a.** to go or come after. *Please follow me to your table.* **b.** to walk or move along. *Follow this path to the park.*

food /fōōd/ *n.* anything taken in by plants and animals that makes them live and grow. *Spinach is a healthful food.*

foot•ball /fōōt′ bôl′/ *n.* **a.** a game played by throwing, kicking, and running with a ball. *Wear your helmet when you play football.* **b.** the oval ball used in this game. *Jason will pass the football to me.*

for /fôr/ *prep.* **a.** with the purpose of. *We are going for a bike ride.* **b.** sent or given to. *This letter is for you.* **c.** because of. *We jumped for joy.*

fork /fôrk/ *n.* a pointed tool used for lifting food or hay. *You can't eat soup with a fork.*

found /found/ *v.* past tense of **find**. to come upon. *I found your boot in the closet.*

fox /fŏks/ *n.* (**fox•es** *pl.*) a wild animal like a dog but with a bushy tail. *A fox may live in a den.*

free /frē/ *adj.* **a.** loose; not tied down. *We tried to catch the free end of the dog's leash.* **b.** not costing anything. *Our neighbor gave us free tickets.*

fresh /frĕsh/ *adj.* **a.** newly made, grown, or gathered. *Mother baked fresh bread this morning.* **b.** clean. *Breathe this fresh air.*

frisk•y /frĭs′ kē/ *adj.* (**frisk•i•er, frisk•i•est**) lively and playful. *Pat's frisky cat plays with yarn.*

frog /frŏg/ *n.* a small animal with webbed feet that lives near water. *A frog can jump far.*

from /frŭm/ *prep.* **a.** out of. *We live thirty miles from town.* **b.** beginning with. *The party will last from two to four.*

front[1] /frŭnt/ *n.* **a.** a part that faces forward. *The front of the house faces the street.* **b.** the first part. *The pilot sits in the front of the plane.*

front[2] /frŭnt/ *adj.* located in the front. *We stood on the front porch.*

frown[1] /froun/ *v.* to make a face that shows displeasure. *Why did you frown during the movie?*

frown[2] /froun/ *n.* a facial expression that shows displeasure. *My mom had a frown on her face when I came home late.*

fry /frī/ *v.* (**fries, fried, fry•ing**) to cook in hot oil over direct heat. *Fry these vegetables lightly to keep them crisp.*

full /fŏŏl/ *adj.* (**full•er, full•est**) having as much or as many as possible; able to hold no more. *The bus is full of people.*

game /gām/ *n.* **a.** a way to play that follows rules. *Let's have a game of tag.* **b.** the things needed to play a game. *Where is your game of checkers?*

girl /gûrl/ *n.* (**girls** *pl.*) a female child. *Their new baby is a girl.*

give /gĭv/ *v.* (**gives, gave, giv•en, giv•ing**) to hand over; to let have. *I will give this game to Ernesto.*

glad /glăd/ *adj.* **a.** happy; pleased. *We are glad that you could come.* **b.** willing, ready. *He will be glad to help you.*

glass /glăs/ *n.* (**glass•es** *pl.*) **a.** a hard substance that can be seen through. *Glass is used in windows.* **b.** a container for drinking. *Please hand me a water glass.* **c.** a pair of lenses to correct sight. *Erin wears glasses to help her see better.*

gloss•y /glô′ sē/ or /glŏs′ ē/ *adj.*
(**gloss•i•er, gloss•i•est**) smooth and
shiny. *The glossy paper is really
smooth.*

glove /glŭv/ *n.* a covering for your
hand. *Mom wore a glove to plant
flowers.*

go /gō/ *v.* (**goes, went, gone, go•ing**)
a. to get to another place. *Let's go to
your house.* **b.** to work or run. *The car
won't go.*

go•ing /gō′ ĭng/ *v.* present tense of go.
Are you going to Tracie's party?

gold•en /gōl′ dən/ *adj.* made of gold.
The palace has a golden ceiling.

gone /gôn/ or /gŏn/ *v.* past tense of go.
My grandpa has gone fishing.

good /good/ *adj.* (**bet•ter, best**) **a.** of
high quality; better than the usual kind.
I saw a good movie last night. **b.** well-
behaved. *Our teacher says that we are
a good class.*

goose /goos/ *n.* (**geese** *pl.*)
a swimming bird that looks
like a duck, but has a
larger body and a longer
neck. *The male goose
is called a gander.*

goose

Pronunciation Key

ă	pat	ŏ	pot	th	thin
ā	pay	ō	toe	*th*	*th*is
âr	care	ô	paw, for	hw	which
ä	father	oi	noise	zh	vision
ě	pet	ou	out	ə	about,
ē	be	oo	took		item,
ĭ	pit	oo	boot		pencil,
ī	pie	ŭ	cut		gallop,
îr	pier	ûr	urge		circus

got /gŏt/ *v.* (**gets, got,** or **got•ten,
get•ting**) **a.** received. *Our class got new
desks.* **b.** brought. *I got Mom a glass of
water.*

grade /grād/ *n.* **a.** class or year in
school. *The fifth grade is in room 210.*
b. a slope in a road. *The road up the
mountain has a steep grade.*

grand /grănd/ *adj.* **a.** large; beautiful;
costing much money. *The queen lived
in a grand palace.* **b.** fine; wonderful.
You'll have a grand time at the party.

grass /grăs/ *n.* a plant with thin leaves,
found in lawns or pastures. *He will
mow the grass.*

grate¹ /grāt/ *v.* (**grates, grat•ed,
grat•ing**) to break something down into
small pieces by rubbing it against a
rough surface. *He grated the onions
and mixed them in with the meat.*

grate² /grāt/ *n.* a metal covering. *The
men replaced the grate over the hole.*

➤ **Grate** sounds like **great**.

grease¹ /grēs/ *n.* a thick, oily substance. *There is grease in the frying pan.*

grease² /grēs/ *v.* to coat or rub with grease. *I will grease the skillet.*

great /grāt/ *adj.* (**great•er, great•est; great•ly** *adv.*) **a.** large in size or number; big. *A great crowd of people was at the carnival.* **b.** more than is ordinary or expected. *You did a great job in cutting down the tree.* **c.** important; skilled; famous. *There have been many great presidents in our history.*

➤ **Great** sounds like **grate**.

grow /grō/ *v.* (**grows, grew, grown, grow•ing**) **a.** to become larger; to increase. *Our baby is growing so fast!* **b.** to live in a certain place. *Palm trees grow in the tropics.* **c.** to raise by planting seeds and caring for. *We grow tomatoes in our garden.*

gruff /grŭf/ *adj.* (**gruff•er, gruff•est**) harsh or stern. *His gruff voice scared me.*

grump•y /grŭm′ pē/ *adj.* (**grump•i•er, grump•i•est**) grouchy. *The grumpy man became happy.*

guess¹ /gĕs/ *v.* (**guess•es, guessed, guess•ing**) to form an opinion without being sure. *When I forgot my watch, I had to guess the time.*

guess² /gĕs/ *n.* (**guess•es** *pl.*) an opinion formed without being sure. *That was a good guess.*

hand¹ /hănd/ *n.* the part of the arm below the wrist. *I write with my left hand.*

hand² /hănd/ *v.* to give or pass. *Please hand me the keys.*

hang /hăng/ *v.* (**hangs, hung, hang•ing**) **a.** to fasten or be fastened from above. *Let's hang the wash on the line.* **b.** to droop; bend down. *The branches hang down after the heavy snowfall.*

hard¹ /härd/ *adj.* **a.** not soft. *Ice is hard.* **b.** not easy. *That ball was hard to catch.*

hard² /härd/ *adv.* with effort. *We worked hard for the team.*

has•n't /hăz′ ənt/ has not. *The school bus hasn't come yet.*

hatch /hăch/ *v.* (**hatch•es, hatched, hatch•ing**) to emerge from an egg or cocoon. *The bird's egg might hatch today.*

have /hăv/ *v.* (**has, had, hav•ing**) **a.** to own; to possess. *They have a new house.* **b.** to cause to. *Have him play another song.* **c.** to accept; to take. *Have an apple.* **d.** to experience. *I hope he had a nice time.*

head /hĕd/ *n.* **a.** the part of the body that contains the eyes, ears, nose, and mouth. *Don't bump your head.* **b.** the top or front part. *I was at the head of the line.*

health /hĕlth/ *n.* the condition of the body or mind. *The doctor checked my health.*

hear /hîr/ v. (hears, heard, hear•ing) **a.** to take in sound with the ears. *I hear a funny noise.* **b.** to listen to. *We like to hear good music.*

➤ **Hear** sounds like **here**.

help[1] /hĕlp/ v. to aid; to assist. *Please help me wash the dog.*

help[2] /hĕlp/ n. aid or assistance. *Sarah gave me some help with my homework.*

her[1] /hûr/ adj. of or belonging to a girl or woman. *Donna lost her key.*

her[2] /hûr/ pron. that girl or woman. *Rosa took the bag with her.*

here /hîr/ adv. **a.** in or at this place. *We like living here.* **b.** to or into this place. *Please come here.*

➤ **Here** sounds like **hear**.

here's /hîrz/ here is. *Here's the book I want you to read.*

he's /hēz/ he is; he has. *He's my best friend.*

hide /hīd/ v. (hides, hid, hid•den or hid, hid•ing) to put or keep out of sight. *Let's hide the gifts quickly.*

hill /hĭl/ n. land that is higher than the land around it, but not so tall as a mountain. *From the top of the hill, we could see for miles.*

hit /hĭt/ v. (hits, hit, hit•ting) to give a blow to; to strike. *Chris hit the ball over the net.*

hob•by /hŏb' ē/ n. (hob•bies pl.) something you do for fun. *Sue's favorite hobby is sewing.*

Pronunciation Key

ă	pat	ŏ	pot	th	thin
ā	pay	ō	toe	th	this
âr	care	ô	paw, for	hw	which
ä	father	oi	noise	zh	vision
ĕ	pet	ou	out	ə	about,
ē	be	ŏŏ	took		item,
ĭ	pit	ōō	boot		pencil,
ī	pie	ŭ	cut		gallop,
îr	pier	ûr	urge		circus

hold /hōld/ v. (holds, held, hold•ing) **a.** to take and not let go. *I was asked to hold the baby.* **b.** to keep in a certain position. *Hold your head high.*

hor•net /hôr' nĭt/ n. a large wasp. *The hornet stung Joe.*

horse /hôrs/ n. a large, hoofed animal used for riding and pulling loads. *A colt is a young male horse.*

horse

hour /our/ *n.* **a.** sixty minutes. *There are twenty-four hours in a day.* **b.** a certain time. *The doctor's office hours are from ten to four.*

➤ **Hour** sounds like **our**.

house /hous/ *n.* a building where people live. *Our house is made of bricks.*

house•fly /hous′ flī′/ *n.* (**house•flies** *pl.*) a common two-winged flying insect. *There's a housefly in that spiderweb.*

how /hou/ *adv.* **a.** in what way. *How do you boil an egg?* **b.** to what degree or amount. *How hot is it outside?* **c.** in what condition. *They asked me how I felt.*

hunt /hŭnt/ *v.* to search; to try to find. *We all hunted for the lost ball.*

hush /hŭsh/ *v.* (**hush•es, hushed, hush•ing**) to make still or quiet. *See if you can hush the baby.*

I'm /īm/ I am. *I'm going to be eight years old on my next birthday.*

in•side[1] /ĭn sīd′/ or /ĭn′ sīd′/ *adv.* within; not outside. *When it rains, we play inside.*

in•side[2] /ĭn sīd′/ or /ĭn′ sīd′/ *adj.* inner. *My jacket has an inside pocket.*

in•to /ĭn′ too/ *prep.* **a.** to the inside of. *She walked into the room.* **b.** to the form of. *Water turns into ice in cold weather.*

is•n't /ĭz′ ənt/ is not. *This shirt isn't large enough.*

join /join/ *v.* to become part of a group. *Jill will join the drama club.*

joke /jōk/ *n.* something said or done to make someone laugh. *Rob told a funny joke.*

joy /joi/ *n.* happiness. *He had the joy of seeing his son learning to read.*

jug /jŭg/ *n.* a big bottle with a narrow mouth. *They brought a jug of milk from the farm.*

jump /jŭmp/ *v.* (**jumps, jumped, jumping**) to leap off the ground. *It was fun to watch the horses jump over the fences.*

just[1] /jŭst/ *adj.* fair; honest. *That was the only just way to decide.*

just[2] /jŭst/ *adv.* **a.** exactly. *You did that just right!* **b.** a short time ago. *I just saw her there.* **c.** only. *We get just one turn at bat.*

keep /kēp/ *v.* (**keeps, kept, keep•ing**) **a.** to hold on to; to save. *Tanisha wants to keep all her old schoolwork.* **b.** to let stay; to have. *Toby can keep his socks in the top drawer.*

kick[1] /kĭk/ *v.* to hit with the foot. *The restless horse kicked the stall.*

kick[2] /kĭk/ *n.* a blow made by the foot. *Marika gave the ball a hard kick.*

king /kĭng/ *n.* **a.** the male ruler of a country. *Some kings wear crowns.* **b.** a person or thing best in its class. *The lion is known as the king of the jungle.*

king·dom /kĭng′ dəm/ *n.* a country, land, or territory ruled by a king or queen. *The queen declared a holiday throughout the kingdom.*

kiss[1] /kĭs/ *v.* (**kiss•es, kissed, kiss•ing**) to touch with the lips as a sign of love or greeting. *The girl kissed her mother and left for camp.*

kiss[2] /kĭs/ *n.* (**kiss•es** *pl.*) a touch with the lips. *His aunt gave him a kiss.*

kit·ten /kĭt′ n/ *n.* a young cat. *The kitten chased a butterfly around the garden.*

kitten

know /nō/ *v.* (**knows, knew, known, know•ing**) **a.** to understand; have knowledge about. *Do you know how to knit?* **b.** to be aware of; realize. *I didn't know they had moved away.*

➤ **Know** sounds like **no**.

late /lāt/ *adj.* (**lat•er, lat•est; late•ly** *adv.*) **a.** happening after the usual time. *I was late for school.* **b.** near the end of a certain time. *It's too late to shop.*

leg /lĕg/ *n.* the part of the body used for standing and walking. *We put our pants on one leg at a time.*

lem·on /lĕm′ ən/ *n.* a juicy, yellow, sour fruit. *The lemon made Alex pucker.*

let /lĕt/ *v.* (**lets, let, let•ting**) to allow; to permit. *Please let me go to the park.*

let·tuce /lĕt′ əs/ *n.* a green, leafy vegetable. *I like lettuce on hamburgers.*

line /līn/ *n.* **a.** a long thin mark. *Draw a line on the paper.* **b.** a row of persons or things. *We stood in a line.*

lit·tle[1] /lĭt′ l/ *adj.* **a.** small. *An elephant is big and an ant is little.* **b.** not much. *There is little food in the house.*

lit·tle[2] /lĭt′ l/ *n.* a small amount. *Patricia showed the teacher a little of her poetry.*

live[1] /lĭv/ *v.* (**lives, lived, liv•ing**) **a.** to have one's home; to reside; dwell. *Theo lives on Camden Street.* **b.** to be alive; to have life. *Most plants need sun to live.*

live[2] /līv/ *adj.* alive; having life. *We saw a live parrot at the zoo.*

lock[1] /lŏk/ *n.* a device for fastening a door, drawer, etc. *Do you have a key that will fit this lock?*

lock[2] /lŏk/ *v.* to fasten with a lock. *Lock the door when you go out.*

log /lôg/ or /lŏg/ *n.* a long piece of a tree that has been cut down. *Logs are cut into smaller pieces for building and for firewood.*

log

long /lông/ or /lŏng/ *adj.* **a.** having great distance or length of time. *It's a long walk to the bus stop.* **b.** having a certain length. *The room is twelve feet long.*

look /lŏok/ *v.* (**looks, looked, look•ing**) **a.** to use or turn the eyes in order to see. *Look both ways before you cross the street.* **b.** to search. *We looked all over for my library book.*

lot /lŏt/ *n.* a large amount; many. *We have a lot of books in our room.*

loud /loud/ *adj.* having sound of high volume. *The radio is too loud.*

love[1] /lŭv/ *n.* **a.** a deep, fond, affectionate feeling. *Helping people is a way of showing love.* **b.** a great liking. *He has a love of books.*

love[2] /lŭv/ *v.* (**loves, loved, lov•ing**) **a.** to have a deep affection for. *My parents love me.* **b.** to like very much. *Emily loves to play soccer.*

low /lō/ *adj.* **a.** not high; not tall. *A skyscraper is tall; most houses are low.* **b.** soft; not loud. *The kitten gave a low purr.*

luck /lŭk/ *n.* good fortune. *We had the luck to get the best seats.*

lunch /lŭnch/ *n.* (**lunch•es** *pl.*) a light meal eaten around the middle of the day. *We have lunch at noon.*

made /mād/ *v.* (**makes, made, mak•ing**) **a.** put together; built, formed, or shaped. *Dad made dinner tonight.* **b.** caused. *The flowers made Mom happy.* **c.** earned. *I made five dollars selling books.*

mall /môl/ or /măl/ *n.* a shopping area with many stores. *We shop at our local mall.*

man /măn/ *n.* (**men** *pl.*) an adult male person. *Mr. Green is a nice man.*

man•y /měn' ē/ *adj.* (**more, most**) a great number of. *Many children were late to school because of the snow.*

map[1] /măp/ *n.* a flat picture or chart of a part of the surface of Earth. *Maps show where to find towns, rivers, and roads.*

map[2] /măp/ *v.* (**maps, mapped, map•ping**) to plan using a map. *Let's map out the path we will take.*

marsh /märsh/ *n.* (**marsh•es** *pl.*) soft, wet land; a swamp. *There's an alligator in the marsh.*

may /mā/ *v.* (**might**) **a.** to be allowed to. *May I be excused?* **b.** to be likely to. *It may snow this morning.*

meat /mēt/ *n.* the flesh of an animal used as food. *My favorite meat is turkey.*
➤ **Meat** sounds like **meet**.

meet /mēt/ *v.* (**meets, met, meet•ing**) **a.** to come face to face with; to come together. *I'll meet you at the corner.* **b.** to be introduced to. *How did you meet her?* **c.** to gather as a group or club. *Our dance class meets on Tuesdays.*
➤ **Meet** sounds like **meat**.

mel•on /měl' ən/ *n.* a large, juicy fruit with a hard rind. *This melon tastes sweet!*

mile /mīl/ *n.* a measure of distance that is equal to 5,280 feet. *We drove two hundred miles on the first day of our trip.*

Pronunciation Key		
ă pat	ŏ pot	th **th**in
ā pay	ō toe	*th* **th**is
âr care	ô paw, for	hw **wh**ich
ä father	oi noise	zh vi**s**ion
ě pet	ou **ou**t	ə **a**bout,
ē be	ŏŏ took	it**e**m,
ĭ pit	ōō boot	penc**i**l,
ī pie	ŭ cut	gall**o**p,
îr pier	ûr **ur**ge	circ**u**s

milk[1] /mĭlk/ *n.* a white drink that comes from cows or other animals. *I always drink milk with my lunch.*

milk

milk[2] /mĭlk/ *v.* to get or draw milk from. *The farmer milks his cows twice a day.*

mime[1] /mīm/ *n.* someone who acts out a story without talking. *It's fun to watch the mime in the park.*

mime[2] /mīm/ *v.* (**mimes, mimed, mim•ing**) to act out a story without talking. *Do you have talent to mime?*

miss /mĭs/ *v.* (**miss•es, missed, miss•ing**) **a.** to fail to hit, reach, or get. *Her arrow missed the target by ten feet.* **b.** to feel sadness at the absence of someone or something. *We missed our dog while we were away.*

mod•el[1] /mŏd′ l/ *n.* **a.** a small copy of something. *Mr. Hill made a model of the bridge.* **b.** a person who wears clothes to show to others. *The model will look great in a blue suit.*

mod•el[2] /mŏd′ l/ *v.* to wear clothes to show to others. *Pam was asked to model a new coat.*

mom /mŏm/ *n.* a short word for mother. *My mom has a good job.*

moon /mo͞on/ *n.* the body that shines in the night sky. *A full moon looks like a big circle.*

moose /mo͞os/ *n.* (**moose** *pl.*) an animal with large antlers that is the largest member of the deer family. *We saw a moose in Canada.*

more /môr/ or /mōr/ *adj.* greater in number or amount. *You have more crayons than I do.*

morn•ing /môr′ nĭng/ *n.* the earliest part of the day, ending at noon. *We eat breakfast every morning.*

moth /môth/ or /mŏth/ *n.* an insect that usually flies at night and is very much like a butterfly. *The moths fluttered around the porch light.*

moth

move /mo͞ov/ *v.* (**moves, moved, mov•ing**) **a.** to change place or position. *Please move to another desk.* **b.** to go to another place to live. *My family wants to move to the beach.*

much[1] /mŭch/ *adj.* (**more, most**) large in amount or degree. *We have so much homework to do!*

much[2] /mŭch/ *n.* a great amount. *I didn't get much at the store.*

mud /mŭd/ *n.* soft, wet, sticky dirt. *The car wheels got stuck in the mud.*

mule /myo͞ol/ *n.* a work animal that is part horse and part donkey. *Mules can carry heavy loads.*

must /mŭst/ *v. aux.* to have to. *You must come home at six.*

my /mī/ *pron.* of or belonging to me. *I'll meet you at my house.*

my•self /mī sĕlf′/ *pron.* (**our•selves** *pl.*) **a.** one's own self. *I guessed the answer by myself.* **b.** one's usual self. *When I was sick, I didn't feel like myself.*

name /nām/ *n.* a word or words to call a person, place, or thing. *His name is Ahmed.*

nap•kins /năp′ kĭnz/ *n.* plural of **napkin.** pieces of cloth or paper to wipe your mouth and hands while eating. *Please put the napkins on the table.*

neat /nēt/ *adj.* clean; in order; tidy. *A neat store is a nice place to shop.*

need /nēd/ *v.* (**needs, need•ed, need•ing**) to require; to have to have. *Most plants need lots of sunshine to grow.*

next /nĕkst/ *adj.* **a.** nearest; closest. *My best friend sat next to me.* **b.** just after; coming at once. *The next thing we will do is math.*

nib•ble[1] /nĭb′ əl/ *v.* (**nib•bles, nib•bled, nib•bling**) to take small bites of food. *The bird likes to nibble on bread.*

nib•ble[2] /nĭb′ əl/ *n.* a small bite of food. *I took a nibble of the cookie.*

nice /nīs/ *adj.* (**nic•er, nic•est**) **a.** agreeable; pleasant. *Did you have a nice time at the picnic?* **b.** showing skill and care. *Kathy does a nice job of painting.*

no[1] /nō/ *adv.* the opposite of yes. *I voted "no" in a loud voice.*

no[2] /nō/ *adj.* not any. *The dog had no food until we got home.*

➤ **No** sounds like **know.**

nod /nŏd/ *v.* (**nods, nod•ded, nod•ding**) to bow the head and raise it quickly to say "yes" or "hello." *He nodded and waved to his friend.*

noise /noiz/ *n.* a sound. *Our car is making a strange noise.*

noon /no͞on/ *n.* the middle of the day; twelve o'clock in the daytime. *Our school serves lunch at noon.*

note•book /nōt′ bo͝ok′/ *n.* a book for notes of things to be learned or remembered. *I always carry a notebook to class.*

noth•ing /nŭth′ ĭng/ *n.* **a.** not anything. *We saw nothing we liked in that shop.* **b.** zero. *Six taken from six leaves nothing.*

now /nou/ *adv.* at the time being talked about at present. *Carlos is opening the window now.*

ny•lon /nī′ lŏn′/ *n.* a strong, man-made cloth or plastic. *My jacket is made of nylon.*

oc•to•pus /ŏk′ tə pəs/ *n.* (**oc•to•pus•es** or **oc•to•pi** *pl.*) a sea animal having a soft body and eight arms called tentacles. *An octopus uses its arms to grasp things.*

o•dor /ō′ dər/ *n.* a strong smell. *The garbage had a bad odor.*

off /ôf/ or /ŏf/ *adv.* **a.** away. *That hill is a long way off.* **b.** away from its present place. *Take your coat off.* **c.** not running; not on. *Please turn off the television.*

oil /oil/ *n.* a slippery liquid, such as motor oil or olive oil. *Don't spill the oil on the floor.*

old /ōld/ *adj.* having lived or existed for a length of time. *An old tree has a thick trunk.*

or /ôr/ *conj.* a word used to express a choice or a difference. *Do you want soup or salad?*

ouch /ouch/ *interj.* used to express sudden pain. *Bret cried, "Ouch!" when he stubbed his toe.*

our /our/ *pron.* of or belonging to us. *We ate our lunches outside.*
> **Our** sounds like **hour**.

out /out/ *adv.* away from the inside or center. *The cat ran out when we opened the door.*

out•side¹ /out sīd′/ or /′out′ sīd′/ *n.* the outer side. *Clean the outside of the windows.*

out•side² /out sīd′/ or /′out′ sīd′/ *adv.* outdoors. *Put the dog outside.*

own¹ /ōn/ *v.* to have; possess. *Who owns that blue car?*

own² /ōn/ *adj.* belonging to oneself. *Kate has her own room.*

pack /păk/ *v.* (**packs, packed, pack•ing**) put carefully in a box or trunk. *My brother packed my suitcase for me.*

pants /pănts/ *n.* plural of **pant**. a piece of clothing that covers each leg separately. *I wear pants to school.*

park¹ /pärk/ *n.* a piece of land where people can come to rest, play, or enjoy nature. *We saw a herd of deer in the park.*

park

park² /pärk/ *v.* to put or leave in a certain spot. *Park the car in the garage.*

par•ka /pär′ kə/ *n.* a heavy jacket with a hood. *The skier wore a parka.*

part /pärt/ *n.* a piece or section; some; less than all. *Would you like part of my orange?*

par•ty /pär′ tē/ *n.* (**par•ties** *pl.*) a gathering of people to have a good time together. *We had fun at the birthday party!*

peak /pēk/ *n.* **a.** the pointed top of a mountain. *We hiked up to a snowy peak.* **b.** the highest point. *It rained hardest during the storm's peak.*

pen /pĕn/ *n.* **a.** a tool used for writing in ink. *My pen has blue ink.* **b.** a closed place to keep animals. *That pig lives in a pen.*

pick /pĭk/ *v.* (**picks, picked, pick•ing**) **a.** to choose. *I picked a poem to recite to the class.* **b.** to pull off. *He picked the peaches all afternoon.*

pies /pīz/ *n.* plural of **pie**. baked goods made of fruit, meat, or pudding within a crust. *My mother bakes pies for the holidays.*

pike /pīk/ *n.* (**pike** or **pikes** *pl.*) **a.** a bony fish. *Lee caught a pike from the lake.* **b.** a big road. *He drove up the pike.*

pipe /pīp/ *n.* a long tube through which a liquid or gas may flow. *The pipes beneath the ground carry gas from Texas to Chicago.*

plain /plān/ *adj.* simple; not fancy in appearance. *Tracy wore a plain blue dress.*

Pronunciation Key

ă	pat	ŏ	pot	th	**thin**
ā	pay	ō	toe	*th*	**th**is
âr	care	ô	paw, for	hw	**which**
ä	father	oi	noise	zh	vision
ĕ	pet	ou	**out**	ə	about,
ē	be	o͞o	took		item,
ĭ	pit	o͞o	boot		pencil,
ī	pie	ŭ	cut		gallop,
îr	**pier**	ûr	**urge**		circus

---

plant[1] /plănt/ *n.* a living thing that is not an animal. *Flowers, fruits, and vegetables are plants.*

plant[2] /plănt/ *v.* (**plants, plant•ed, plant•ing**) to put into the ground so that it will grow. *The farmer planted corn.*

plate /plāt/ *n.* a thin, flat piece of metal or plastic. *The plate on the door displays his name.*

plat•ter /plăt′ ər/ *n.* a large dish used for serving food. *The platter held three baked fish.*

play[1] /plā/ *v.* (**plays, played, play•ing**) **a.** to take part in a game or activity for fun. *Children like to play tag.* **b.** to perform on a musical instrument. *I can play the piano.* **c.** to act on the stage. *Jennifer wants to play the queen.*

play[2] /plā/ *n.* a story written to be acted out. *The hero has the most lines in the play.*

please /plēz/ *v.* (**pleas•es, pleased, pleas•ing**) **a.** to bring happiness to. *My father's cooking pleases the family.* **b.** to be so kind as to. *Please help me.*

pleat /plēt/ *n.* a flat fold made in cloth. *Mom ironed the pleat on my skirt.*

plum /plŭm/ *n.* a small, soft, juicy fruit. *He picked a wild plum.*

pond /pŏnd/ *n.* a little lake. *We can fish in the pond.*

point¹ /point/ *n.* **a.** a sharp tip, such as on a needle or a pencil. *I broke the point of my pencil.* **b.** a unit of scoring in a game. *The correct answer will earn one point.*

point² /point/ *v.* to aim at something; to show which one. *Point to the dog you want.*

pop•corn /pŏp′ kôrn′/ *n.* kernels of corn that burst open when heated. *Do you like butter on your popcorn?*

porch /pôrch/ or /pōrch/ *n.* (**porch•es** *pl.*) a covered area along the outside of a house. *I like to sit on the porch.*

pressed /prĕst/ *v.* past tense of **press**. made smooth; flattened. *She pressed the leaf with a book.*

prize /prīz/ *n.* a thing won in a contest. *Tony won the prize for spelling the most words correctly.*

pry /prī/ *v.* (**pries, pried, pry•ing**) to raise or move by force with a lever. *Can you pry the lid off this paint can?*

pud•dle /pŭd′ l/ *n.* a small pool of liquid, such as water. *The dog splashed in the puddle.*

pull /pŏŏl/ *v.* to move something by force toward oneself; to tug. *Pull the rope up the hill.*

put /pŏŏt/ *v.* (**puts, put, put•ting**) to place; set. *I will put the plates on the table.*

rad•ish•es /răd′ ĭsh əz/ *n.* plural of **radish**. crisp, red or white roots of a garden plant, eaten as a raw vegetable. *The chef put radishes in the salad.*

rain¹ /rān/ *n.* drops of water that fall from clouds. *The rain splashed on the sidewalk.*

rain² /rān/ *v.* to fall in drops from the clouds. *Look how hard it is raining!*

read /rēd/ *v.* (**reads, read, read•ing**) **a.** to get the meaning from print or writing. *Do you like to read books?* **b.** to speak out loud something printed or written. *Please read your story to the class.*

re•al /rē′ əl/ or /rēl/ *adj.* **a.** actual; true; not imagined; not made up. *My uncle told us a real story about his trip to Brazil.* **b.** genuine. *Her necklace is made of real pearls.*

ride /rīd/ *v.* (**rides, rode, rid•den, rid•ing**) **a.** to sit on a moving animal or bicycle. *Can you ride a horse?* **b.** to go in a car, bus, or train. *How long does it take to ride to the city?*

ring[1] /rĭng/ *n.* **a.** a metal circle worn on the finger as jewelry. *The stone in that ring is a diamond.* **b.** a circular band for holding things. *Put the napkins in the napkin rings.*

ring

ring[2] /rĭng/ *v.* (**rings, rang, rung, ring•ing**) to make a clear sound. *Did the bell ring?*

road /rōd/ *n.* a way or path between places; highway. *This is the road to my friend's house.*

roast[1] /rōst/ *v.* (**roasts, roast•ed, roast•ing**) to cook with dry heat. *Dad is going to roast the turkey for dinner.*

roast[2] /rōst/ *adj.* roasted; cooked by dry heat. *We eat gravy on our roast beef.*

roast[3] /rōst/ *n.* a cut of meat for roasting. *We enjoyed the roast for dinner.*

robe /rōb/ *n.* a long, loose garment. *After his shower, he put on a robe.*

rock[1] /rŏk/ *n.* a hard mineral; a stone. *Can you skip a rock across the creek?*

rock[2] /rŏk/ *v.* to move back and forth. *I like to rock in a rocking chair.*

room /ro͞om/ *n.* **a.** a closed space inside a building. *Jan walked into the front room.* **b.** extra space. *Leave room on your paper for your name.*

root[1] /ro͞ot/ or /ro͝ot/ *n.* the part of a plant that holds it in place and takes in food for it. *We eat some roots, such as carrots and beets.*

root[2] /ro͞ot/ *v.* **a.** to dig up. *The pigs rooted up the garden and made a mess.* **b.** to support or cheer for. *We root for Mike's team.*

row•boat /rō′bōt′/ *n.* a small boat propelled by oars. *We like to take the rowboat on the lake.*

rub /rŭb/ *v.* (**rubs, rubbed, rub•bing**) to move back and forth against something. *The wheel of my bike rubs the fender.*

rug /rŭg/ *n.* a covering for a floor; a carpet. *He has a round rug in his room.*

rush /rŭsh/ *v.* (**rush•es, rushed, rush•ing**) to move quickly, often with force. *The water rushed over the falls.*

sad /săd/ *adj.* (**sad•der, sad•dest**) unhappy. *We were sad when Jo left.*

safe /sāf/ *adj.* free from harm or danger. *We were safe in the house during the storm.*

said /sĕd/ *v.* past tense of say. *Su Li said she would come.*

sal•ad /săl′ əd/ *n.* lettuce or other raw vegetables served with a dressing. *I like tomatoes in my salad.*

sat /săt/ *v.* past tense of sit. *We sat on the sofa.*

save /sāv/ *v.* (**saves, saved, sav•ing**) **a.** to rescue; to make safe from danger. *We saved the cat that was up in the tree.* **b.** to put away; keep. *I save stamps for my collection.*

saw¹ /sô/ *n.* a tool or machine used to cut. *Dad used his saw to build a birdhouse.*

saw² /sô/ *v.* past tense of **see**. *I saw the Big Dipper last night.*

say /sā/ *v.* (**says, said, say•ing**) **a.** to speak; put into words. *What did he say to you?* **b.** to give as an opinion. *I really can't say which I like best.*

says /sĕz/ *v.* (**say, said, say•ing**) present tense of **say**; expresses in words. *My teacher says our test is Friday.*

scarf /skärf/ *n.* (**scarfs** or **scarves** *pl.*) a long piece of material worn around the neck. *The scarf kept my neck warm.*

scoot•er /skōō′ tər/ *n.* a vehicle that has a footboard and an upright handlebar. *Alex rides his scooter on the sidewalk.*

sea /sē/ *n.* the ocean. *We walked on the beach by the sea.*

➤ **Sea** sounds like **see**.

sea

seat /sēt/ *n.* **a.** a thing to sit on; a place to sit. *We do not have enough seats for the party.* **b.** the part of anything that is used for sitting. *Brian tore the seat of his pants.*

seek /sēk/ *v.* (**seeks, sought, seek•ing**) to try to find; to look for. *Julie wants to seek a new job.*

seem /sēm/ *v.* to look like; to appear to be. *The new family next door seems very nice.*

seen /sēn/ *v.* a form of see. *Have you ever seen an elephant?*

send /sĕnd/ *v.* (**sends, sent, send•ing**) to cause or order to go. *Let's send a card to our teacher.*

shag•gy /shăg' ē/ *adj.* (**shag•gi•er, shag•gi•est**) covered with long, coarse, or tangled hair. *We washed the shaggy dog with lots of shampoo.*

shark /shärk/ *n.* a large ocean fish that eats other fish. *A shark has strong, sharp teeth.*

she /shē/ *pron.* that girl or woman. *She likes to read.*

she's /shēz/ she is; she has. *She's going to help us bake a cake.*

shift¹ /shĭft/ *v.* (**shifts, shift•ed, shift•ing**) to move or change from one place or position to another. *Let's shift the books from the top shelf to the bottom shelf.*

shift² /shĭft/ *n.* a time during which a group works. *The factory shift ends at four o'clock.*

shine /shīn/ *v.* (**shines, shone** or **shined, shin•ing**) **a.** to give off light. *That light shines right in my eyes.* **b.** to make bright; to polish. *I helped my sister shine the pots and pans.*

shin•y /shī' nē/ *adj.* (**shin•i•er, shin•i•est**) bright. *We saw the shiny car quickly.*

shiv•er /shĭv' ər/ *v.* to shake because it is cold. *I usually shiver at the winter parade.*

shoe /shoo/ *n.* an outer cover for the foot. *My new shoes are waterproof.*

Pronunciation Key

ă	pat	ŏ	pot	th	**th**in
ā	pay	ō	toe	*th*	**th**is
âr	care	ô	paw, for	hw	**wh**ich
ä	father	oi	n**oi**se	zh	vi**si**on
ĕ	pet	ou	**ou**t	ə	**a**bout,
ē	be	ŏŏ	t**oo**k		it**e**m,
ĭ	pit	ōō	b**oo**t		penc**i**l,
ī	pie	ŭ	cut		gall**o**p,
îr	pier	ûr	**ur**ge		circ**u**s

---

shoe•lace /shoo' lās'/ *n.* a strip of leather or other material for tying a shoe. *I have red shoelaces in my new shoes.*

shop /shŏp/ *n.* a small store. *We have a good hobby shop on our street.*

shore /shôr/ or /shōr/ *n.* the land at the edge of a lake, sea, or river. *We like to play in the sand at the shore.*

short /shôrt/ *adj.* **a.** not long or tall. *I look short next to my big brother.* **b.** not having enough. *When we passed out the worksheets, we were three short.* **c.** not having a long vowel sound. *The e in* pet *is a short vowel.*

shout /shout/ *v.* to call out loudly. *We shouted into the tunnel to hear the echo.*

shov•el /shŭv' əl/ *n.* a tool with a long handle and a scoop for digging or lifting things. *Pete used a shovel to dig up the tree.*

sick /sĭk/ *adj.* not well; having a disease. *Michelle stayed in bed when she was sick.*

sing /sĭng/ *v.* (**sings, sang, sung, sing•ing**) to make music with the voice. *Let's sing a round.*

sink[1] /sĭngk/ *v.* (**sinks, sank, sunk, sink•ing**) **a.** to go down. *The sun sinks in the west.* **b.** to make something go under. *That wave will sink the toy boat.*

sink[2] /sĭngk/ *n.* a kitchen or bathroom fixture. *He washed the dishes in the sink.*

size /sīz/ *n.* **a.** the amount of space that a thing takes up. *Look at the size of that elephant!* **b.** one of a series of measures. *Which size paintbrush do you need?*

sketch /skĕch/ *n.* (**sketch•es** *pl.*) a simple, rough drawing that is made quickly. *The artist drew sketches of the people in the park.*

sky /skī/ *n.* (**skies** *pl.*) the air high above the world; the space overhead. *Birds fly high in the sky.*

sleep[1] /slēp/ *n.* the resting of body and mind; the state of not being awake. *I had a good night's sleep.*

sleep[2] /slēp/ *v.* (**sleeps, slept, sleep•ing**) to be asleep; to rest the body and mind. *I am going to sleep at Melanie's house tonight.*

sleep•ing /slē′ pĭng/ *v.* present tense of sleep.

sleeve /slēv/ *n.* the part of clothing that covers the arm. *The sleeve of my uniform has a patch.*

slip /slĭp/ *v.* (**slips, slipped, slip•ping**) to slide suddenly. *Don't slip on the wet sidewalk.*

slow[1] /slō/ *adj.* not moving fast or quickly. *The bus ride to school is so slow.*

slow[2] /slō/ *v.* to go slower. *A driver slows down and stops for a red light.*

slow•ly /slō′ lē/ *adv.* moving in a manner that is not fast or quick. *Because it was so hot outside, he slowly mowed the lawn.*

small /smôl/ *adj.* **a.** not big; little. *A cub is a small bear.* **b.** not important. *We won't worry about that small detail.*

smock /smŏk/ *n.* a loose covering to protect clothing. *The artist wears a smock when she paints.*

smooth /smōōth/ *adj.* having no bumps or rough spots. *The smooth highway made driving a pleasure.*

sneak•ers /snē′ kərz/ *n.* plural of **sneaker**. tennis shoes; running shoes; shoes with rubber soles, used for sports. *I bought new basketball sneakers.*

sneakers

sneeze /snēz/ *v.* (**sneez•es, sneezed, sneez•ing**) to have a sudden force of air come through your nose. *Please cover your nose when you sneeze.*

soil /soil/ *n.* the top layer of the earth's surface in which plants grow. *This soil is good for growing peanuts.*

some /sŭm/ *adj.* **a.** a certain one, but not named or known. *Some girl called while you were out.* **b.** a number of. *Have some nuts.*

➤ **Some** sounds like **sum**.

son /sŭn/ *n.* a male child. *My son looks just like me.*

➤ **Son** sounds like **sun**.

soon /sōōn/ *adv.* (**soon•er, soon•est**) before long. *Dinner will be ready soon.*

sound /sound/ *n.* vibrations you can hear. *We heard a strange sound.*

soy /soi/ *n.* short for soybean. *Soy sauce is made from soy.*

soy•bean /**soi′** bēn/ *n.* a bushy plant; the seed of the plant. *I will plant a soybean and watch it grow.*

space /spās/ *n.* **a.** the area in which the planets and stars exist. *Earth travels in space around the sun.* **b.** room; a place. *There is no more space for passengers in the crowded train.*

spell /spĕl/ *v.* (**spells, spelled, spell•ing**) to put the letters of a word in the right order. *Some words are tricky to spell.*

spice /spīs/ *n.* a seasoning used to add flavor to food. *Pepper is a spice.*

Pronunciation Key

ă	pat	ŏ	pot	th	thin
ā	pay	ō	toe	*th*	*th*is
âr	care	ô	paw, for	hw	which
ä	father	oi	noise	zh	vision
ĕ	pet	ou	out	ə	about,
ē	be	ōō	took		item,
ĭ	pit	ōō	boot		pencil,
ī	pie	ŭ	cut		gallop,
îr	pier	ûr	urge		circus

spin /spĭn/ *v.* (**spins, spun, spin•ning**) to turn around fast. *Can you see the wheel spin?*

spot /spŏt/ *n.* a mark; a stain; a speck. *There are ink spots on this paper.*

spray¹ /sprā/ *n.* water or another liquid flying through the air. *The spray of the water got my shirt wet.*

spray² /sprā/ *v.* to cause water or another liquid to fly through the air. *Spray the flowers with the water hose.*

squall¹ /skwôl/ *n.* **a.** a sudden and loud cry. *Chad's squall woke me up.* **b.** a sudden storm with strong wind and often heavy rain. *The squall caused our tent to fall.*

squall² /skwôl/ *v.* to cry suddenly and loudly. *The spider caused the baby to squall.*

stain¹ /stān/ *v.* to make a discolored spot; to soil. *Ink will stain your shirt.*

stain² /stān/ *n.* a discolored or soiled spot. *There's a grass stain on my white pants.*

stalk /stôk/ *n.* the long, main stem of a plant. *Corn grows on a stalk.*

stall /stôl/ *n.* a space for an animal in a barn or stable. *My horse sleeps in her stall.*

star /stär/ *n.* **a.** a large body in space that we see as a small point of light on a clear night. *Our sun is a star that is close to Earth.* **b.** a shape with five or six points. *Our country's first flag had thirteen stars.*

star•fish /stär′ fĭsh′/ *n.* (**star•fish•es** or **star•fish** *pl.*) a small sea animal with a body shaped like a star. *We found a starfish on the beach.*

start /stärt/ *v.* (**starts, start•ed, start•ing**) to begin. *What time does the game start?*

stay /stā/ *v.* **a.** to remain. *Let's stay until four.* **b.** to keep on being. *It will stay cold all winter.*

stood /stŏŏd/ *v.* (**stand, stands, stand•ing, stood**) past tense of **stand**. *The sailors stood on the deck.*

stop /stŏp/ *v.* (**stops, stopped, stop•ping**) **a.** to prevent. *We want to stop crime.* **b.** to come to a halt. *Why did that car stop out front?*

store /stôr/ or /stōr/ *n.* a place where things are sold. *Salim bought a hammer in the hardware store.*

stork /stôrk/ *n.* a large bird with long legs, a long neck, and a long bill. *The stork had a leaf in its bill.*

storm /stôrm/ *n.* strong winds often accompanied by heavy amounts of rain, snow, hail, or sleet. *In summer a storm can bring thunder and lightning.*

stream /strēm/ *n.* a brook, creek, or small river. *The stream bubbled over the rocks.*

street /strēt/ *n.* a road in a city or town. *This street is always crowded during rush hour.*

stump /stŭmp/ *n.* the base of a tree that is left after the tree trunk is cut. *The tree stump is only two feet high.*

such /sŭch/ *adj.* **a.** so much; so great. *The game was such fun that we hated to stop.* **b.** of a certain kind. *Good ball players such as José are hard to find.*

sun /sŭn/ *n.* the star that gives us light and heat. *The sun sets in the west.*

➤ **Sun** sounds like **son**.

sun•ny /sŭn′ ē/ *adj.* (**sun•ni•er, sun•ni•est; sun•ni•ly** *adv.*) bright with sunshine. *Let's play outside while it's still sunny.*

swamp /swŏmp/ *n.* a soft, very wet piece of land. *Moss hangs from the trees in some swamps.*

swing[1] /swĭng/ *v.* (**swings, swung, swing•ing**) to move back and forth while being suspended from above. *I like to swing at the playground.*

swing[2] /swĭng/ *n.* a seat, hung by ropes or chains, on which to move back and forth. *There's a swing on Grandma's porch.*

tack•le[1] /tăk′ əl/ *n.* **a.** the equipment used for catching fish. *Fishing tackle is sold at the bait store.* **b.** the act of grabbing hold of and throwing to the ground. *His tackle kept me from running away.*

tack•le[2] /tăk′ əl/ *v.* (**tack•les, tack•led, tack•ling**) to grab hold of and throw to the ground. *Football players tackle each other.*

tail /tāl/ *n.* the part of an animal's body at the end of its backbone, especially a growth that sticks out beyond the body. *My dog has a bushy tail.*

➤ **Tail** sounds like **tale**.

tail

	Pronunciation Key	
ă pat	ŏ pot	th **thin**
ā pay	ō toe	*th* **this**
âr care	ô paw, for	hw **which**
ä father	oi noise	zh vision
ĕ pet	ou out	ə about,
ē be	ŏŏ took	item,
ĭ pit	ōō boot	pencil,
ī pie	ŭ cut	gallop,
îr pier	ûr urge	circus

tale /tāl/ *n.* a story. *The teacher told us a tale about a talking turtle.*

➤ **Tale** sounds like **tail**.

talk /tôk/ *v.* (**talks, talked, talk•ing**) to speak; to say words. *Can the baby talk yet?*

tall /tôl/ *adj.* **a.** high; not short. *There are many tall trees in the forest.* **b.** being a stated height. *My brother is five feet tall.*

tape[1] /tāp/ *n.* a narrow strip or band of cloth, plastic, etc. *The doctor put tape around my sore ankle.*

tape[2] /tāp/ *v.* to fasten with tape. *Evan will tape the pieces of paper onto the box.*

teach /tēch/ *v.* (**teach•es, taught, teach•ing**) to show how to do something; to help learn. *I like to teach children how to sing.*

teeth /tēth/ *n. pl.* more than one tooth. *Did you brush your teeth this morning?*

tell /tĕl/ v. (**tells, told, tell•ing**) **a.** to say; to talk about. *Tell us a story.* **b.** to make known. *Don't tell the answer to anyone.*

than /thăn/ or /thən/ conj. compared to or with. *Kim is taller than Janet.*

thank /thăngk/ v. to say or show you are pleased and grateful. *I want to thank Grandfather for my game.*

that's /thăts/ that is. *That's the best movie I have ever seen.*

the /thə/ or /thē/ article. that one or those. *Did you find the pen or the pencils I lost?*

them /thĕm/ pron. the ones spoken about. *We saw them working on the house.*

then /thĕn/ adv. **a.** at that time. *They came at two o'clock, but I was gone by then.* **b.** soon after. *We went to the movies, and then we came home.*

there's /thârz/ there is. *There's a skunk in our yard under the shed.*

these /thēz/ pron., adj. plural of this. *Give me three of these flowers.*

they /thā/ pron. the ones spoken about. *Liz and Dennis said they would come.*

thim•ble /thĭm' bəl/ n. a metal or plastic cap worn on the finger to push a sewing needle. *Mom wears a thimble when she sews.*

think /thĭngk/ v. (**thinks, thought, think•ing**) **a.** to use the mind to reach decisions, form opinions, etc. *I can't think when there is noise all around me.* **b.** to have in mind as an opinion, idea, etc.; to believe. *She thought she knew the answer.*

those /thōz/ pron., adj. plural of that. *Those are the ones we need.*

thread /thrĕd/ n. a fine strand of cotton, silk, wool, or nylon used in sewing. *I'll use blue thread to sew the quilt.*

thumb /thŭm/ n. **a.** the short, thick finger on the hand. *Little Jack Horner stuck his thumb into his pie.* **b.** something that covers the thumb. *Someone cut the thumbs off my mittens.*

toe /tō/ n. one of the five end parts of the front of the foot. *Rita wiggled her toes in the mud.*

➤ **Toe** sounds like **tow**.

told /tōld/ v. past tense of tell. *I told him how to get there.*

too /tōō/ adv. **a.** also; in addition. *If you go to the game, we will go, too.* **b.** more than enough. *The sheet is too big for the bed.*

➤ **Too** sounds like **two**.

took /tōōk/ v. past tense of take. *Mom took us fishing.*

tooth /tōōth/ n. (**teeth** pl.) one of the hard, bonelike parts in the jaw used for chewing. *The dentist filled a cavity in my tooth.*

torn /tôrn/ v. a form of **tear**. *Angie had torn her skirt.*

tow /tō/ v. to tug; to pull something by a rope or chain. *Our car can tow your boat.*

➤ **Tow** sounds like **toe**.

tow•el /tou' əl/ n. a piece of cloth or paper for drying something wet. *After showering, I use a soft towel.*

town /toun/ *n.* (**towns** *pl.*) a community larger than a village but smaller than a city. *The people in our town are proud of it.*

toy /toi/ *n.* (**toys** *pl.*) an object to play with. *I got my sister a toy kitten.*

train /trān/ *n.* a line of connected railroad or subway cars. *Many people take a train to work.*

train

tree /trē/ *n.* a large plant having a woody trunk with branches and leaves at its upper part. *Forests are made up of many trees.*

trucks /trŭks/ *n.* plural of **truck**. four-wheeled vehicles with beds for carrying loads. *The trucks hauled the furniture.*

try /trī/ *v.* (**tries, tried, try•ing**) to attempt. *Try to answer all of the questions.*

tum•ble[1] /tŭm′ bəl/ *n.* a fall in which you roll. *The cat took a tumble down the steps.*

tum•ble[2] /tŭm′ bəl/ *v.* to fall or roll. *We tumble in the leaves.*

Pronunciation Key

ă	pat	ŏ	pot	th	**th**in
ā	pay	ō	toe	*th*	**th**is
âr	care	ô	paw, for	hw	**wh**ich
ä	father	oi	noise	zh	vi**s**ion
ĕ	pet	ou	**ou**t	ə	about,
ē	be	o͞o	took		item,
ĭ	pit	o͞o	boot		pencil,
ī	pie	ŭ	cut		gallop,
îr	pier	ûr	urge		circus

twine /twīn/ *n.* a strong string. *The bales of hay are wrapped with twine.*

twist[1] /twĭst/ *v.* (**twists, twist•ed, twist•ing**) to move with a turning motion. *My office chair can twist.*

twist[2] /twĭst/ *n.* a turn or curve, such as in a road. *The twist in the road is very sharp.*

ug•ly /ŭg′ lē/ *adj.* (**ug•li•er, ug•li•est**) unpleasant to any sense. *His mask was very ugly and scary.*

un•til[1] /ŭn tĭl′/ *prep.* **a.** up to the time of; till. *I slept until noon today.* **b.** before the time of. *He could not stop working until midnight.*

un•til[2] /ŭn tĭl′/ *conj.* **a.** up to the time that. *We waited for you until the show was about to begin.* **b.** before. *She would not serve dinner until everyone was seated.*

veg•e•ta•ble /vĕj′ tə bəl/ or /vĕj′ ĭ tə bəl/ *n.* an edible plant. *Corn is a vegetable.*

voice /vois/ *n.* sounds made by the vocal chords in the throat. *The singer has a beautiful voice.*

wag•on /wăg′ ən/ *n.* a four-wheeled vehicle for carrying loads usually pulled by a tractor, a horse, or a person. *Dad pulled us in the red wagon.*

wagon

wait /wāt/ *v.* to stay or stop until something happens or someone comes. *Wait for me at the park.*

walk¹ /wôk/ *v.* (**walks, walked, walk•ing**) to go on foot at a normal rate. *We walk to school every day.*

walk² /wôk/ *n.* **a.** the act of walking. *We took a walk after dinner.* **b.** the distance covered in walking. *It is not a long walk to the park.*

wall /wôl/ *n.* the side of a room, house, or other building. *That wall has no windows in it.*

want /wŏnt/ or /wônt/ *v.* (**wants, want•ed, want•ing**) to wish for. *I want a new coat.*

was /wŭz/, /wŏz/, or /wəz/ *v.* past tense of is. *He was sick.*

wash /wŏsh/ or /wôsh/ *v.* (**wash•es, washed, wash•ing**) to clean with water or another liquid. *He will wash the dishes for us.*

was•n't /wŭz′ ənt/ was not. *The test wasn't hard.*

wave¹ /wāv/ *n.* **a.** a high ridge that moves across the surface of a body of water. *Waves make the ocean exciting.* **b.** the moving of the hand in greeting. *She gave a wave as she passed us.*

wave² /wāv/ *v.* to move back and forth. *We will wave the flag at the parade.*

we /wē/ *pron.* us; ourselves; the persons speaking. *We are friends.*

week /wēk/ *n.* a period of seven days, especially from Sunday to Saturday. *This is the third week of the month.*

well¹ /wĕl/ *n.* a hole dug in the ground to get water, oil, or gas. *The water from our well is good and cold.*

well² /wĕl/ *adv.* (**bet•ter, best**) in a good or pleasing way; with skill. *He did the job well.*

well[3] /wĕl/ *adj.* not sick; healthy. *Alla feels well today.*

went /wĕnt/ *v.* past tense of go. *We went downtown.*

were•n't /wûrnt, **wûr'** ənt/ were not. *We weren't at the party on Saturday.*

whale /hwāl/ *n.* a huge sea mammal that looks like a fish and breathes air. *When a whale comes up for air, it blows a spout of water vapor.*

what /hwŏt/ *pron.* **a.** which thing or things. *What did you forget?* **b.** that which; the thing that. *I know what you mean.*

what's /hwŏts/ what is. *What's that bird in the tree?*

wheel /hwēl/ or /wēl/ *n.* a circular frame that turns on a central axle. *My bike's wheel is broken.*

when[1] /hwĕn/ *adv.* at what time. *When may we go?*

when[2] /hwĕn/ *conj.* after. *You may go when the work is done.*

where's /hwârz/ where is. *Where's my blue sweater?*

which /hwĭch/ *pron.* what one. *Which of those boys is your friend?*

while[1] /hwīl/ *n.* a length of time. *Can you wait a while for my answer?*

while[2] /hwīl/ *conj.* during the time that. *Come and see our house while you are here.*

whis•per /**hwĭs'** pər/ or /**wĭs'** pər/ *v.* to say something very softly. *We whisper in the library.*

Pronunciation Key

ă	pat	ŏ	pot	th	**th**in
ā	pay	ō	toe	*th*	**th**is
âr	care	ô	paw, for	hw	**wh**ich
ä	father	oi	noise	zh	vi**s**ion
ĕ	pet	ou	**ou**t	ə	**a**bout,
ē	be	o͝o	t**oo**k		it**e**m,
ĭ	pit	o͞o	b**oo**t		penc**i**l,
ī	pie	ŭ	cut		gall**o**p,
îr	pier	ûr	**ur**ge		circ**u**s

---

who /ho͞o/ *pron.* **a.** what person or persons. *Who gave you that book?* **b.** that. *The person who asked for the book is not here.*

who's /ho͞oz/ who is. *Who's going to be in our group?*

why[1] /hwī/ *adv.* for what reason. *Why did you come to see me?*

why[2] /hwī/ *conj.* the reason for which. *I know why Adam left.*

wig•gle /**wĭg'** əl/ *v.* (**wig•gles, wig•gled, wig•gling**) to move side to side with quick, short motions; to squirm. *A worm can wiggle.*

will /wĭl/ *v.* (**would**) am, is or are going to. *We will see you next week.*

win /wĭn/ *v.* (**wins, won, win•ning**) **a.** to gain a victory. *Do you think our team can win?* **b.** to get or earn. *Nina's pig may win a ribbon at the fair.*

wind /wĭnd/ *n.* air that is moving. *The wind is from the north.*

wing /wĭng/ *n.* the part of a bird or insect that keeps and moves it in the air. *A hawk can spread its wings and glide.*

wing

wink /wĭngk/ *v.* to close and open one eye quickly as a kind of signal. *Aunt Emily winked at me behind Mom's back.*

wish¹ /wĭsh/ *v.* (**wish•es, wished, wish•ing**) to want; to have a desire for. *I wish he could come.*

wish² /wĭsh/ *n.* (**wish•es** *pl.*) something wanted. *Did your wish come true?*

with /wĭth/ or /wĭth/ *prep.* in the company of. *They went with Uncle Charles.*

wood /wood/ *n.* the hard inside part of a tree, beneath its bark. *Oak and walnut are hard woods.*

wood•peck•er /wood′ pĕk′ ər/ *n.* a bird that uses its bill to drill holes in trees. *We heard the woodpecker pecking at the tree.*

wool /wool/ *n.* **a.** the soft, curly hair of a sheep. *Wool is shaved from sheep in the spring.* **b.** the yarn or cloth made from the hair of a sheep. *In winter he wore a cap of wool.*

wrench /rĕnch/ *n.* (**wrench•es** *pl.*) a tool to tighten nuts and bolts and other things. *The plumber used a wrench to fix the pipe.*

zone /zōn/ *n.* a special area. *Drive slowly through the school zone.*

The **Writing Thesaurus** provides synonyms—words that mean the same or nearly the same—and antonyms—words that mean the opposite—for your spelling words. Use this sample to identify the various parts of each thesaurus entry.

- **Entry words** are listed in alphabetical order and are printed in boldface type.
- The abbreviation for the **part of speech** of each entry word follows the boldface entry word.
- The **definition** of the entry word matches the definition of the word in your **Spelling Dictionary**. A **sample sentence** shows the correct use of the word in context.

- Each **synonym** for the entry word is listed under the entry word. Again, a sample sentence shows the correct use of the synonym in context.
- Where appropriate, **antonyms** for the entry word are listed at the end of the entry.

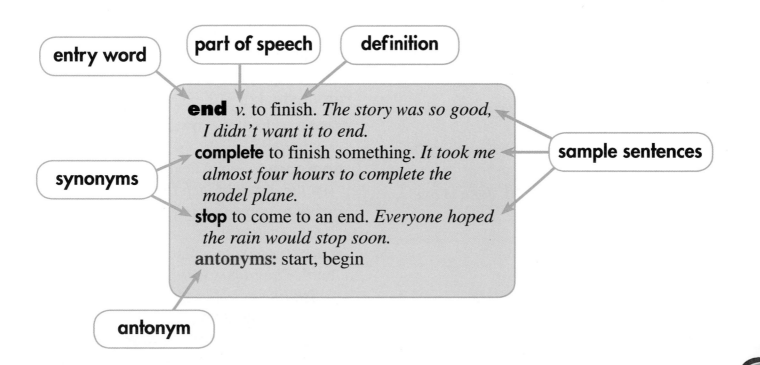

ask *v.* to try to find out or get by using words. *Let's ask Mr. Fulton how to get there.*

inquire to find out by asking. *Did you inquire about the price of stamps?*

invite to ask someone to join you. *Mom said I could invite two friends to sleep over.*

question to ask over and over. *The principal will question them again about the broken window.*

antonym: answer

bring *v.* to carry from somewhere else. *Please bring my book with you.*

carry to take from one place to another. *That truck can carry a heavy load.*

fetch to carry something to someone. *My dog likes to fetch the ball.*

get to bring something to someone. *Dad asked me to get him a cup of tea.*

boy *n.* a male child. *We have only one boy in our family.*

lad a young boy. *The hero of many folk tales is a young lad.*

son someone's male child. *Jake is one of the Smiths' three sons.*

antonym: girl

box *n.* a case for holding things. *Please put the tools back in the box.*

carton a cardboard box. *Orange juice sometimes comes in a carton.*

crate a large wooden box. *The big machine was packed in a crate.*

call *v.* to shout; to cry out. *Did Lani hear you call her?*

name to give a name to. *Let's name the puppy Spot.*

phone to call on the telephone. *I'll phone you when I'm ready to go.*

summon to order to come. *Did the police summon that driver to appear in court?*

cold *adj.* having a low temperature; not warm. *January is a cold month.*

cool somewhat cold. *The cool air felt good.*

freezing without heat. *When the fire went out, the cabin was freezing.*

icy very cold, like ice. *The icy wind made my eyes water.*

antonym: hot

come *v.* to move toward. *Come over to my house.*

approach to come near. *It was scary to see the cat approach the baby bird.*

arrive to come to a place. *His plane will arrive at 10:00.*

reach to come to a place after trying hard. *The racers were glad to reach the finish line.*

antonyms: go, leave

cry *v.* to weep; to shed tears. *We heard the baby cry.*

bawl to cry loudly. *The toddler started to bawl when he couldn't find his mother.*

sob to cry with short, quick breaths. *The sad movie made the girls sob.*

whimper to cry with low, weak sounds. *Some dogs whimper when they're left alone.*

antonym: laugh

cup *n.* a small, hollow container used for drinking. *Pour some milk into my cup, please.*

mug a cup that often holds hot liquid. *I plan to buy Aunt Sue a fancy coffee mug for her birthday.*

trophy a cup-shaped prize. *Our football team won a trophy last year.*

dark *adj.* not light; having little or no light. *I like to look at stars on a clear, dark night.*

dim not very bright. *The dim light in the hallway made it hard to see.*

gloomy dark and unpleasant. *The sun doesn't shine on gloomy days.*

antonym: light

done *adj.* completed; finished. *Take the cake out of the oven when it's done.*

over ended. *When will the play be over?*

through finished with. *Sandy was through reading her book.*

drink *v.* to take a liquid into the mouth and swallow it. *Do you drink much milk?*

gulp to drink quickly. *The coach told the players not to gulp water.*

sip to drink a little at a time. *You should sip the hot soup slowly.*

dry *adj.* not wet or moist. *The ground was dry before the rain came.*

arid having little or no water. *It's surprising to see flowers growing in the arid desert.*

thirsty needing water. *Working in the hot sun made Ned thirsty.*

waterless without water. *Sometimes I use waterless hand cleaner.*

antonym: wet

eat *v.* to take food into the mouth, chew it, and swallow it. *We eat beans for lunch.*

consume to eat up. *Elephants consume a lot of food.*

nibble to take little bites at a time. *Rabbits like to nibble on lettuce.*

snack to eat between meals. *I like to snack on popcorn after school.*

end *n.* the point at which something either begins or stops. *A piece of string has two ends.*

close the point at which something stops. *Our class sang at the close of the show.*

ending the last part. *The movie had a happy ending.*

tip the top point. *The tip of the iceberg stuck out of the water.*

end *v.* to finish. *The story was so good, I didn't want it to end.*

complete to finish something. *It took me almost four hours to complete the model plane.*

stop to come to an end. *Everyone hoped the rain would stop soon.*

antonyms: start, begin

fall *v.* to drop from a higher place. *Leaves fall from trees.*

collapse to fall down or fall apart. *Heavy snow on the roof made the building collapse.*

sink to drop down. *The leaky boat began to sink.*

topple to fall over. *Don't pile the blocks too high or they will topple.*

antonym: rise

fat *adj.* having much flesh; plump. *Those cows are fat.*

chubby round and plump. *The baby has chubby cheeks.*

heavy weighing a lot. *Your dog is too heavy to sit on my lap.*

overweight weighing more than is normal. *Eating too much fast food may make you overweight.*

antonym: thin

fit *adj.* in good condition. *My sister is running to get fit.*

healthy in good health. *The doctor said that Ann was healthy enough to go back to school.*

strong in good condition. *Eating spinach helps build strong bones.*

antonyms: unhealthy; weak

fly *v.* to move through the air by using wings. *Birds fly.*

glide to move smoothly and easily. *The plane seemed to glide through the air.*

soar to fly very high. *We watched the eagle soar above the treetops.*

free *adj.* loose; not tied down. *We tried to find the free end of the dog's leash.*

independent not under the control or rule of others. *The United States is an independent country.*

untied loose; not tied. *Mark tripped over his untied shoelace.*

front *n.* the first part. *The pilot sits in the front of the plane.*

bow the front part of a boat. *The bow of the boat cut through the water.*

face the front part of the head. *Hannah had a funny look on her face.*

head the top or beginning of something. *It took a long time to get to the head of the line.*

antonyms: back, rear

girl *n.* a female child. *Their new baby is a girl.*

daughter someone's female child. *The king's daughter is a princess.*

lass a young girl. *The brave lass tamed the dragon.*

give *v.* to hand over; to let have. *I will give this game to Ernesto.*

donate to give money or goods. *It felt good to donate some of my toys to Toys for Tots.*

present to give to. *The general will present medals to the soldiers.*

provide to give something needed. *The PTA will provide food for the party.*

antonyms: get, receive, take

glad *adj.* happy, pleased. *We are glad that you could come.*

cheerful feeling and acting happy. *That song always makes me cheerful.*

delighted very pleased. *We were delighted that our team won the game.*

joyful happy. *Holidays are joyful times.*

antonyms: sad, unhappy, upset

good *adj.* of high quality; better than the usual kind. *I saw a good movie last night.*

excellent extremely good; the best. *Sandy is an excellent piano player.*

nice very good. *We had nice weather for the picnic.*

positive good; hopeful. *Mr. Adams got a positive report from his doctor.*

antonyms: bad, poor

grow *v.* to become larger; to increase. *Our baby is growing so fast.*

expand to get larger; to take up more space. *Water will expand when it's heated.*

swell to increase in size. *A bad toothache made my jaw swell.*

antonym: shrink

hard *adj.* not easy. *That ball was hard to catch.*

difficult hard to do. *Tony does some difficult skateboard tricks.*

tough very hard. *It's really tough to row a boat by yourself.*

antonyms: simple, easy

help *n.* the act of doing what is useful. *Sarah gave me some help with my homework.*

aid help in doing something. *Rico needed the aid of a cane when he broke his leg.*

assistance help. *Lily blew up all the balloons without assistance.*

hit *v.* to give a blow to; to strike. *Chris hit the ball over the net.*

bat to hit with a bat. *Which player will bat next?*

beat to hit over and over. *The boy beat the locked door.*

bump to hit lightly. *Don't bump your head on the car door.*

hold *v.* to take and not let go. *I was asked to hold the baby.*

grip to hold onto. *It was hard to grip the slippery fish.*

hug to put the arms around and hold. *My grandpa likes to hug me.*

keep to have and not give up. *Kara decided to keep one of the puppies.*

hunt *v.* to search; to try to find. *We all hunted for the lost ball.*

chase to follow and try to catch. *I saw your cat chase a mouse.*

seek to look for. *The prince set out to seek his fortune.*

track to follow in order to find. *It's easy to track an animal that leaves its prints in the snow.*

jump *v.* to leap off the ground. *It was fun to watch the horses jump over the fences.*

hop to jump on one foot or on both feet together. *Robins, rabbits, and kangaroos are all animals that hop.*

skip to jump over. *My friend and I like to skip rope at lunch time.*

just *adv.* exactly. *You did that just right.*

perfectly just right. *The line she drew was perfectly straight.*

precisely exactly. *The bell rings at precisely nine o'clock.*

know *v.* **a.** to understand; have knowledge about. *Do you know how to knit?* **b.** to be aware of; realize. *I didn't know they had moved away.*

comprehend to understand. *It's hard to comprehend why you don't like baseball.*

realize to be aware of. *Do you realize that Jane's birthday is Friday?*

recognize to see and know. *Morrie didn't recognize the lady who said hello.*

late *adj.* happening after the usual time. *I was late for school.*

delayed late coming or going. *Our flight may be delayed because of the storm.*

overdue not on time. *The train was two hours overdue.*

tardy late. *I was tardy because I didn't get up on time.*

antonym: early

lock *v.* to fasten with a lock. *Lock the door when you go out.*

bolt to lock with a bolt. *Please bolt the barn door so the animals can't get out.*

hook to lock with a hook. *Did you hook the screen door?*

look *v.* to use or turn the eyes in order to see. *Look both ways before you cross the street.*

peek to look at quickly or secretly. *Don't try to peek at your presents.*

stare to look directly at for a long time. *People stopped to stare at the strange bird.*

watch to look at carefully for a long time. *My parents let me watch TV after I finish my homework.*

many *adj.* a great number of. *Many children were late to school because of the snow.*
countless too many to count. *There are countless shapes of snowflakes.*
lots of a large number. *Lots of kids in my class like vegetables.*
numerous a large number of. *That actor has won numerous awards.*
antonym: few

meet *v.* to come face to face with; to come together. *I'll meet you at the corner.*
face to meet bravely. *It was brave of Red Riding Hood to face the wolf.*
gather to get together. *The marchers will gather at the park before the parade.*
join to get together with. *Selma's family might join us for Thanksgiving dinner.*

neat *adj.* clean; in order; tidy. *A neat store is a nice place to shop.*
orderly in order. *The class waited in an orderly line.*
organized kept in good order. *My desk is so well organized that I can find anything I need.*
antonyms: dirty, messy, untidy

new *adj.* just made or born; not old. *The new puppies can't leave their mother.*
latest newest. *Have you heard the latest news?*
modern not old. *We live in a modern house.*
recent fairly new. *I got my favorite author's most recent book at the library.*
antonym: old

nice *adj.* agreeable; pleasant. *Did you have a nice time at the picnic?*
enjoyable pleasant. *We had an enjoyable holiday.*
kind nice to others. *It was kind of you to help me fix my scooter.*
likable pleasant; easy to like. *Anya is so likable that she has many friends.*
antonyms: unpleasant, awful, terrible

old *adj.* having lived or existed for a long time. *An old tree has a thick trunk.*
ancient having lived or existed a long time ago. *King Tut lived in ancient times.*
elderly old in years. *Our elderly dog is fourteen years old.*
used not new. *My uncle bought a used car.*
antonyms: young, new

part *n.* a piece or section; some; less than all. *Would you like part of my orange?*

item one thing in a group. *One item I need to buy is a notebook.*

portion a part or share of something. *I can't eat a large portion of meat.*

segment a section. *Part of a line is called a segment.*

share one part. *Each of us did our share of the work.*

antonyms: whole, all

put *v.* to place; set. *I will put the plates on the table.*

deposit to put away. *Luis went to the bank to deposit money .*

insert to put into something. *You need to insert the coin in the slot.*

lay to put in a place. *Birds lay their eggs in nests.*

antonym: take

rain *n.* drops of water that fall from clouds. *The rain splashed on the sidewalk.*

cloudburst a sudden, heavy rain. *The cloudburst surprised us, and we all got wet.*

downpour heavy rain. *The streets were flooded after the downpour.*

shower a light rain. *A gentle spring shower helps grass and flowers grow.*

rain *v.* to fall in drops from the clouds. *Look how hard it is raining!*

drizzle to rain very lightly. *I put up my umbrella when it began to drizzle.*

pour to rain very hard. *We came inside when it started to pour.*

sprinkle to rain in small drops. *When it sprinkled, there were little drops of water on the sidewalk.*

sad *adj.* unhappy. *We were sad when Jo left.*

miserable very unhappy. *Lola was miserable when she lost her favorite scarf.*

sorrowful not happy. *The story's sorrowful ending made me cry.*

sorry not glad about. *The children were sorry to see summer end.*

antonyms: happy, glad, joyful

safe *adj.* free from harm or danger. *We were safe in the house during the storm.*

secure safe and comfortable. *My little brother's blanket makes him feel secure.*

unhurt not harmed. *Juan was lucky to be unhurt when he fell off his bike.*

antonyms: dangerous, unsafe

save *v.* to put away; keep. *I save stamps for my collection.*

collect to gather things that are alike. *Ned used to collect toy dinosaurs.*

hold keep for a while. *I'm afraid that I'll get in trouble if I hold your place in line.*

store to put away. *Squirrels store acorns for the winter.*

say *v.* to speak; put into words. *What did he say to you?*

declare to say strongly. *Maya declared that she would never eat squash.*

exclaim to speak in an excited way. *"We won! We won!" he exclaimed.*

recite to say from memory. *We recite the Pledge of Allegiance in school.*

tell to put into words. *Tell us everything about your trip.*

send *v.* to cause or order to go. *Let's send a card to our teacher.*

e-mail to send over the Internet. *Please e-mail me your new cell phone number.*

mail to send by mail. *I'll mail the letter today.*

ship to send by ship, train, truck or plane. *The company will ship the computer in two days.*

antonyms: get, receive

shine *v.* to give off light. *That light shines right in my eyes.*

glow to give off a soft light. *A cat's eyes glow in the dark.*

sparkle to shine brightly. *The jewels sparkled in the sunlight.*

twinkle to shine with flashes of light. *Stars twinkle in the sky.*

short *adj.* not long or tall. *I look short next to my big brother.*

brief not long. *The president's speech was brief.*

low not high. *There is a low fence around our yard.*

antonyms: tall, long

shout *v.* to call out loudly. *We shout into the tunnel to hear the echo.*

cry to call out. *Sal heard a swimmer cry for help.*

scream to make a loud, sharp cry. *Did you scream when you saw the mouse?*

yell to shout. *Don't yell when the baby is sleeping.*

sick *adj.* not well; having a disease. *Michelle stayed in bed when she was sick.*

ill sick. *I feel ill because I ate too much candy.*

unwell not well. *Eddie felt unwell, so he stayed home from school.*

antonyms: well, healthy

sleep *v.* to be asleep; to rest the body and mind. *I am going to sleep over at Melanie's house tonight.*

doze to sleep lightly. *Grandpa started to doze during the show.*

hibernate to sleep for a long time. *Some bears hibernate all winter.*

nap to sleep for a short time. *Mom likes to nap while the baby sleeps.*

small *adj.* not big; little. *A cub is a small bear.*

narrow not wide. *The puppy got loose through a narrow space under the fence.*

tiny very small. *Tom Thumb was so tiny that he lived in a thimble.*

wee very little. *The wee kittens were very cute.*

spot *n.* a mark; a stain; a speck. *There are ink spots on this paper.*

dot a tiny round spot. *My favorite dress has pink dots on it.*

smudge a dirty mark. *Alan's dirty fingers left a smudge on the wall.*

speck a small spot. *There was a speck of dirt on my glasses.*

stay *v.* **a.** to remain. *Let's stay until four.* **b.** to keep on being. *It will stay cold all winter.*

linger to stay after something is over. *Don't linger on the playground after school.*

stop to stay somewhere for a while. *It's a long trip, so we'll stop at a hotel overnight.*

wait to stay until someone comes or something happens. *I'll wait at the bus stop for you.*

antonym: leave

stop *v.* to come to a halt. *Why did that car stop out front?*

end to stop. *The party will end at four o'clock.*

pause to stop for a while. *Remember to pause and think before you answer the question.*

quit to stop. *My aunt finally quit smoking.*

antonyms: go, start

store *n.* a place where things are sold. *Salim bought a hammer at the hardware store.*

drugstore a store where medicine and other things are sold. *Martin got some cold pills at the drugstore.*

market a special store. *Maybe Alan will stop at the fish market on his way home.*

shop a small store. *The clerk at the jewelry shop was very friendly.*

supermarket a large store that sells food and household supplies. *Blueberries are on sale at the supermarket this week.*

talk *v.* to speak; to say words. *Can the baby talk yet?*

chat to talk in a friendly way. *Karl and I had a nice chat on the telephone.*

converse to talk with. *It's hard to converse with someone when you don't speak the same language.*

discuss to talk about with someone. *We met to discuss plans for the party.*

tell *v.* to say; to talk about. *Tell us a story.*

announce to make known. *I am happy to announce that you are the winner.*

inform to give information. *The teacher will inform us about the contest rules.*

report to tell about. *You have to report the accident to the police.*

state to tell. *The judge asked the man to state his name.*

try *v.* to attempt. *Try to answer all the questions.*

strive to try hard. *I always strive to do my best in school.*

struggle to try very hard. *Vera had to struggle to climb the steep hill.*

walk *v.* to go on foot at a normal rate. *We walk to school every day.*

hike to walk a long way. *We had to hike five miles to the camp.*

march to walk in step with others. *Eleven bands will march in the parade.*

stroll to walk slowly. *It's a beautiful day to stroll through the woods.*

strut to walk in a proud way. *The proud rooster liked to strut around the yard in the morning.*

want *v.* to wish for. *I want a new coat.*

hope to want very much. *I hope I get a part in the class play.*

long to wish for very much. *The children long for their grandparents who are far away.*

well *adv.* in a good or pleasing way; with skill. *He did the job well.*

nicely in a pleasing way. *The baby was nicely dressed.*

properly in the right way. *Their rowboat wasn't tied up properly, so it drifted away.*

antonym: poorly

went *v.* past tense of go. *We went downtown.*

left went away. *The circus left town last week.*

traveled went from one place to another. *Lee's grandparents traveled to China last year.*

antonym: came

wish *n.* something wanted. *Did your wish come true?*

dream something a person wishes for. *Michael's dream is to visit all fifty states.*

goal something wanted and worked for. *Susan's goal is to learn to speak Spanish.*

hope a wish for something. *It's our hope that the puppies find good homes.*

Index

proper noun, 51, 89, 127, 164, 165, 203, 241

publishing, 17, 23, 29, 35, 51, 55, 61, 67, 73, 79, 89, 93, 99, 105, 111, 117, 127, 131, 137, 143, 149, 155, 165, 169, 175, 181, 187, 193, 203, 207, 213, 219, 225, 241

punctuation. *See also specific kinds of punctuation*
editing checklist, 51, 89, 127, 165, 203, 241

Q

question mark, 88, 193
quotation marks, 51, 89, 127, 165, 203, 241

R

r-controlled vowels. *See* **vowels**
reading skills
analogies, 16, 40, 54, 98, 130, 154, 168, 174, 180, 186, 224
antonyms, 22, 28, 30, 42, 60, 92, 94, 110, 112, 132, 170, 188, 214, 232
categorizing words, 28, 30, 34, 54, 56, 60, 68, 72, 136, 144, 156, 188, 206, 208, 212, 224, 230
complete the sentence/ paragraph, 45, 116, 121, 161, 176, 180, 202, 223
(*see also* **context clues**)

reading skills, (cont.)
context clues, 16, 34, 40, 54, 60, 66, 72, 78, 92, 98, 104, 110, 116, 130, 136, 142, 148, 154, 168, 174, 186, 192, 206, 212, 218, 224, 230
making inferences, 66
rhyming words
(*see* **rhyme**)
standardized test practice, 48–49, 86–87, 124–125, 162–163, 200–201, 238–239
synonyms, 22, 30, 40, 62, 66, 104, 174, 192, 205, 211, 223
word meaning, 72, 182
realistic story, 175
related words. *See* **synonyms**
review, 45–47, 83–85, 121–123, 159–161, 197–199, 235–237
revising, 17, 23, 29, 35, 51, 55, 61, 67, 73, 79, 89, 93, 99, 105, 111, 117, 127, 131, 137, 143, 149, 155, 165, 169, 175, 181, 187, 193, 203, 207, 213, 219, 225, 241

rhyme
identifying, 15, 18, 19, 24, 26, 27, 32, 37, 38, 42, 45, 53, 68, 77, 78, 80, 83, 91, 100, 101, 107, 109, 115, 119, 121, 123, 132, 138, 142, 153, 156, 159, 160, 167, 173, 176, 184, 185, 191, 197,

rhyme, (cont.)
identifying, (cont.) 198, 205, 208, 211, 214, 223, 235
using in poetry, 35, 187

S

science and spelling. *See* **spelling across the curriculum**
sensory words, 127, 143
sequence, 213, 241
setting, 111, 149, 207
slash (proofreading mark), 17
social studies and spelling. *See* **spelling across the curriculum**
sorting words, 10–11
al, 52, 57, 85
compound words, 228, 233
consonant blends, 58, 63, 128, 133
consonant digraphs, 190, 195, 210, 215, 216, 221
contractions, 178, 183
homophones, 222, 227
inflectional endings, 140, 145, 146, 151
/k/, 114, 119
long a, 90, 95
long and short /oo/, 152, 157
long e, 96, 101
long i, 102, 107
long o, 108, 113
nk/ng, 64, 69
/oi/, 134, 139
/ou/, 172, 177

Credits

Photography: Cover image © George C. Anderson Photography; p. 3 © Jupiter Images; p. 4 top © Jupiter Images; p. 4 bottom © iStockphoto.com/Tom Hahn; p. 5 top © iStockphoto.com: Ira Bachinskaya; p. 5 bottom © iStockphoto.com/felinda; p. 6 top © iStockphoto.com/Bernd Klumpp; p. 6 bottom © Jupiter Images; p. 7 top © Jupiter Images; p. 7 bottom © iStockphoto.com/Sue Jackson; p. 8 © iStockphoto.com/cotesebastien; p. 9 © iStockphoto.com/Marilyn Nieves; p. 10 top © George C. Anderson Photography; p. 10 bottom © 2001–2009 Smart Technologies ULC. All rights reserved; p. 11–13 © George C. Anderson Photography; p. 15 © Fancy/Alamy; p. 16 © Jupiter Images; p. 19 © iStockphoto.com/Jeryl Tan; p. 21 © iStockphoto.com/Jeanell Norvell; p. 22 © iStockphoto.com/Carmen Martinez Banus; p. 25 © iStockphoto.com/felinda; p. 27 © image100/Alamy; p. 28 © Liu Jin/AFP/Getty Images, Inc.; p. 31 © iStockphoto.com/Katie Fletcher; p. 33 © iStockphoto.com/Fertnig Photography; p. 34 © Datacraft–Sozaijiten/Alamy; p. 37 © Image Source Black/Alamy; p. 39 © Jupiter Images; p. 40 © Stephanie Rausser/Iconica/Getty Images, Inc.; p. 43 © Sam Diephuis/Corbis; p. 45 © iStockphoto.com/Stefanie Timmermann; p. 46 © Blend Images/Alamy; p. 50 © iStockphoto.com/dra_schwartz; p. 53 © Jupiter Images; p. 54 © John Lund/Drew Kelly/Blend Images/Corbis; p. 57 © Phillip Spears/Getty Images, Inc.; p. 59 © Purestock/Getty Images, Inc.; p. 60 © iStockphoto.com/Jane Norton; p. 63 © iStockphoto.com/Laura Stone; p. 65 © Blend Images/Alamy; p. 66 © Joshua Ets-Hokin/Photodisc/Getty Images, Inc.; p. 69 © iStockphoto.com/Marilyn Nieves; p. 71 © Jose Luis Pelaez, Inc./Blend Images/Corbis; p. 72 © Stockbyte/Getty Images, Inc.; p. 75 © iStockphoto.com/Yory Frenklakh; p. 77 © iStockphoto.com/Pam Rowell; p. 78 © iStockphoto.com/Arthur Kwiatkowski; p. 81 © iStockphoto.com/Daniel Keeler; p. 83 © Lorie Leigh Lawrence/Alamy; p. 84 © iStockphoto.com/Bernd Klumpp; p. 88 © iStockphoto.com/Stefan Klein; p. 91 © iStockphoto.com/Fertnig Photography; p. 92 © Cultura/Alamy; p. 95 © NASA/JPL-Caltech/University of Wisconsin; p. 97 © iStockphoto.com/Miguel Angelo Silva; p. 98 © iStockphoto.com/Carmen Martinez Banus; p. 101 © Alaska Stock LLC/Alamy; p. 103 © iStockphoto.com/Brandon Clark; p. 104 © iStockphoto.com/Suprijono Suharjoto; p. 107 © iStockphoto.com/Grafissimo; p. 109 © iStockphoto.com/Clint Spencer; p. 110 © Panorama Stock RF/Photolibrary; p. 113 © Thomas Barwick/Digital Vision/Getty Images, Inc.; p. 115 © iStockphoto.com/iofoto; p. 116 © Comstock Images/JupiterImages; p. 119 © iStockphoto.com/Sue Jackson; p. 121 © iStockphoto.com/aldomurillo; p. 122 © iStockphoto.com/Rich Legg; p. 126 © iStockphoto/Stefan Witas; p. 129 © iStockphoto.com/Ira Bachinskaya; p. 130 © Gib Martinez/Alamy; p. 133 © Ariel Skelley/Getty Images, Inc.; p. 135 © iStockphoto.com; p. 136 © iStockphoto.com/Jill Chen; p. 139 © Gabe Palmer/Alamy; p. 141 © Creatas/Jupiter Images; p. 142 © iStockphoto.com/Lisa Valder; p. 145 © Diana Bier Arazola/Alamy; p. 147 © Laura Dwight/Corbis; p. 148 © Monashee Frantz/OJO Images/Getty Images, Inc.; p. 151 © Creatas/Jupiter Images; p. 153 © Jupiter Images; p. 154 © Jupiter Images; p. 157 © Jose Luis Pelaez, Inc./Blend Images/Corbis; p. 159 © iStockphoto.com/Simon Masters; p. 160 © iStockphoto.com/Michael Braun; p. 164 © iStockphoto.com/Samuel Kessler; p. 167 © iStockphoto.com/Jeff Gynane; p. 168 © iStockphoto.com/DNY59; p. 171 Photo Courtesy of University of California/Riverside; p. 173 © Marek Zuk/Alamy; p. 174 © iStockphoto.com/Arthur Kwiatkowski; p. 177 © iStockphoto.com/zoomstudio; p. 179 © Jose Luis Pelaez, Inc./Blend Images/Corbis; p. 180 © iStockphoto.com/Steve Byland; p. 183 © iStockphoto.com/Carlos Alvarez; p. 185 © iStockphoto.com/Rick Rhay; p. 186 © Christie's Images/SuperStock; p. 189 © Jacob Andrzejczak/WireImage/Getty Images, Inc.; p. 191 © iStockphoto.com/Jaren Wicklund; p. 192 © iStockphoto.com/AVTG; p. 195 © Chad Slattery/Stone/Getty Images, Inc.; p. 197 © Digital Vision; p. 198 © iStockphoto.com/Jane Norton; p. 202 © Dana Menussi/The Image Bank/Getty Images, Inc.; p. 205 © Danita Delimont/Alamy; p. 206 © Jupiter Images; p. 209 © iStockphoto.com/Tobias Helbig; p. 211 © iStockphoto.com/Tom Hahn; p. 212 © iStockphoto.com/AlexVarlakov; p. 215 © iStockphoto.com/northlightimages; p. 217 © iStockphoto.com/cotesebastien; p. 218 © iStockphoto.com/ArtisticCaptures; p. 221 © iStockphoto.com/Editorial2; p. 223 © iStockphoto.com/Liz Leyden; p. 224 © Creatas/Jupiter Images; p. 227 © iStockphoto.com/miteemaus5; p. 229 © Richard Cummins/Corbis; p. 230 © iStockphoto.com/Bryngelzon; p. 233 © Corbis/SuperStock; p. 235 © iStockphoto.com; p. 236 © Jupiter Images; p. 240 © Ariel Skelley/Getty Images, Inc.; p. 251 © iStockphoto.com/Bernd Klumpp; p. 252 © Alaska Stock LLC/Alamy; p. 253 © Jupiter Images; p. 254 © iStockphoto.com/Elena Workman; p. 255 © iStockphoto.com/Tom Hahn; p. 257 © iStockphoto.com/Arthur Kwiatkowski; p. 258 © iStockphoto.com/Brandon Clark; p. 261 © Jupiter Images; p. 262 © iStockphoto.com/Pam Rowell; p. 265 © iStockphoto.com/narvikk; p. 267 © iStockphoto.com/Marti57900; p. 269 © iStockphoto.com/jamiestokes; p. 270 © iStockphoto.com/Fertnig Photography; p. 271 © image100/Alamy; p. 272 © Bruce Walsh/University of Arizona; p. 274 © iStockphoto.com/Rick Rhay; p. 277 © Blend Images/Alamy; p. 278 © iStockphoto.com/YinYang; p. 280 © iStockphoto.com/Carlos Alvarez; p. 283 © iStockphoto.com/Liz Leyden; p. 285 © Comstock/Getty Images, Inc.; p. 286 © John Anderson/Alamy; p. 288 © iStockphoto.com/cotesebastien.

Illustrations: Alessia Girasole: 24, 30, 36, 42, 56, 62, 68, 74, 80, 94, 100, 106, 112, 118, 132, 138, 144, 150, 156, 170, 176, 182, 188, 194, 208, 214, 220, 226, 232